Vic (V.P.) Walker was born in Lincoln in 1930, educated at the Lincoln School, and worked for the *Lincolnshire Chronicle* from 1948 to 1952 and the *Western Daily Press* in Bristol from 1952 to 1954.

He moved to Greece in late 1954 intending to spend a year as editor of *Athens News*, the English-language daily, on his way to Australia: instead, he spent fifteen years with *Athens News* while working also as the Athens correspondent of the *Sydney Morning Herald* and Melbourne *Herald* group.

Since 1963 he has represented The Journal of Commerce (New York) and since 1969 has been an editor in the English-language department of the Athens News Agency. He has written regularly or occasionally for newspapers in Europe, the United States, Canada and South Africa, including the *Financial Times* and the *International Herald Tribune*, and he contributes to specialist publications on shipping, industrial relations, tourism and economic matters in general.

COLLINS INDEPENDENT TRAVELLERS GUIDE

MAINLAND GREECE

VICTOR WALKER

Series Editor Robin Dewhurst

Collins
8 Grafton Street, London
1988

Note
Whilst every effort has been made to ensure that prices, hotel and restaurant recommendations, opening hours and similar factual information in this book are accurate at the time of going to press, the Publishers cannot be held responsible for any changes found by readers using this guide.

William Collins Sons & Co Ltd
London · Glasgow · Sydney
Auckland · Toronto · Johannesburg

First published in 1988
Reprinted 1988
© Victor Walker 1988

Maps by Kevin Jones Associates

BRITISH LIBRARY CATALOGUING IN PUBLICATION DATA
Collins Independent Travellers Guide to Mainland Greece.
1. Greece—Description and travel—1951
—Guide-books
914.95′0476   DF716

ISBN 0 00 410972 4

Typeset by Ace Filmsetting Ltd, Frome, Somerset.
Printed and bound in Great Britain by Mackays of Chatham.

Contents

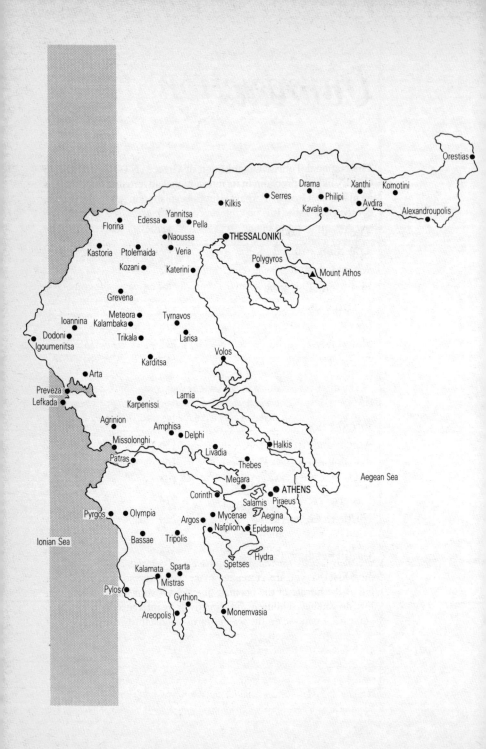

Introduction

The National Tourist Organisation of Greece (NTOG, or EOT in Greek), likes to proclaim in its international advertising that 'there is no place like Greece'. Perhaps! But the explanation lies in the people, not the geography. It is possible, of course, to visit Greece for the sea and sunshine and to divide an enjoyable holiday between the public rooms of a hotel and its stretch of private beach. But even then, only the practising misanthropist will fail to establish a personal relationship with the Greeks who cater to his needs.

This is as true today, when the visitor is one among eight million, as it was a quarter of a century ago when he was one among eighty thousand. The Greeks are a perverse people: they seem unable to appreciate that the tourist is no more than a single strand in a golden fleece, insist on regarding him as an individual, and retain the curiosity that has always been their most engaging characteristic. For the visitor, this implies an obligation to respond.

The discovery waiting to be made is that obstacles to communication exist only in the mind; that there is a world to explore, requiring only a readiness to converse. And this readiness is not a matter of language, but of attitude. The Greeks are not chauvinistic about their language. They do not expect the foreigner to learn Greek, no matter how long he stays or how often he visits. They appreciate that it is spoken only in a tiny corner of the world and, if born and brought up in the communities abroad, they often will not bother to learn it properly themselves. This turns them into linguists.

Though the Greeks learn English more intensively than in the past, because of membership of the European Community, tourism and the number of jobs for which English is a prerequisite, they still want to use their facility for the simple pleasure of communication. And the mere fact that you are a foreigner makes you interesting. If you do not fall at the hurdle of the opening questions - your name, where you live, do you have children and, directly or by inference, how much do you earn - you are on the way towards an instant friendship.

You then arrive at the waterjump. If you expect your new acquaintance to talk to you of England or America, London or New York, let alone sheep farming in the Mendip hills, the conversation will fade into awkward silences and you will politely be left to your own devices. Reasonably and inevitably, your potential friend expects to be met in the middle, to receive something in exchange for his knowledge of your language. He needs from you intelligent questions and a degree of informed comment on his own country, its characteristics and quirks, and at least the broader political, economic and social issues around which mealtime talk will revolve in his own home.

Make the effort (this book will help you), and you have turned the key to understanding Greece without even leaving your hotel. To open the door and slip through, you have to move about a little in the country itself. Do not just see Athens and the main town of your chosen island but, at least in passing, visit the bustling little provincial cities; observe the industries as well as the antiquities, and go to where the grapes grow, as well as where the wine is drunk.

You will find a country that is undergoing rapid, but superficial, change. The main effect, at one level, is to help you see it more easily: new or improved roads lead into the interior, and there are hotels where only a few years ago you had to rely on family hospitality or unfold a tent. Greece is making a determined attempt to turn itself into a European country, to modernise its structures and institutions and to de-Balkanise itself socially and politically. The challenge has been accepted, but the process is not altogether painless.

The immediate result has been the emergence of tensions in society that were not present before, or were not obvious. Where *avrio* ('tomorrow') was once a way of life, the Greeks are now looking for tangible results as of yesterday. Freed from the pressures of a day-to-day struggle for survival, they have subjected themselves to ambitions that can be unnerving in their imprecision. Not so long ago, contentment was a regular income sufficient to ensure food, clothing and shelter, an occasional night out and a few gold sovereigns under the mattress in case of illness. Now, freed from the treadmills of a poor country, the Greek family wants at least one car and a country cottage to escape to at weekends; it wants an assurance of affluence and the leisure to enjoy it, today and indefinitely.

The Greeks were told, and most of them believed, that this would be the effortless reward of membership of the European Community. Now, seven years later, they are learning better. They are also discovering, from the broken promises of successive governments, that it is more painful to have to retreat from uplands prematurely occupied than it was to gaze at them from the valleys as unattainably utopian. You will not need to be particularly acute to observe the symptoms of discontent. The Greeks in the main retain their politeness towards the foreigner, but they surprise themselves by their rudeness towards one another since losing the contentment of modest aspirations.

Greece as a country and a society is in a state of transition: for the independent traveller, this can only add to its fascination.

History

Through the ages

If there is one single achievement that makes the Greeks unique, it is their retention of a sense of identity through successive 'dark ages'; this is, perhaps, the only consistency to which they can lay an unchallenged claim. As the modern Greek will sometimes permit himself to observe when pushed into an objectionable defensiveness, there were Greeks in Greece, attending theatres, at a time when the tribes of the island that would become Britain were painting themselves with woad, and those in Germany, if not actually swinging from the trees, were at least huddling beneath them clad in animal skins.

The Greeks identify themselves with their precursors to a greater degree than other peoples might choose. But though they remember that they invented democracy, they do not remember that they combined it with the practice of slavery; they recall that they bequeathed to the west the seeds of the Renaissance, but not that they simultaneously persecuted thought under the dictate of political expediency. Whereas they defeated great empires in the name of freedom, they look differently on the establishment of their own ancient colonies and the exploits of Alexander the Great. What the modern visitor sees is some of the physical evidence both of the continuity and the inconsistency: much of it he has to infer, or imagine.

Minoans and earlier

Travelling along the motorway from Athens to Thessaloniki, or visiting the Cyclades islands, you are in countryside where, as much as 9,000 years ago, Neolithic man was already farming the land and rearing livestock. Your Aegean ferry takes you through waters where, in the same general period, according to theories put to the test in 1987, there was already a kind of merchant marine to ship obsidian from outcrops on the island of Milos to settlements in the Peloponnese.

As many years before the birth of Christ as have passed since, the Minoan civilisation was developing on the island of Crete. The palaces of Knossos, Phaestos, Malia and Kato Zakros are silent reminders of the legendary King Minos and the decidedly unpleasant minotaur that Theseus slew, of Cretan dominance of the Aegean, and of the earliest known examples of flush toilets and toplessness in high fashion. In their spare time the Minoans played a kind of backgammon, distant ancestor of the *tavli* in Greek coffee-shops today and of the love of dice among the Romans.

Sometime in the fifteenth century BC, the volcano on the island of Santorini (known also as Thera) blew up, creating the most spectacular of the Aegean islands as well as (possibly) the legend of the Lost Continent of Atlantis. The accompanying earthquakes, tidal waves and dust clouds coincided with, and probably caused, the collapse of Minoan power.

A Minoan city at a site now called Acrotiri was discovered on Santorini just twenty years ago by the late Professor Spyridon Marinatos and has since been partly excavated and roofed over. You enter what appears to be a giant aircraft hangar, and find yourself walking along narrow streets that were populous more than 3,000 years ago, and peering into tiny rooms where families once gathered for dinner. Though by modern standards the houses were mean and poky, frescoes discovered there (now on display in the Athens Archaeological Museum) give a vivid impression of the power of Minoan Crete and the luxury to which the wealthy could aspire.

Professor Marinatos was fatally injured in a fall during the excavations: if Acrotiri was indeed a village of 'Atlantis', a belief based in part on the writings of Plato, his was the last death in the Lost Continent.

And so to Mycenae

With the Minoans on the way out, the opportunity came for the Mycenaeans: Agamemnon, in whose time brave men lived; Helen 'of Troy', who launched the thousand ships; Clytemnestra, Elektra, Orestes and the rest of the ill-fated Atreus family. They are remembered today because the Greeks were already tellers of stories that have inspired playwrights from Aeschylus to Eugene O'Neill.

The gold death masks, portions of armour, gold and silver utensils and tomb furnishings that were discovered in 1876 by Heinrich Schliemann are now in the Athens Archaeological Museum. The beehive tombs themselves, the Lion Gate and the remains of the city are included on every coach tour of the Peloponnese.

From Mycenae came the first form of written Greek, the Linear B script deciphered in 1952 by the late Michael Ventris. Later the Greeks adopted a 24-letter modified version of the Phoenician alphabet, which is essentially the alphabet still in use today. Unlike Linear B, which was of as little help to the creative writer as the Egyptian hieroglyphics, this had seven letters representing vowels. Without it, neither the *Odyssey* and *Iliad* nor the works of the ancient dramatists would have survived. But even in the times of Linear B, it is now known that more than a hundred recognised occupations were represented among the people who used it, inviting speculation whether they might have been organised into some form of trade unions.

This great civilisation was obliterated by the Dorian invasions of the twelfth century BC, and the result was a 450-year so-called 'dark age'. But the term is to some extent a misnomer: the era left no great art or literature, and if there were any exceptional men their names have not survived, but it did see the adoption of the alphabetic writing, Homer as man or firm lived and worked during it, cities sprang up, refugees founded the first Greek colonies on the Asia Minor coast, and the gods set up home on Mount Olympos. In art this was the so-called Geometric Period: its curiously modernistic forms may be seen most concentratedly in the Goulandris Museum in Athens. And out of this relative darkness came Sparta and Athens.

The real Ancient Greece

Together, the Archaic, Classical and Hellenistic Periods carry the story of Ancient Greece from the end of the 'dark age' up to the Roman conquest – from around 700 to 146 BC. These years contain almost everything that makes up the popular concept of Ancient Greece, and need to be signposted:

Archaic (700 to 500 BC): saw the development of city states and of uniform social, religious and political life; the demise of monarchy, except in Sparta, and early experiments with forms of government that included aristocracy, tyranny and degrees of democracy. A sense of Greekness came to be acquired, as seen in the panhellenic athletic contests and the first Olympic Games.

Classical (500 to 323 BC): saw the three Persian invasions, and the battles of Marathon, Thermopylae and Salamis; the Golden Age of Pericles, of the dramatists and the philosophers; the Peloponnesian War and the defeat of Athens by Sparta. Philip II of Macedonia and his son, Alexander the Great, were the dominant figures.

Hellenistic (323 to 146 BC): the decline of Athens and Sparta was accompanied by the development of Greek civilisation overseas. The Romans moved in and took over.

Nothing would have been quite the way it was, and probably would not be quite the way it is today, if there had never been city states in Ancient Greece. They were the product initially of geography. Then as now, or at least until the fever of road construction that began in the early 1950s, Greece was a land divided by mountains and united by the sea. So the city state, consisting of the town and its surrounding countryside up to the next natural barrier, had to be large enough to be defensible but not so populous as to be either ungovernable or too frequently subject to famine.

When the city states outgrew their possibilities, the Greeks went out to colonise: on the coast of what is now Turkey, along the Sea of Marmara and the Black Sea all the way to the Crimea, and westward to Sicily, Italy and the South of France – Marseilles, Nice, Monaco and Naples were all founded by the Greeks. (In the same way, after the Second World War, comparable pressures drove modern Greeks to communities in the United States and Australia and to the factories of West Germany.)

The word for the city state, *polis*, has come down to us as politics, matters concerning the state. Periodic clashes between the ruling class and the common people provided not just experimentation in governmental systems but also the first written codes of law: in Athens in 621 BC one Drakos gave his name to the Draconian code that stipulated death even for minor theft, much as in eighteenth-century England. The Greeks are still experimenting: in the past twenty years they have twice deposed a monarchy (once at the point of a gun and once voluntarily), experienced a dictatorship and instituted two republics, one military and the other civilian.

The Ancient Greeks had the custom of ostracism, despatching into temporary exile even their most distinguished governors if they sniffed a tyranny in the offing. Exile was not then and is not now considered a sentence of political death; rather, it was intended to be a chastening experience and an invitation to acquire circumspection. Though too close a parallel would be misleading, the present century has seen the exile or self-exile of three ruling monarchs and Greece's two greatest modern statesmen, Eleftherios Venizelos and Constantine Karamanlis.

The Ancient Greek demanded and exercised the right to realise his full potential and speak his mind. These same freedoms are enshrined in the 1975 Constitution, clearly if perhaps not quite so forthrightly as when Pericles declared: 'We do not say of a man who takes no interest in politics that he is minding his own business; we say he has no business to be here at all.' Deprivation of these rights was the real agony of the 1967–74 dictatorship, and explains the ongoing demand that Greeks living abroad should be able to vote, in consulates or by post, in general elections in Greece.

Tucked away in the Classical Period is the thirty-year Golden Age of Pericles, from 460 to 429 BC. An incomparable minister of public works before the title was coined, Pericles commissioned the great works of architecture, including the Parthenon, that modern Greece is still living on.

In 27 BC Greece formally became a province of Rome, with Corinth the administrative capital and Athens the principal artistic centre. For Greece, the Pax Romanum represented three centuries of peace and prosperity during which, in many ways, the vanquished conquered the victors. The Greeks taught the Romans philosophy, poetry, sculpture, drama and sciences, and wealthy Roman families competed for the services of Greek cooks and sent their sons to study at Greek universities. In Athens, Hadrian completed the construction of the Temple of Olympian Zeus that had been started 600 years earlier, while the Herod Atticus theatre, now used for performances during the summer Athens Festival, is also Roman.

Nero competed in a rigged Olympiad (it was even more necessary to be accommodating to the superpower then than now). He also dug the first official sod in an attempt to drive a canal through the Isthmus of Corinth, but was thwarted by a combination of the terrain and the priesthood, the latter polishing skills subsequently perfected by bureaucrats with the result that ships had to wait another 2,000 years for the canal's completion.

While many works of art were shipped to Rome by anonymous predecessors of Lord Elgin and Herman Goering, the Romans were also prepared to settle, and pay, for replicas turned out by small- and medium-sized enterprises in Corinth, Patras and Athens itself.

The Roman period also saw the arrival of Christianity in the middle of the first century, with visits by St Paul to Athens, Corinth and Thessaloniki. The Greeks embraced the new faith with reformist passion, all pagan temples were closed, and in AD 393 the Olympics were abolished. Three years later the Goths arrived under Alaric.

But the Greeks did not entirely abandon their old local gods; they converted them to Christianity, and some of them were accorded sainthood. The modern visitor may easily find himself watching a procession of icons on the patronal festival of a saint whose sway extends only to that particular region or island and whose origins are lost in a pagan past.

The thousand years of Byzantium

In 395 the Roman Empire split into the Western and Eastern Empires, with the latter based at Constantinople (present-day Istanbul), the new, Roman name for the Greek city of Byzantium founded by Byzas of Megara after pondering a typically obscure pronouncement by the Oracle of Delphi. Had the Emperor Constantine not moved the capital to the shores of the Bosphorus some seventy years earlier, and had he not been baptised into the Christian faith on his deathbed, Greece would not today be largely populated by men with the name of Constantine (more familiarly, Costa or Dino) and women called Constantina (Costoula or Dina).

From the beginning, however, the Eastern Empire was Greek in spirit, language and religion. Greece itself became a province of Constantinople; Thessaloniki was the Empire's second city, and Athens declined into a minor provincial town.

After the Fourth Crusade in 1204 had disgraced itself by seizing Constantinople as an easier and more remunerative alternative to the Holy Land which it had been formed to liberate, much of Greece was parcelled out among Crusader participants. The Frankish feudal states did not survive long, but left behind them some notable castles in the Peloponnese that are well worth visiting. Rather more remains of the Venetians, who held Crete until the seventeenth century, and Corfu until they were dislodged by Napoleon.

Byzantium awaits the visitor today in the form of churches almost everywhere in Greece, but especially in Athens, Thessaloniki, Kastoria and Arta, and in the monasteries of Meteora and the ruined city of Mistras in the Peloponnese. Its supreme memorial is the self-governing Mount Athos 'Holy Community', to which access for strangers is very restricted. Less tangibly, its echoes linger in the Byzantine chant of church services and, of course, as a somewhat unflattering epithet for anything tortuous or complicated.

The latest dark age

In the early hours of Tuesday, 29 May 1453, Constantinople fell to the Ottoman Turks under Mohammed II. Greece has never been the same since. With Constantinople taken, the Turks swept quickly into Greece; they completed their conquest of the Peloponnese in 1461, and seized Rhodes from the Knights of St John of Jerusalem in 1522 and Crete from the Venetians in 1661. Only the Ionian islands occupied by the Venetians escaped entirely, though in some of the more remote parts of Greece – the Mani at the southern tip of the Peloponnese and the high mountains of Crete and Epiros – Turkish power remained far from absolute.

For Greece as a whole, it was another dark age, lasting for almost 400 years, and it accounts for the enduring hatred felt in Greece for the Turks. Successive uprisings bloodily suppressed, the harvesting of girls for Turkish harems and boys for the élite Janissary corps, and village plane trees that once served as makeshift gallows are indelibly recorded in the popular memory. And yet, through religion, the Greek language and national identity were preserved, as innumerable churches dating from the seventeenth and eighteenth centuries testify. The legend of the village priest with cross in one hand and musket in the other dates from the centuries of Turkish occupation and still helps to preserve the influence of the Church. The fall of Constantinople, by forcing a flight of intellectuals to the west and in particular to Italy, paved the way for the Renaissance. Without the Renaissance it is unlikely that there could have been the same growth of philhellenism in Europe, and without the philhellene movement the Greeks would probably not have regained their freedom through the 1821 Revolution. And even in occupied Constantinople, the Greeks provided the business and administrative class, in a way that the Romans would have understood. They also supplied the Turkish name for the city, Istanbul, a corruption of *eis teen polis*, Greek for 'in the city'. Even today, when a Greek speaks of the 'polis' he is thinking of Constantinople, the 'polis' of Constantine: there is no other city in the world without the need of a proper name.

In present-day Greece, Tuesday is still considered an unpropitious day to start a journey, launch an enterprise or get married, since it was on a Tuesday that the city fell.

Freedom and afterwards

The French Revolution of 1789 provided the impetus, thirty-two years later, for the Greek Revolution of 1821. It was proclaimed in the Peloponnese on or about 25 March, the date subsequently adopted for the principal of Greece's two national days.

Success, at least to a limited degree, came six years later. Acting under the pressure of domestic philhellene agitation, Britain, France and Russia as the 'protecting powers' intervened with the Ottoman Sultan to concede national and political independence for an embryonic Greek state. An unintended naval battle in the Bay of Navarino, in which a tri-national squadron under the command of Vice-Admiral Lord Codrington sank most of the combined Turkish–Egyptian fleet, left the Sultan with no option but to agree. While Pylos is now the only name in use for the town at the head of the bay, the bay itself is written on modern Greek maps either as Navarino or Pylos. Today, Codrington has a street in Athens named after him.

The Battle of Navarino was the decisive encounter in the Greek Revolution. In the context of the 200th anniversary of the birth of Lord Byron, scholars and historians in Greece at least will be offered a new opportunity to examine whether it could have been fought if Lord Byron had not died in Missolonghi three years earlier.

In the inevitable form of street names, the Greeks remember other notable philhellenes of that era: France's Victor Hugo and Alfred de Musset, for example, and America's Samuel Grindley Howe, the Boston doctor who in 1825 became surgeon-general of the Greek Revolutionary forces, raised $60,000 for Greek relief, and as late as 1866 involved himself in one of the abortive attempts to liberate Crete.

But Byron outshone them all, and after his death Greece could no longer be left to its fate. The Greeks may not read Byron, but they have the grace to honour him.

It was not much of a country that gained its independence in 1829. It consisted of the Peloponnese, the southern part of central Greece and a few islands. When the Bavarian Prince Otto (hellenised as Othon) arrived to take up the throne which the protecting powers had created for him, his capital was the backwater Peloponnesian port of Nafplion and Athens was a cluster of hovels at the foot of the Acropolis. But Othon moved his capital to Athens, where a demonstration in 1843 forced him to grant a constitution and in the process gave a name to the open space in front of his palace in which it was staged: Constitution (Syntagma) Square.

The King's submission on the constitutional issue bought him just under twenty years; he was deposed in 1862 and replaced the following year by Prince George of Denmark, of the House of Glucksburg. As a gesture to the new monarch, Britain ceded the Ionian islands, which it had been holding as a protectorate since the defeat of Napoleon.

The rest of the nineteenth century and first two decades of the twentieth were devoted to pursuit of the *megali ithea*, the 'Great Idea', the incorporation of all territories inhabited by Greeks and restoration of Greek power on both sides of the Aegean, behind frontiers broadly matching those of the old Byzantine Empire. It was a dream that started and ended badly but nevertheless gave Greece its present borders.

After thirty years of continual revolts in Crete and parts of Thessaly and Epiros, Greece fought and lost a war with Turkey in 1897. But out of the resulting turmoil sprang the 1909 Revolution and the advent to power of Greece's most revered modern statesman, the Cretan Eleftherios Venizelos. Venizelos pushed through a general modernisation that included the reinforcement of parliamentary government and, above all, turned the army and navy into fighting forces that could look with confidence and relish to their next opportunity.

The faith was justified by the two Balkan Wars of 1912 and 1913 that secured Thessaloniki, most of central and western Macedonia, Ioannina and south Epiros. Together with Crete, which had united with Greece in 1908, and the eastern Aegean islands, Greece emerged from the Balkan Wars with its surface area and population almost doubled.

Most of the older parts of central Athens, the main public buildings, the National (formerly Royal) gardens and the Zappeion Park date from the first half-century of modern Greek freedom.

In 1913 the assassination of George I in Thessaloniki, after a fifty-year reign, brought his son Constantine to the throne. The outbreak of the First World War in 1914 led to a conflict between Constantine and Venizelos that the pro-German King lost. Venizelos took Greece into the war on the side of Britain and France, Constantine was deposed and the Macedonian Front was formed.

Treaties signed in 1919 and 1920 gave Greece eastern and western Thrace as well as a mandate to administer Smyrna, now Izmir, and its hinterland pending a plebiscite. The result was a foretaste on a small scale of what was to occur later in Germany because of the Treaty of Versailles: too much was demanded of the vanquished Turkey for having fought on the losing side. While the Greeks were voting Venizelos out of office and restoring Constantine through a plebiscite, Mustapha Kemal, subsequently Kemal Ataturk, was preparing Turkey for its day of revenge.

The 'Great Idea' in its last flowering led to the Greek–Turkish War of 1922; the Asia Minor disaster; the sack of Smyrna and massacre of its inhabitants; the arrival in Greece of a million and a half refugees whom it took thirty years to assimilate fully and house properly; and, through the Treaty of Lausanne, the return of eastern Thrace to Turkey. Understandably, the Greeks took their defeat badly. The army revolted, Constantine was deposed for a second and final time, and the five political leaders and the army commander-in-chief judged chiefly responsible for the disaster were tried and executed.

The executions opened a schism that led to successive military revolts; the proclamation of a republic that lasted only eleven years; the restoration of the monarchy in 1935 under Constantine's elder son, George II; the flight of Venizelos to exile in France and his death there in 1936; and, in August 1936, the establishment of a dictatorship under General Ioannis Metaxas.

World War, occupation and civil strife

The Second World War began for Greece on 28 October 1940, when Metaxas rejected an Italian ultimatum (his 'No! [*Ochi!*]', gave Greece its other national day). Greek victories over Mussolini in Epiros and Albania, the first to be gained by the allies, forced Hitler to invade in 1941. It is possible to assert, as the Greeks frequently do, that had the Germans not had to rescue their Italian allies the invasion of Russia would have been launched several months before June 1941; then Moscow would have been captured before the onset of winter, and the war might have had a different outcome.

The three-year occupation by German, Italian and Bulgarian forces left Greece in ruins. It was followed almost immediately after liberation by the first of two communist attempts to seize power, in December 1944: the so-called 'December Days', when Greece's freedom was preserved by British troops.

The communists' second attempt, the 'second round', took three years of hard fighting to defeat, despite American assistance under the Truman doctrine of the cold war. Clearly having studied the example of the Janissaries, the communist guerrillas as they melted away across the Yugoslav and Albanian frontiers took with them a round-up of children for indoctrination and training for an eventual third round. These wounds have yet to close completely.

Meanwhile, another referendum had confirmed the monarchy, George II had died and been succeeded by his brother Paul, and the Dodecanese islands, occupied by Italy since 1912, had been ceded to Greece under the terms of the Greek–Italian peace treaty. Greece had thus reached its present dimensions. There is still a hankering for northern Epiros, now part of southern Albania, but this is currently a question of the human rights of the Greek minority, and is not being pursued as a territorial claim.

The Greece you visit

Greece is an archipelago country that, since its final enlargement with incorporation of the Dodecanese islands, has a surface area of 131,944 sq km. In south-east Europe at the southern tip of the Balkan peninsula, it is the only member of the European Community without a land frontier with another member; its closest Community neighbour, Italy, can be reached by ferry across the Adriatic or by land through Yugoslavia. To the north and east, Greece has land borders with Albania (247 km), Yugoslavia (246 km), Bulgaria (474 km) and Turkey (203 km).

Though roughly four-fifths of Greece is mountainous, no part of mainland Greece is more than 100 km from the sea; in central Greece the maximum is 60 km and in the Peloponnese 50 km. Of the twenty-eight mountains above 2,000 metres, the best-known are Olympos (2,917 m), Parnassos (2,457 m), Taygettus (2,407 m) and Athos (2,033 m).

The Peloponnese, which is not regarded as an island although it is severed from the mainland by the Corinth Canal, has an area of 21,439 sq km. The 169 inhabited islands, of which the largest are Crete and Euboia, together total 24,909 sq km, and uninhabited islets another 257 sq km. There is no exact tally of these islets, some of which are little more than dangers to shipping, but the generally accepted figure is around 2,000. Total length of mainland and island coasts is put by the National Statistics Service at 15,020 km.

Two of the larger islands are almost as close to the mainland as the Peloponnese itself: the width of the Corinth Canal is 24.6 m, while the bridge across the Evripos straits to Euboia at Halkis spans a waterline of only 40 m and that joining the mainland to Lefkas in the Ionian islands a canal of a mere 25 m.

Though obviously every inhabited island has at least one harbour, and there are several dozen along the mainland coasts, Greece has seven main ports: Piraeus, Thessaloniki, Patras, Volos, Igoumenitsa, Kavala and, on the islands, Irakleion in Crete.

Greece is not well provided with rivers – it has none that are navigable – but makes maximum use of those it has both for irrigation and hydro-electricity production.

The 1981 census established a Greek population of 9.71 million, compared with 8.76 million in 1971, 8.38 million in 1961 and 7.63 million in 1951. The growth by almost a million in the ten years to 1981 was the result mainly of a decline in post-war emigration and the beginning of a move back by temporary migrants to western Europe. The present population is assumed to be around or slightly above 10 million.

During the thirty years from 1951 to 1981 in which the population of Greece rose by 2.08 million, that of Greater Athens alone (Athens, Piraeus and the suburbs of both cities) rose by 1.64 million, from 1.37 million in 1951 to 3.02 million in 1981. The urban population in its entirety rose by more than the total population increase, as a result of migration from villages and islands. It is the causes and effects of this, along with a relatively low birth-rate, which constitute Greece's 'demographic problem'.

Greece Today

The Greeks today, in 1988, are back at school, compulsorily attending the third year of a course in household economics. When they graduate, hopefully next year or the year after, they will have learned that their country, though unbelievably affluent by the local standards of thirty years ago, is not yet sufficiently rich to be able to afford a welfare state of the Anglo–Danish type and, like its people, must live more or less within its means.

It is not a lesson attended with pleasure, as will almost certainly be brought to your attention during your stay. It requires that living standards must fall, not far perhaps, but for the first time in three decades. The natural reaction is a degree of social unrest, and resistance in the form of strikes. You may well find that if the buses are running the trains are not, and if the banks are open the bakeries are closed. You may also observe indications of unemployment and under-employment. Though nothing compared to the times just after the Second World War when close on a million Greeks were driven to permanent or temporary emigration, it is a persistent problem and for that reason disturbing.

If you were in Greece three or five or seven years ago, you will remark how much more crowded the shops and tavernas were then. Only the video clubs, then a rarity, have blossomed since and are continuing to flourish. The Greeks spend more time at home now, not from choice but of necessity, weighed down by bills and taxes and deprived of the buoyancy of wage increases mandatorily in step with inflation and usually a little ahead. However, to appreciate Greece today a rather longer perspective is needed: say thirty years.

Through the eyes of children

In the immediate aftermath of the Second World War and the Greek civil war, and to a diminishing extent until the early 1960s, only an American relief organisation, the Foster Parents Plan, stood between several thousand Greek families and a possibility that normal deprivation could turn at any moment into actual starvation.

In return for $8 a month, then 240 drachmas, and the occasional parcel of food and clothing, the children supported by the Plan had to write a monthly thank-you letter to their 'foster parent'. The letters were translated in Athens, and copies were kept on file. Through the eyes of children between the ages of five and fifteen from every corner of mainland and Peloponnesian Greece and the large and small islands, they made up a body of testimony of what it was like to be alive and poor in Greece in the days when Britain was painfully emerging from austerity, Germany was rebuilding its gutted cities, Australia was welcoming monthly boat-loads of Greek immigrants, and Greece itself was slowly recovering with the help of aid under the Marshall Plan.

Though the files may no longer exist, the tenor of the letters remains in the mind:

● Yesterday I was beaten when I went to school because I had missed lessons for three weeks. But I couldn't return until the chicken laid an egg, because they laugh at me when I haven't got a pencil.

● Thank you for the second blanket. Now that we have two, my sister and I can sleep in one bed and mother in the other.

● Last week we went to father's grave and laid some flowers. It's just three years since the bandits (communist guerrillas) came and shot him because he wouldn't join them. Mother went straight to bed when we got home, and won't stop crying.

● In reply to your question, yes, we did sell our tobacco, but the merchants paid only half as much as last year. So now we shan't be able to buy a goat, to have milk this winter.

● Last week something terrible happened. Mother got a sudden pain in her side in the morning and went to bed, and in the afternoon she died. The doctor came next day so she could be buried, and now we are going to an orphanage.

By the middle of the 1960s Greece had outgrown the need for this form of direct charity, and 240 drachmas had lost their value. The Plan moved elsewhere. But Greece was still a very poor country. A family expected to spend between a third and a half of its income on rent. Jobs were precious, and the unemployed could look only to their families for support; it was not altogether unusual for unsuccessful beggars, or those whose heart was not in it, to be found dead in shop doorways or public conveniences in the depths of winter. Regardless of what the law said, children in the villages, girls especially, were lucky to finish primary school, and to dream of a university education required a courage divorced from reality. There was no health service, or right to a pension, outside the main towns. As late as the 1967-74 military dictatorship, Brigadier Stylianos Pattakos, a country boy himself, could describe the five-day week as a 'Marxist invention'. The trade unions were docile, in the grip of 'fathers of labour' appointed by government, and a six-day week of sixty hours was far preferable to no work at all. On Saturdays, shops did not close till 10 p.m.

In Athens, the present-day apartment blocks were beginning to be built – for the most part, they date from the 1960s. But the mistake should not be made of attributing them to money: they were the result of poverty. Had the state been wealthier, it could have imposed at least elementary town planning regulations. The blocks would not have been constructed side-by-side along narrow streets, each occupying the site of the one- or two-storey house it replaced with never a thought of greenery, simply because the faster they were completed the sooner the tax was collected.

Greeks had always been ambitious to own their own homes; for the poorer, and particularly for those flooding into Athens from the provinces, the construction of a dozen or more apartments on the site of a former one-family house made this an attainable ambition. The condition was that costs should be held down by building small and cutting standards.

The availability of mortgages, through a specialised state bank and some trade union organisations, helped solve the problem of down-payments. The blocks themselves were built under a system that required little or no capital: the owner of a site would exchange it for one or two of the more desirable of the apartments to be built and then move into a rented home for a couple of years, while construction would be financed from the down-payments and ongoing instalments paid by prospective apartment purchasers as the work progressed. Final payments, due on presentation of the key, represented the builder's profits – provided he had managed to keep out of debt.

It meant that apartments were purchased while the block still existed only on paper, or as a hole in the ground; work could begin only when enough down-payments had been received to finance the cost of cement and reinforcing rods. Obviously those who bought the apartments had little control over quality; they were committed to the purchase, had scant hope of recovering their money in the event of a dispute with the builder and, in any case, were concerned above all to move in as quickly as possible to avoid the double haemorrhage of payments and temporary rent which, as likely as not, was driving them into debt.

One result of this lack of planning, and above all of the lack of greenery, was seen in July 1987, when more than 1,000 inhabitants of the 'cement city' which Athens has become died of the effects of a heatwave compounded by air pollution.

Had the purchasers been wealthier, they would not have herded themselves into the apartments out of desperation. They would also have been able to afford the time and money for commuting from satellite towns that the governments would have had the budgetary facility to create. The few architects with vision and a sense of responsibility who saw and drew attention to what was happening to Athens were simply advised to be 'practical'.

The face of change

A quarter of a century ago, the Greeks had heard of television but not yet seen it, dreamed of owning radiograms and considered themselves fortunate if they had a small radio and a separate gramophone. In much of the countryside there was still no electricity. The farmers, with the cooperative movement and collective cultivation emerging only slowly, and with no means of borrowing from banks, either sold their crops at the prices offered or lived by barter among their neighbours.

The city Greek had a 'quarter-pillar' of ice delivered to his home in the morning to help preserve food. Unless it could be done in a saucepan, the housewife took the family's midday meal to the baker for cooking; if she had an oven, she could afford to use it only on Sundays. There were so few cars that Panepistimiou Street, the main Athens thoroughfare, could accommodate two-way traffic with a double tramline down the centre and still have room for bus terminals. The villages were still effectively managed by the old triumvirate of priest, schoolteacher and gendarme; the first two taught acceptance as a spiritual and temporal duty, and the third ran sheepdog on the flock.

Politically, Greece was in the grip of the stern conservative movement, sometimes under one name and sometimes another, that had won the civil war but found difficulty in coming to terms with peace. It correctly assumed that recovery could result only from hard work and foreign investment, and that the latter required compliance with the will of the USA as the new and this time indispensable 'protecting power'. In the allocation of budget resources, successive governments gave absolute priority to electrification, road construction, irrigation and the creation of an industrial infrastructure. Hospitals, universities, public transport and pensions were luxuries that could be deferred.

If this was scarcely a populist policy, elections could usually be won with the help of priest, schoolteacher, gendarme, trade union official, the armed militia (now disbanded) and, if need be, judicious manipulation of the military vote. In any case, it hardly mattered if the occasional election was lost, since the centrist opposition differed only in degree, the Communist Party was in exile until its legalisation in 1974, and the last of the Aegean island internment camps were still a functioning threat. A most effective weapon, cheap and ubiquitous, was the 'certificate of political reliability'. This was a police document testifying, in effect, that its holder was untarnished by left-wing associations; without one, it was impossible to obtain a job in the public sector, a passport or, for a time, even a driving licence.

Eventually, of course, these pressures had to be relaxed. Almost inevitably, the moment was delayed beyond the point of safety. Constantine Karamanlis, who held it all together during eight years that changed the face of Greece and made its ultimate admission to the European Community 'club' a realisable vision, was manoeuvred out of office by the Palace in 1963. Greece descended into political chaos, and in 1967 the fallen fruits of power were picked up by the Colonels; they did not even need to shake the tree.

You should be careful in discussing the dictatorship with casual acquaintances: the scars still itch, and bleed easily. For one thing, there is the question of whether, and to what extent, the Greeks resisted. On the morning after the tanks rolled into central Athens the Greeks discovered from their radios that they had lost their freedom, theoretically their most prized possession. Helen Vlachou – who preferred to close her daily newspaper, *Kathimerini*, rather than submit to censorship – caught the mood of that morning in her book *House Arrest* (1971):

'The night's work had been perfectly timed, admirably well executed, and of a lightning rapidity; but the next day the shrugging indifference of the population of Athens helped it more than military efficiency had done. The people in the streets did not show any kind of concern, did not seem to care one way or the other. It was not a victory for anybody, man or party; it was an all-round defeat for all politicians of all denominations, a philosophically accepted overthrow of a situation that evidently did not appeal to the majority. "Let them have a go," was the feeling of the day.'

The triumvirate of middle-ranking officers – Colonels George Papadopoulos and Nicholas Makarezos, and Brigadier Stylianos Pattakos – had one supreme flaw: they knew how to seize power, and hold on to it, but not what to do with it afterwards. The plot and its execution were everything; they proved themselves simple opportunists, without policy or programme.

The trio held power from April 1967 to November 1973, when they were overthrown by a second junta led by the sinister commander of the Military Police, Brigadier Dimitrios Ioannidis. In more than six years, ruling by the formula 'decide and decree' and with neither Parliament nor public opinion to consider, they had failed to solve even one of the 'structural problems' of Greece's economy and society that still torment elected governments.

Some Greeks will insist that the task was inherently impossible for any dictatorship; others take the view that for this failure alone the three and Ioannidis are deservedly serving sentences of life imprisonment, though these were imposed for the seizure of power, not its misuse.

Certainly they were given a credit of time, by the Greeks and internationally. With some honourable exceptions – far fewer than those who afterwards laid claim to resistance activity – the Greeks preferred to fight back with humour. One of the classic dictatorship jokes may be more revealing than its authors intended. A man on a crowded bus taps a fellow passenger on the shoulder. 'Excuse me, sir, but do you happen to be in the army?' 'No!' 'Perhaps you have a brother in the army?' 'No!' 'Or a son?' 'No!' 'Then in that case, sir, would you mind not standing on my foot?'

The ordinary Greeks had their livings to earn, and their children to educate. They knew how easily they could find themselves ordered to live on an Aegean island, dependent on a family that would be both hungry and harassed because of them. It should cause little surprise if they left the heroics to those who were safely out of the country. But this is not always the way it is told today.

Be careful also when you talk to Greeks about the Polytechnic, the uprising of students at the Athens Polytechnic in November 1973 which was, beyond doubt, the supreme act of resistance, but at the same time was peculiarly inappropriate in its timing and unfortunate in its results.

Bending to pressures from outside Greece, Papadopoulos had already appointed a civilian government that, on the Turkish model and under his guidance as first President of the newly-established Greek republic, would supposedly lead the country back in careful stages towards parliamentary rule. It was this government, and Papadopoulos, which the uprising overthrew; it brought to power a man, Ioannidis, who cared nothing for world opinion and had no fear of killing. There were no more outbreaks of resistance.

Many Greeks had said from the beginning that it was pointless to resist the dictators since in the end they would fall by themselves, thus demonstrating their awareness of their own history. They were proved right in July 1974 when the Ioannidis junta suicided. After it had brought Greece to the edge of a war with Turkey that could have led only to disaster, wiser officers brushed it aside and requested the formation, without conditions, of a civilian government.

Karamanlis returned in triumph from eleven years of self-exile in Paris to restore and consolidate government by the people. Armed with the authority of successive election victories and an unequalled international prestige, he jumped the queue in Brussels and secured Greece's accession to the European Community ahead of Spain and Portugal.

This second time round he lasted for six years. In 1981, failing to appreciate that the 'great change' that had become a national longing had already been made inevitable, though not yet manifest, by Community membership, the Greeks voted for socialism. For four years they were handsomely rewarded; then the bill was presented, late in 1985, and is now being paid.

Since 1974 Greece has been a republic; in a plebiscite late that year 70 per cent of Greeks voted against the monarchy, confirming in a free vote the outcome of a rigged referendum staged by the Colonels the year before. The monarchy, really, had only itself to blame: King Paul, who had succeeded his brother George II, forced the 1963 resignation of Karamanlis shortly before his own death, and two years later his son, Constantine, did the same to the Centrist Prime Minister George Papandreou, the late father of the present Prime Minister Andreas Papandreou. Constantine himself went into exile in December 1967 after the failure of an ill-planned attempt to overthrow the dictatorship that, in any case, was undertaken too late to earn his redemption; he had to fight his 1974 campaign from London. In the circumstances, it was surprising that even three out of every ten Greeks voted for him.

Under the 1975 Constitution, presidents are elected by Parliament for five-year terms: that of the present head of state, Christos Sartzetakis, expires in 1990.

The political situation

In view of the Greeks' obsession with politics and their sense of deprivation if a year goes by without an election – general, local or European Parliament – it may seem strange at first that they are only now beginning to acquire a recognisable party system. In a country where everything is politicised, the professional politician can sometimes appear curiously apolitical to those accustomed to equate politics with parties of principle.

Except for the Communist Party of Greece (KKE), which until 1974 was illegal anyway and depended on front organisations, all the parties now represented in the 300-seat, single-chamber Greek Parliament were formed after the fall of the dictatorship.

The conservative New Democracy party, which Karamanlis set up as his vehicle for the 1974 elections, has already established a local record: it has survived three changes of leadership with only minor defections and without a change of name. Its nucleus was the pre-dictatorship National Radical Union, which Karamanlis had created in 1955.

The present ruling party, the Panhellenic Socialist Movement (PASOK), was formed in 1974 by Andreas Papandreou, the Prime Minister, from the left wing of what his father George Papandreou had named the Centre Union when he established it for the 1961 general elections. There is nothing yet to indicate that PASOK will emulate the New Democracy party in outlasting its founder.

The kind of party with which the older, non-communist, Greeks have been brought up, and feel comfortable with, consists of a gathering of Deputies, solidly based in their own constituencies, who have adapted to the parliamentary system the precepts of the racecourse.

Usually, but not necessarily, within the broad confines of right, left or centre, the Deputies identify the one among their peers with the most promising actual or potential track record and place their loyalty at his disposal for as long as he goes on winning. They are students of form, which in politics is graced by the name of charisma, rather than of content. Thus Karamanlis was succeeded as New Democracy leader by George Rallis, who lost one election and went. The same fate awaited Rallis's successor, Evangelos Averof, and would have befallen the present leader, Constantine Mitsotakis, if he had not come close to victory in 1985, and if, by then, New Democracy had not been running short of heirs of the older generation.

Political fluidity is assisted by the absence of a party tradition and the method of leadership elections. The 'parliamentary group', namely the party Deputies, chooses the party leader, and there is no such thing as an annual party conference. Even the architecture of the Parliament building helps party positions to be trimmed: the semi-circular chamber provides benches to be slid along, rather than floors to be crossed.

New Democracy, recognisably conservative under Karamanlis, today follows the policies of the liberal centre in which Mitsotakis served a long apprenticeship. Thanks to the dictatorship, the old right is now associated in the popular mind with neo-fascism, draws a steady three to five per cent of the vote in general elections, is without representation in Parliament and can safely be ignored. For economic rather than political reasons, the ruling Socialists have swung sharply into social democratic channels since 1985, abandoning at least temporarily the policies that brought them two successive election victories in the hope of eventually obtaining a third. This is not found at all confusing: on the contrary, it is the way things have always been.

There is a comparable instability about the voting system. Traditionally, the one under which the next elections will be fought is decided by the government in power a few months before polling day. Since the Second World War, the Greeks have tried all the tested systems: the British winner-takes-all (hurriedly dropped after one experience); simple proportional representation; reinforced proportional representation, and the dictatorship's gun-on-the-table ('Please, sir, would you move your revolver from that pile of papers so that I can take one and vote against you?').

Reinforced PR, which gives bonus seats to the larger parties, appears to have become established, but there is no legal impediment to a switch to the simple PR system demanded by the Communists and the minor parties. The government will decide, shortly before Parliament is prorogued, on the basis of whether it can reasonably hope for another overall majority under the present system or should reconcile itself to leadership of a coalition and therefore let the smaller parties into Parliament.

Nevertheless, changes are under way, presented as reform. In particular, Deputies have had their wings clipped. The number of seats won by each party is still determined by the votes received, but which of the candidates will actually be returned to Parliament is decided by their positions on the party tickets, which in turn is a matter for the leader. Also, in the name of transparency, parties now receive financing from the state budget, in the form of 1,000 million drachmas shared out annually among those represented in Parliament, in return for which they are required to reveal their other sources of income. Transparency, however, has not yet been extended to campaign spending. Parliaments are elected for four years. If the present government can endure its current adversities, the next general elections will be held in the early summer of 1989.

The national issues

Taking it for granted that you do not intend to adopt a vow of silence while in Greece, there are two issues on which it would certainly be useful to be able to converse intelligently. They are not only at the forefront of Greek attention but, to a remarkable extent, above and outside the daily political battle. They are *Ta Turkika* and *Ta Kypriaka*, matters connected with Turkey and Cyprus. They are closely interwoven, and it is unlikely that either can be solved except as part of a package.

Ta Turkika   Despite the legacy of smouldering animosity, the present confrontationary situation in Greek–Turkish relations arises directly from the events of a single year, 1974. On a winter's day early in the year the Prime Minister of the Ioannidis junta went to Kavala in northern Greece to announce, with the equivalent of a clash of cymbals and roll of kettledrums, that Greece had struck it rich.

An international consortium of oil companies working under a Greek state concession, he proclaimed, had located immense quantities of commercially exploitable oil offshore near the island of Thassos – the so-called 'Prinos' field. Oil had indeed been found, but not of a particularly good quality (it was heavily larded with sulphur) and not in particularly large quantities (an estimated nine million tons). It was enough to cover about 10 per cent of Greece's annual requirements until the early 1990s. And it was enough to whet the appetite of its neighbour across the Aegean.

At that time, not one Greek in 100,000 would have known what you were talking about if you had tried to interest him in the 'continental shelf'. Now, it is you who will be expected to be familiar with the *ifalokripida*. Weather maps on Greek television show an Aegean Sea that has no eastern shore; beyond the Greek islands, nothing. In fact, of course, there is the whole Anatolian coast of Turkey, at some points only an easy swim from the closest Greek islands. So who owns the continental shelf?

On the basis of a 1958 Geneva Convention and the 1982 Law of the Sea, the Greeks do, since islands have their own continental shelves. Turkey, which has not ratified the Law of the Sea (but neither has the United States), responds that the Aegean is a special situation since the mainland coast of Turkey is as long as that of Greece. Refusing to concede 97 per cent of the shelf to Greece under the Law of the Sea formula, it demands half on the principle of equity, and proposes political negotiations on a division.

The Greeks are ready to go to the International Court of Justice at The Hague, but solely for demarcation of the shelf under the provisions of the 1982 law. The result is a stalemate, broken by occasional flares of crisis. In effect, each country has had to desist from further exploration outside its own territorial waters, for fear of starting a war, and whatever oil the shelf may contain remains undiscovered.

More emotively, to the Greeks the Aegean, with its 2,000 Greek islands, is a Greek archipelago through which the Turks are free to pass, but no more. To the Turks, it is intolerable that they should be confined to the eastern edges of a 'Greek lake'.

The dispute provides an obvious temptation for Turkey to occupy the islands east of the mid-Aegean, including the Dodecanese group, Chios, Samos, Mytilene, Limnos and Samothrace. Convinced that Turkey would if it could, and asking why else it has an 'Army of the Aegean' along the Anatolian coast supplied with landing-craft, the Greeks have fortified the islands and spend a greater proportion of their gross national product on defence than any other NATO country except the United States.

Inability to resolve the main dispute has encouraged the emergence of secondary issues. Thus, *ta Turkika* today also embraces questions of airspace and civilian air corridors over the Aegean, command control on and over the sea, the militarisation of Greek islands close to the Turkish coast (Greece insists on the supremacy of the unwritten law of self-defence), and allegations by Ankara concerning Greece's treatment of the Muslim minority in Thrace.

But the brush with disaster in the spring of 1987, when the two countries came closer to war than at any time since 1974, was over oil exploration. The Turks moved a seismic research ship into the North Aegean, the Greeks said it would be 'prevented' if exploration were carried out beyond Turkish territorial waters, and Ankara responded that force would be met with force. In the end, the vessel engaged in no tests outside Turkish waters, and the countries' Prime Ministers embarked on a form of 'dialogue' through an exchange of letters. But the letters addressed one issue only: the continental shelf.

The shelf remains at the heart of the dispute, the most likely spark of a war in cold blood, and the essential component of any eventual package agreement.

In the watershed year of 1974, as the late Archbishop Makarios once told them pointedly from a balcony overlooking Constitution Square, the Greeks recovered their democratic freedoms but the cost was paid by Cyprus. In July of that year the Ioannidis junta mounted a coup in Cyprus intended to depose and murder the Archbishop and make the island part of Greece – the old dream of *enosis* (union) which had been quietly abandoned in favour of statehood once the British had left in 1960.

The Turkish response, justifiable under the treaties that established the independence of Cyprus, was to invade and occupy the northern third of the island to protect the 18 per cent Turkish-Cypriot minority of the population. Greece and Turkey stood on the edge of war, the junta collapsed, and Karamanlis returned.

The Turks did not withdraw from Cyprus once the danger of *enosis* had been averted; instead, they are still there in defiance of the United Nations. They have established an 'independent state' in the north of the island that only Turkey itself recognises, have introduced thousands of settlers from the mainland to take over expropriated Greek-Cypriot property, and have built up an armed presence that is a clear threat to the rest of the island. Athens has warned that any attempt to move south will lead to a Greek–Turkish war.

The Cyprus stalemate explains Greece's determination to erect barriers against any improvement of Turkish relations with the European Community and, above all, to block Turkish membership. To the Greeks, the only military threat they face comes from Turkey, from a member of the alliance that they believe to be favoured by the USA and NATO because of its geographic proximity to the USSR and its supposedly greater strategic and numerical contribution to western defence. In these circumstances, a degree of anti-Americanism is understandable. But this never extends to the individual American visitor; the Greeks personalise their politics, not their animosities.

Current economic distress

As you move about the country, you will almost certainly become aware – from strikes, protest marches and conversation – that Greece is attempting to 'stabilise' its economy. Three months after winning a second four-year term under the slogan 'even better days to come' (a slogan which quickly became a dependable music-hall joke), the socialist government was forced to initiate an austerity programme amounting to adoption of basic New Democracy policies that the electorate had just been persuaded by Mr Papandreou to reject.

Internationally, Greece was approaching the position where it could no longer borrow the $3,000 million a year that it then needed to cover its foreign deficits and loan servicing. Domestically, the government faced one of the highest public sector deficits in western Europe (18 per cent of gross domestic product) and a 25 per cent inflation rate matched by wage indexation (the automatic adjustment of incomes to the consumer price index) that was making Greek products unsaleable abroad and vulnerable on the home market to European Community imports.

The government faced the choice of either restoring the competitiveness of Greek products internationally, or re-erecting the old tariff barriers that had had to be dismantled with Community accession. Despite campaign promises of a referendum on continued Community membership, there was really no choice at all: far too much money was coming in from Brussels to make withdrawal a practical option, and without withdrawal there could be no return to protectionism. The stabilisation programme adopted in October 1985 had the apparently modest aims of reducing the foreign borrowing requirement to the amount needed to service existing debt, bring inflation down to 10 per cent, and cut the public sector deficit also to 10 per cent of gross domestic product, by 1988.

In pursuit of these aims, the drachma was first devalued and then allowed to depreciate by the difference between Greek and average Community inflation so as to make exports more competitive and imports more expensive (and also your holiday cheaper in terms of your own currency). Indexation was watered down by the imposition of ceilings well below inflation on permissible wage increases, taxes were increased, and the public utilities and state corporations (electricity, water, telephones, the post office and most forms of public transport) were required to come closer to balancing their budgets by charging more for their services.

Inevitably, this placed a disproportionate burden on lower- and middle-income Greeks, especially on those living on wages, salaries and pensions. The result was a predictable discontent. New Democracy, unable to attack the policies directly since it had advocated them, could only complain that they were not accompanied by cuts in state spending and did not address the larger problem of development through stimulation of domestic and foreign investment and reducing the size of the public sector by privatisation. Certainly there has been only insignificant investment for at least the past ten years, but whether this is due to a shortage of money or a lack of trust in the socialist state is a matter of dispute.

If the failure of PASOK's policies becomes apparent during 1988, and presuming that the government will be unable to divert attention from the economy through some kind of triumph over the Turks, New Democracy may reasonably anticipate an early opportunity to test its own theory. This is that once the socialist parenthesis has been closed Greek and foreign investment will pour in for the creation of new industries and the modernisation of services. Unemployment will be eradicated and Greece will become the Switzerland of the Mediterranean.

In Greece, one does not do things by halves.

Black and shades of grey

There are three permanent peculiarities of the Greek economy, which stem from a deep-seated contradiction in the Greek character and the readiness of successive governments to swim with the current.

● Every Greek dreams of owning his own business, or at least of being self-employed. If he has to settle for something less, he wants to work for the state.

● Though Greece owes all its very considerable industrialisation over the past quarter-century to private enterprise, every government since the collapse of the dictatorship has sought votes through expansion of the public sector.

● Greece has a black economy that is not only unusually large by any standards but those of Italy, but that is also the mainstay of state budgets to which, theoretically, it makes no contribution. Greece would very probably be bankrupt if it were not for tax evasion.

The black economy is something which you, as a visitor, will make contact with at every turn of the road. On a beach, you will rent a chair and sunshade from someone of whom the tax authorities know nothing. Buy something from a small shop, not a supermarket, and you will probably see your money go into an ever-open till underneath a cash register that is there only in case of inspection. If you need to visit a doctor, do not expect a receipt. If you have the misfortune to break a tooth or lose a filling you may be offered two prices, one with and the other without a receipt.

Bowing to the inescapable, the government taxes members of the liberal and fix-it professions – in essence all the self-employed from physicians to plumbers and from engineers to electricians – on the basis of their declarations only if they are above an assumed minimum income that is arbitrarily determined. Effectively, therefore, all income above the minimum level may well be untaxed: to the victors go the spoils. Addressing a Foreign Press Association lunch a few years after the collapse of the dictatorship, a conservative Finance Minister lamented the fact that, 'to the ordinary Greek, tax evasion is a form of national resistance.' He should scarcely have found this surprising.

Between black and white there is a large grey area. Agricultural income in practice and bank interest by law are exempt from tax, the former because of the difficulty and cost of collection rather than any remaining poverty gap, and the latter because otherwise the Greeks would not save the money the government needs to borrow to finance budget deficits. (Supposedly farmers are taxed, but the exempt allowances are set so high that few admit to reaching the ceiling.)

Greek wage and salary earners and pensioners, meanwhile, taxed to the limits of their endurance, cannot see all that much difference between the plumber who gives them no receipt and the neighbour who lives comfortably on the tax-free 18 per cent annual interest, paid monthly, from his nest-egg of five million drachmas that he probably accumulated through tax evasion in the first place. It scarcely gives the dodger a bad name.

The Greek who cannot work for himself wants to work for the state because of security of tenure and a guaranteed pension after thirty-five years of service, regardless of age. The wider public sector now embraces all the utilities, all forms of public transport except taxis and some coastal ferries, 90 per cent of the banking system and, through nationalisation and the creation of state and local authority enterprises, an increasing proportion of manufacturing. Though New Democracy talks of privatisation, when it was in government it too proved unwilling to forgo the political advantage of expanding the public sector.

Even the Greek who has achieved his ambition of personal incorporation into the public sector will very possibly have a second part-time job in the evening. A bank clerk may keep the accounts of a small business; teachers give 'cramming' lessons, and also turn up as taxi drivers and hotel pianists; your wine waiter could be a lawyer in a state corporation by day. Greeks collect jobs as a security against total unemployment, and because aspirations are higher than salaries. The working hours make it feasible, and the income from the secondary occupation, normally, is not declared; if it were, Greeks would probably stay at home and watch television. The money they now earn would not circulate, and the government would have to look elsewhere for the income from indirect taxes, essentially on consumption, which today accounts for close on two-thirds of budget revenues.

Shortly after the 1981 general election the government successfully outlawed the holding of two jobs in the public sector, but recoiled from its own proposal to extend the prohibition to two jobs in the private sector, or one in each. Though hours are staggered to some extent to relieve traffic congestion, Greeks employed in the public sector can expect to go to their offices around 7.30 or 8 a.m., work through without a formal break, and be home for the day by 3 p.m. Lunch and siesta still leave time for a second job before the 11 p.m. late-show at a cinema or the 1 a.m. closure of the cafés.

This explains how a Greek with a wife and two children, earning a good average salary of 80,000 to 100,000 drachmas a month of which from 20 to 30 per cent goes on tax and another 20 per cent on mortgage payments, can afford to engage a language tutor for his children, run a car, spend weekends at his country home, dress himself and his family in imported clothes, and eat well at home and frequently in restaurants. He can also buy a video recorder that costs more than twice as much as in London; the government pockets the *120 per cent* tax, and does not enquire where he found the money.

If he has been a little too ostentatious, he may run foul of life-style criteria when he reports his income. He will then, complainingly, pay the extra tax demanded on the basis of the way he lives, but will insist that the money he has been caught spending came from bank interest. Since banking secrecy is strict in Greece, the assertion is not open to challenge. Any pricking of conscience is quickly anaesthetised by observance of the prodigality with which governments spend tax money, *his* money, in ways that he can easily persuade himself are scandalously wasteful, and that New Democracy now tells him are indeed deplorable. The man outside the system is encouraged to seek not its destruction but his own niche inside it, so as not to be left behind by his neighbours.

The black and grey economies do not simply keep the white one going; they are also the great social safety valve.

The Greek and the family

Though family ties have weakened in the quarter-century that has seen Greece change from a basically agricultural country to one standing on the tripod of agriculture, manufacturing and services, they remain powerful by European comparisons. Traditionally, the family that sticks together in Greece lives in a village, goes to church in a group on Sundays and saints' days, may hold a council to decide anything from the purchase of a cow to a suitor's application for the hand of a daughter, and considers itself collectively responsible for the well-being of all its members. At its worst, this can lead to 'honour killings' and vendettas, of which rare and isolated incidents occur even now in Crete. At its best, it means that the family looks to its own resources, not to the state, when one of its members becomes unemployed, ill or disabled. Twenty-five years ago it had no alternative.

That the Greek family today is in a state of transition and gradual attenuation is explained by the drift to the cities, the growth of a welfare state and the changing position of women.

● **Population drift.** In the thirty years between the census of 1951 and that of 1981, the population of Greater Athens grew by 1.64 million to 3.02 million. With the population of the whole country around 10 million, broadly one Greek in three is an Athenian. Much the same happened in Thessaloniki, and to a lesser extent in the other main cities. There was never any mystery about the reasons for the drift of population to the urban centres: job opportunities, greater financial security and the availability of state services. And at the end of the day, somewhere to go at night.

Clearly, this had to be fought. If the villages were to be abandoned, who would feed the rest of the country? If the lesser islands were depopulated, who would keep out the Turks? There was occasional talk, apparently serious, of imposing a licence requirement for a move to Athens, or some form of 'internal migration tax'. Fortunately, Karamanlis and his successors, including in this instance the Colonels, were wiser than those who offered free advice from coffee-shop tables. They chose the developmental route: new roads, electrification, irrigation, secondary schools first and then universities, rural clinics at least if not full hospitals, and subsidised transport to counter isolation. The process is continuing today in the form of administrative decentralisation. But while it has halted the drift, it has not reversed it, and families remain separated.

● **The welfare state.** Though this is definitely a misnomer in comparison, for example, with Britain or Denmark, Greece may already have overtaken such socially retarded countries as the USA and West Germany. The government's ambition, close to realisation, is that no Greek should be without some form of national insurance cover, providing at least health care and a basic old age pension; less than twenty years ago, this was still the prerogative of the urban worker.

Unemployment relief is patchy, with entitlement to benefit and duration of cover strictly circumscribed. The point has yet to be reached where even those qualifying for maximum family allowances could live better on relief than if they were working. Also, the national health service exists rather on paper than in the realities of new hospitals. However, malnutrition in its various disguises is no longer a common cause of death, and anyone in need of hospital treatment can be sure at least of a bed in a corridor. The Greek in need can now look to state as well as to family.

You may wonder, however, why you are accosted by so many beggars – in crowded buses, the underground to Piraeus and at street corners. Without doubt, some are simply exercising the only profession they have ever known, on beats they have found remunerative, and are unwilling to deprive their regular clients of the opportunity of contentment through charity. At Christmas and Easter they are reinforced by gipsies with babies, some of the latter allegedly rented. But regardless of what you may hear about blind beggars changing into their rags in the stock exchange toilets when the markets close (even the Greeks who give most regularly will often insist that they are being taken), there are undoubtedly isolated pockets of genuine hardship. Whether you give or not is your decision: you will be invited, but at least you will no longer be pestered.

● **The ascent of woman.** The old family was patriarchal in concept, and Greece was a man's world. A family that bred prolifically but with the wrong balance would say it had 'two sons and five burdens', and pitying glances would be cast on the husband of such a wife. The sons had it both good and bad. It would be unthinkable that they should assist with the household chores, clean their own shoes or fetch their slippers. In the fields, the girls picked and they carried, assisted by their donkeys; afterwards, they relaxed in the coffee-shops while their sisters cooked. But they had a price to pay. The daughters had not only to be provided with dowries but married off first; a son would be regarded as disloyal to his family, the worst of charges, if he took a wife before he had secured husbands for his sisters. It made for late marriages, and incessant subdivisions of family land into smaller and smaller holdings.

Women acquired the right to vote only in 1952, and the first woman Deputy took her seat in Parliament the following year – the honour of electing her, in a by-election, went to Thessaloniki; the Parliament elected in 1985 consists of 289 men and 11 women.

The battle for sex equality has already been won legislatively, and remains to be fought only in the psychology of the Greeks. Sex discrimination in career opportunities and at the place of work has been outlawed, and the principle of equal pay established. There are women judges and professors as well as taxi and bus drivers, and women's branches of the police and armed forces; women are theoretically subject to conscription too, but have not been heard to complain over the fact that only volunteers are taken. Women have acquired the right to separate ownership of property after marriage and, in the event of divorce, an equal share of communal property acquired during marriage. They may also, if they wish, retain their maiden names. Other legislation has removed adultery from the category of criminal offences, so making divorce easier, and has placed controls on the 'exploitation' of the female body in advertising.

Far more importantly, all legal underpinning has been removed from the dowry system, while the establishment of thousands of low-cost day-nurseries has made it possible for married women in practice to make use of the equal opportunities provided for them in theory. At the same time, there has been a widening appreciation that the most durable form of dowry, and the only one protected against inflation, is a working wife's salary and eventual pension.

● **The result.** The family today, in the tribal sense, is no longer an economic necessity. It has been dispersed, among towns and villages and from the family home into the cells, in both senses, of small apartments.

And yet it survives. On holiday weekends and in the summer it reunites in the village of origin. In ways that the state cannot, it looks after its own: family influence will be used to find young Costas a job or get him a posting closer to home during his conscription, and it is a rare parent who will be consigned to an old people's home if there is a corner in the city apartment where a bed can be unfolded at night. The difference is that it is now a matter of blood, not survival. To many a modern Greek, his family has become a useful organisation to belong to, but there is definitely life outside.

Religion and the church

Like the family, and because of the same liberation process, the Church too is in a state of flux. Statistically, of every 1,000 Greeks 974 are Christians, and of these 967 belong to the Greek Orthodox Church. Orthodoxy is the established religion and other faiths and creeds are tolerated on condition that they refrain from proselytism – a mandatory abstention that appears to be ignored only by Jehovah's Witnesses.

The Greek Church is autocephalous, divided into seventy-eight dioceses, headed by an Archbishop of Athens and All Greece, and governed by a synod of the hierarchy of which all serving bishops are members. Day-to-day administration is handled by a small 'permanent holy synod' of twelve senior bishops and the Primate. The separate Church of Crete, the bishoprics of the Dodecanese and the Holy Community of Mount Athos are spiritually and administratively subject to the Ecumenical Patriarchate of Constantinople.

The Greek Church derives its income from its very considerable real estate and directly from the state budget; in certain civil matters it is subject to the Ministry of National Education and Religious Affairs. Married men may be ordained as priests, but celibacy is a requirement for higher office.

That said, it becomes a question of influence and power, and of why the Church is being drained of both.

A reformist movement is believed to exist among a section of the clergy, but appears to be dormant: nothing has been heard for several years, for example, of the proposed liberalisation of priestly dress and appearance. Thus the priest continues to be seen only in black ankle-length cassock and pillbox hat, full-bearded and with hair uncut. You may occasionally observe a priest driving a car or sitting, in his canonicals, enjoying a glass of wine in a taverna. But you will not find one serving on a local authority as an elected member, or getting out among his parishioners in ways you would expect at home.

Aloofness at a personal level, at a time of rapid changes in society, has been accompanied by misfortune in the choice of issues on which the Church has taken a stand in relations with the state. Two particularly significant and popular reforms instituted since the socialist election victory in 1981, both initially resisted by the Church hierarchy but finally accepted under threat, introduced civil marriage as a second ceremony or an alternative to religious rites, and legalised abortion.

Civil marriage, apart from relieving the irreligious of compulsory hypocrisy, had the side-effect of legitimising the position of thousands of Greeks in the communities abroad who, having been married only in civil ceremonies, were regarded under Greek civil law and in the eyes of the Church as unmarried when they came to Greece; their children were therefore illegitimate, and had only restricted inheritance rights.

Legalisation of abortion amounted simply, but emotively, to recognition of an existing situation. Though figures of 250,000–300,000 abortions a year and 'three abortions for every live birth' quoted during debate on the legislation were obviously no more than estimates, there has never been any doubt that abortion was, and is, the most common form of birth control and family planning in Greece. The Church understandably regards it as tantamount to murder, but could offer only doctrinal arguments to the basic observation that if the embryo was going to be slaughtered anyway at least the mother should be protected from the danger of botched interventions carried out secretly, and both parents should be protected from the risk of blackmail. The only real losers from legalisation were those doctors who saw their income fall, as the fees for abortions plummeted and also became reportable for tax.

It is partly in deference to the Church that even now, despite AIDS, the condom is neither mentionable on television, advertised nor displayed for sale: *profylaktika* is still a whispered purchase, whether from a chemist or a newspaper and cigarette kiosk.

In 1987 the Church again found itself on the losing side in an argument with the state over compulsory distribution of unexploited agricultural land. Technically, the dispute was over whether the land should go to individual landless farm workers or to farm cooperatives, but this was a finer point lost on most Greeks, to whom it seemed simply that the Church was resolved to keep what it held.

Not surprisingly, given its militant traditions, the Church does not support pacifism, and accepts the need for continued conscription. The lack of a 'but' to soften the 'yes' costs it sympathy.

In the last thirty years the Church has lost much of its authority within a rapidly developing society, and has seen its regular Sunday congregations become increasingly elderly. Even Easters are no longer what they used to be: the midnight resurrection services on the Saturday, held in the open air, are still heavily attended, but few now stay longer than ten minutes to hear the *Christos Anesti* ('Christ is

Risen'), light their white candles, exchange kisses and set off fire-
works. And a growing number of them go to church after, not before,
they have eaten their Easter soup – the traditional breaking of the
Lenten fast that only their grandparents will have observed. Athens
municipality has ceased to drape the street lamps in black tulle on
Good Friday and lovers of classical music, to whom Holy Week was
an annual oasis in the desert of Greek television and radio, no longer
enjoy a respite from soap operas and politics.

If you had been travelling in a crowded bus in Athens a few years
ago, and a priest had got on, you would have remarked the alacrity
with which the passengers competed to offer him a seat. Now, unless
he is very old and of saintly appearance, his entry has the peculiar
effect of turning a humdrum city street, observable through the
windows, into a fascinating panorama. Eventually, someone will
catch his eye, and the offer will be made; the fact that a younger priest
will occasionally reject it may well be a good sign for the future.

The impact of tourism

The rapid changes in Greece over the past thirty years have been
accompanied, and to some extent influenced, by the growth of tourism
from a movement of a few hundred thousand to close on eight million
a year. But first, a clarification: to the Greek National Statistics
Service, a tourist is anyone entering Greece on a foreign passport,
including Greeks from the communities abroad and foreign businessmen operating out of Athens who, if they happen to travel monthly,
become twelve tourists a year. But while this may swell the numbers,
it scarcely affects the growth rates. It certainly does not alleviate the
responsibilities which you, the holidaymaker pure and simple, must
share for what you have wrought.

Thirty years ago you came to Greece by boat from Marseilles (there
were no ferries from Italian east coast ports to Patras), by the old
Simplon Orient Express (the part of it that ended in Athens and not
Istanbul), or by air to Athens, the only Greek destination to which you
could fly. If you were adventurous, you might then hazard the twenty-
four-hour voyage from Piraeus to Rhodes or Corfu; otherwise, you
would settle for a visit to one of the offshore islands – Aegina, Poros,
Hydra or Spetses. There were no day cruises. In Athens you had a
choice among six de-luxe hotels; in Rhodes or Corfu you had to settle
for much less.

In those days you did not come for the swimming, and probably did
not come at all unless you were drawn by the antiquities. If you did
pack a swimming costume, you took your dip from a free public beach
that did not provide any facilities.

In Athens at least, you could eat well – possibly better than today in terms of quality and service. Apart from your hotel there were about a dozen really excellent restaurants (barely half of them in existence today among the scores of new ones), and in the evening Plaka awaited you. Since the restaurants relied on Greek business they had to be good.

You could not have dreamed of a cruise. Andreas and George Potamianos, whose Epirotiki Lines is today the world's largest family-owned cruise-ship company, had still to purchase the long-gone Semiramis that, waddling across to Myconos, became the first Greek cruise-liner ever to sail out of Piraeus on a regular schedule.

In the villages, you were such a rare sight that you could expect to be greeted by old ladies with cries of *Evghè* ('Glory be!'), on the assumption that you were one of the legendary tribes, known sometimes as 'Lordi' and sometimes as 'Imiluds'. Since you were presumed normally to ride a horse, you would at least be offered a donkey. In short, you made no impact on the economy or on Greek society.

But now, to accommodate you, hotels have been built in every corner of the mainland and on all but the tiniest of the islands. There is no part of Greece you cannot reach easily, safely and quickly. You have become a principal support of the Greek economy: you bring in more than $2,000 million a year, double the contribution of the Greek merchant marine and half as much as Greece's total exports.

By coming earlier and staying later (from Easter to October instead of June to late August), you are the great safety valve against unemployment. The Greeks who serve you would be delighted to see you in the winter also, but in the meantime are prepared to consider themselves employed if they have well-paid jobs for seven months of the year.

Because of you, at least a smattering of English has become almost essential for a young Greek seeking a job in any of the businesses or services with which you are likely to come into contact. European Community accession has accelerated and expanded this process, but you began it. You have also brought with you some of your modern ways, and to some extent have disfigured the landscape and disoriented society.

Possibly the worst and best thing you did was to make the ordinary young Greek feel, first, a sense of inferiority and then, when he sat down and thought about it, a determination to reach your standards. It was not your fault that you made him feel poor in his own country; you could not be expected to live austerely just because he had to, especially when you were on holiday. But he looked at your ample wardrobe (you yourself travelled in style in those days) and thought of his one Sunday suit. He contrasted your meals with what he got at home, and observed the equanimity with which you paid bills that would have bankrupted him for a month. He did not always appreciate that when you hailed a taxi for a thirty-mile drive it was because you had no idea where to find a bus.

As you grew in numbers, the socialist and communist parties pounced on the opportunities you offered. One of the central themes of their campaign against European Community accession (others included the alleged interdependence of the Community and NATO and the unpreparedness of the Greek economy) was that membership would turn Greece into 'the holiday camp of Europe' and the Greeks into 'a nation of waiters'. For considerations that were never made entirely clear, this was presented as the ultimate degradation.

With similar innocence, and equally unknowingly, you were also chipping away at what some Greeks regarded as their moral standards. What was normal for your beaches was revolutionary indeed for theirs. Before your arrival, the bikini was unknown. Now you have imposed the monokini, and it is only a matter of time before your *pan-kat* (the Greek for skinny dipping, from the words for above and below, *epano* and *kato*) bursts out of its Myconos beach-heads. Before you came, a nipple in a photograph could get a newspaper editor arrested. Just look at the kiosks now!

You helped to liberate young girls and widows, the former from their chaperone brothers and the latter from everlasting black. You even taught the Greeks to drink between meals, and introduced them to beer; just about the last barrier still to fall is that against public drunkenness. Before tourism, one small nineteenth-century brewery in central Athens covered Greece's total needs in beer and still relied for solvency on the manufacture of household ice. Wine was the daily drink with meals, and ouzo the only aperitif. Beer was for celebrations, whisky was exclusive to snob bars, and the customary order at a café or cinema, if not coffee, was a lemonade, ice cream or cake.

Now, it is an underprivileged family indeed that does not make its regular contribution to keeping Scotland afloat. Beer is drunk as often as wine. Even the coffee has changed, from what was then Turkish and subsequently rechristened Greek to ordinary instant. Though Greek coffee by law is available wherever any coffee is served, not one of the cavernous coffee-shops of central Athens which used to serve no other form, and which were the places where politicians gathered to consult the electorate across a table, has survived your invasion.

On the principle that nothing can be envisaged until it has been seen, hotels of concrete and glass had to be erected along beaches and in tiny bays before it was appreciated what they were doing to the landscape. Controls then followed, but the eyesores remain.

So too does the neon lighting, in which the economical Greeks invested only because word-of-mouth requires a common language. Thirty years ago Plaka in Athens was a peaceful nineteenth-century haven; fifteen years ago it was a garish nightmare, in which every nightclub and taverna competed against its neighbour with the brightness of its lights and the volume of its amplifiers; today, because even you were frightened away along with the Greeks, it is becoming quiet and tranquil again.

In summary, you have rescued the economy, provided sufficient jobs to make emigration unnecessary, helped to narrow the divisions between Athens and the rest of Greece by going everywhere and needing to be supplied with the means of spending your money, ruined some of the most beautiful landscapes, inculcated discontent, promoted communism and, on the islands at least, built a new Greece more or less in your own image. God bless and shame on you!

Where to from here?

What changes may you expect to see in Greece in the next five or ten years? Agriculture, already breathing with new lungs, will switch more decisively towards the luxury and early-season products that fetch the best prices on European markets, with a further increase in the role of the cooperative movement in production, processing and marketing. There will be a greater consolidation of holdings, and the old-style peasant farmer will become still more of an anachronism. Thanks also to the European Community's Integrated Mediterranean Programmes, the provinces will become visibly more affluent and better provided with services, and the so-far tentative beginning of a population move back from the towns should be gathering speed.

Hopelessly unviable traditional industries – the ones that are floundering – will have to sink, and their place be taken by smaller enterprises based on modern technology and less dependent on proximity to urban conglomerations. This is already happening, and should accelerate once investors gain confidence that the present swing away from extreme socialism is not just a tactical manoeuvre. So you will see industry where now there is only agriculture.

Having ceased to equate the tourism industry with goat-breeding as equal indicators of backwardness, and through appropriate use of Community funds, the Greeks should be well on the way to creating the infrastructure that will permit them to mount a challenge for the upmarket segment of the tourist movement: conventions, incentive travel, special-interest tours and business deriving from the exploitation of spas and yachting. As reliance on cut-price package tours is reduced, more good hotels will be built outside Athens and the main resorts, offering services of the standards demanded by those prepared to pay for them. More of you will be visiting Greece through time-share arrangements, legalised only in 1986.

On arrival, you will find considerable improvements at Athens and provincial airports, even if the proposed new Athens International

Airport is still in its third decade on the drawing boards. You will drive your own or your hired car along safer motorways and, if your choice is a coach tour, will be carried in far greater comfort. The yachtsmen among you will have more and larger marinas to choose from, and even the humble ferries to the islands should have been replaced, under fleet renewal plans, by ships of rather higher standards. Already the Athens air is improving, and the *nephos*, the notorious smog, strikes less frequently.

Unless the opportunities are to be wasted again, you should also find a larger foreign presence throughout Greece. This is a somewhat contentious subject, and no government since the dictatorship can take particular pride in the way it has been handled. Geographically, as a Community country abutting the Balkans and close to the Middle East, Greece ought to be at once a crossroads for the movement of trade, a manufacturing centre for exports in all three directions, and an international banking, insurance and general business centre of the kind that Beirut once was. So far it is none of these things, to the distress of the real philhellenes.

The greatest single obstacle to internationalisation has taken the form of over-regulation, attributable as much to an ingrained, psychotic fear of foreign competition as, in recent years, to socialist precepts. Under Community pressure, a start has been made on dismantling the barriers to the free movement of goods and services, and those that remain will presumably have to go by, or soon after, 1992 as the unified internal market becomes a reality.

For the moment, the foreign presence is largely a matter of banks, a steady 250 'offshore' companies, shipping services provided in Piraeus, and a few restaurants and bars opened by Community nationals who have been prepared to demand their rights and present a thick skin to bureaucratic obstructionism.

Athens could easily accommodate and serve a far larger foreign community; it has the quality housing and office accommodation, foreign schools, adaptable workforce and management potential represented by the thousands of Greeks brought up or educated abroad and fluent in languages. It has the infrastructure in terms of air links and telecommunications. Even the climate is propitious.

If you find the Greeks have overcome their xenophobia and have begun to think of themselves as Europeans, you will know that the country is not just at the end of the runway but has actually taken off.

Attitudes towards the law

Though it has no serious crime problem, Greece is notoriously not a law-abiding country, for reasons that spring from history and are reinforced by tradition. Despite a common tendency to exaggerate the degree to which the 400 years of Turkish hegemony that ended more than 150 years ago may still be blamed for modern attitudes, the period of 'the yoke' was one in which, for the ordinary Greek, the only available expression of patriotism between revolts was quiet defiance. He learned the importance of stubborn non-cooperation, and outlooks that have become part of the national subconscious are difficult to eradicate. He learned also to distinguish between laws that must be obeyed, and those that can safely be ignored.

The axiom that bad money drives out good has been demonstrated more than once in Greece (barely twenty years ago the most respected currency, welcome in restaurants and alone acceptable in sale and purchase of real estate, was the British gold sovereign); Greek experience suggests that something similar may apply to legislation. One result of European Community membership and economic difficulties has been the emergence of 'productivity' as the catchword of the moment. For Parliament, productivity is measured by the yardstick of laws enacted. Provided their number is sufficiently impressive, the 300 Deputies can feel themselves secure against accusations of indolence; the content and enforceability of the laws are of lesser importance.

Names and language Thousands of shops in Athens and the resort islands flout a law that was passed with a flourish of trumpets but will probably never be applied; the conflict arose out of concern for the Greek language. As the tourist movement grew in numbers and expanded in destinations, it was only natural that shopkeepers, restaurateurs, proprietors of fast-food outlets and bar and nightclub owners should be moved by their sense of politeness and business acumen to anglicise themselves. This led to expressions of concern among academics and in the correspondence columns of the quality press, which in the early 1980s found an echo in Parliament. The conviction spread that a stand must be taken, the tide must be turned – the names must be *Greek*.

It was not the kind of suggestion to be opposed frivolously, especially since a similar campaign was being fought in France at that time. When realism collided with patriotism, it was no contest. Language is at least as sensitive an issue in Greece as in France. It is commonly asserted that Greece as a nation might not have survived 'the 400 years' but for the secret schools, mostly run by village priests, which preserved the Greek language. It is less than a century since the last language riots in Athens, over the encroachment of spoken 'demotic' Greek into the preserves of the formal *katharevousa*. Even in the last fifteen years there has been sometimes bitter argument over the adoption of demotic by the state services and the simplification of written Greek through the use of a single uniform accent to indicate stress.

It was therefore only to be expected that once the new threat from foreign names had been identified, legislation should follow. Parliament decreed that, from a specified date, all foreign names above business premises or in neon advertising would become illegal unless surmounted by a larger sign giving the name in Greek. The final date for compliance, though several times extended, has long since passed. Nothing has changed, and there has not been one reported instance of prosecution.

Knowing which

When a country wallows in legislation, the trick is to identify which law is being applied at any particular moment. A driver may park his car on the pavement outside his home for years with perfect impunity, and then receive three tickets within a week and possibly find his plates removed as well. So he seeks out another pavement, until his own recovers its immunity.

At another moment, he may find it temporarily expedient to wear the seatbelts that are legally compulsory at all times. When word spreads that decibels are being measured again, boys with their first motorcycles replace the silencers that take away half the fun. Similar whispers tell householders when it would be safer to put out their rubbish in specially purchased black plastic sacks instead of supermarket carrier-bags.

Of greater relevance to the tourist, it has been quietly impressed on the individual policeman that his ambitions will not be furthered if he allows himself actually to notice certain things that in law he is required to prevent, such as toplessness on beaches anywhere, or nudity even on the most remote.

In Athens there are now more than twenty cinemas, five of them in the immediate vicinity of Omonia Square, showing totally illegal hard-core pornography from 9 a.m. to midnight, for very low admission fees. They used to be raided at regular intervals, but now a policeman is more likely to be found in the audience than clamping handcuffs on the projectionist. The pornographic magazines displayed by Athens kiosks are equally illegal, though only a shop that sold them in the privacy of a back room, away from the gaze of children, would today run any risk of being raided.

Much of the blame or credit for these changing attitudes lies with tourism, and Greece's reluctance to expose itself to adverse publicity abroad. Also, the advent to power in 1981 of the first socialist government in Greek history has brought with it an increased emphasis on personal freedom. This is seen in the view now taken of homosexuality and also in the protest marches, once a rarity, that disrupt Athens traffic two or three nights a week in fine weather. The government may appear to be more unpopular than any of its predecessors, but in fact it is simply less protected from sidewalk dissent.

The law and the sidewalk

The pavements of Athens offer a wealth of testimony to some modern Greek characteristics. Not many years ago, a Scottish policeman on holiday in Athens accepted a challenge to stroll 200 yards in central Athens and mentally collate the summonses that could have

been served under British law. He said afterwards he regretted he had
not studied higher mathematics: there were potholes of apparent
venerability; new excavations unprotected by fencing and without
warning lights; loose paving slabs; all manner of obstructions; danger-
ously low awnings and traffic signs; and litter everywhere, except in
the baskets provided by the municipality.

The offences were no less actual under Greek law; they were simply
not part of the legislation that was being enforced then, or ever since.
They also said something for the lack of planning and coordination to
which the Greeks will readily plead guilty; the municipality may justifiably observe that as soon as it fills in holes left by one public utility
new ones are opened in the same place by another, but when it does
send in its teams to repair a pavement there is no question of providing
a temporary walkway.

In protecting oneself from crimes committed not on but by the
streets of Athens, the most valuable attribute is an alert subconscious
that remembers more than it conveys to the attention. But this takes
time and repeated passage along the same route. In the interim, it is
advisable to forget about conversation. Try to look up, down and
sideways at the same time, and pack an elastic bandage before setting
out for Greece.

The Athens municipality itself, with the best of intentions, has
made a significant contribution to pedestrian insecurity. In compensation for the paucity of parks and gardens, it has planted thousands of
trees along almost every street. Unfortunately, those employed to
prune them have either been issued with short ladders or have not had
their attention drawn to differences in height between the average
tourist and the average Athenian.

One last word on walking: it would be reckless to assume that the
safest place to cross a street is the place designated. Greek traffic lights
are provided with the usual little men, known locally as Gregory and
Stamatis from puns on the words for 'Move it!' and 'Stop!' When red
Stamatis gives way to green Gregory, you still wait to make sure the
traffic has really stopped before venturing on to the pedestrian crossing, and then you really go *grigora*. Pedestrian crossings without traffic
lights should be regarded as purely decorative.

You can also very easily be run over by a motorcyclist for whom an
uncongested pavement is an irresistible temptation in a traffic jam.
Supposedly, the pavement is for use only as a vehicle park, but to push
a motorcycle would be unmanly. Similar care is needed when using
the so-called pedestrian malls.

A no-banana republic

The Greeks' casual attitude towards legality – 'if there is a law,
there must be a window' – can lead them to an equally casual acceptance of bad legislation that elsewhere would be laughed out of the
statute book. Consider, for example, the big banana, which to the
Greek state is the modern equivalent of the yellow peril.

Until the 1967 military coup, Greece was a monarchy with bananas, though not necessarily, as some Greeks would have you believe, a banana monarchy. One of the triumvirate of middle-ranking officers who led the coup was Brigadier Stylianos Pattakos, the junta's first Interior Minister. Seeking popularity on his home island of Crete, where some fifty or sixty families were then producing between 600 and 800 tonnes a year of a lemon-flavoured mini-banana which nobody wanted to buy, the Brigadier placed a total ban on banana imports. For his rather more serious offences, Pattakos is now serving a life sentence in the Athens Korydallos jail, but as of the middle of 1987 Greece was still resisting European Community pressure to liberate the banana.

That all elected governments since 1974 have been adamant on this point is attributable to pressure exerted by the powerful apple lobby, which markets – but does not always succeed in selling – about 280,000 tonnes of apples a year. It has persuaded successive Commerce Ministers that if the Greeks were exposed to full-sized bananas the apples would rot on the trees. The big banana did make a brief comeback, as a holiday treat, at Christmas 1977. In three months the Greeks tucked away a normal full year's supply, 50,000 tonnes, and gave the government indigestion. Subsequently, even appeals based on alleged deprivation of human rights were brushed aside.

The travel industry lore maintains that the trail of Greeks on holiday in Europe can be followed by their banana skins. A banana brought back is an appreciated gift even for a teenager, for whom it could be a first experience of the forbidden fruit. A banana brought back? Yes, there is a one-kilo rule: the allowance for anyone entering Greece. Excess bananas are liable to confiscation, unless eaten in the presence of a Customs officer.

You could, of course, try a well-tested method of small-scale evasion that arises naturally from Greek attitudes. You enter Customs carrying an obvious two kilos, to which your attention is drawn. 'Yes,' you agree, 'For me and my wife.' And where is the lady? You point vaguely towards a banana-less woman some distance in front of you. Your real wife, with her two kilos, does the same. Result: four kilos, and a bad law bent.

The Greeks can sometimes be a surprisingly patient people.

Crime – and the lack of it

Crimes 'against the person' are definitely not something you need worry about while in Greece. You may have your pocket picked, especially on a crowded bus, but it is almost inconceivable that you should be mugged.

Consider the average householder. Increasingly, he is learning to secure his apartment with expensive steel-lined doors imported from Italy, triple locks and safety chains. But he is moved by fear of burglary, which is common; not of assault, which is rare. Affluent New Yorkers on Aegean cruises have been known to ask if the gold earrings worn through pierced lobes for formal dinners can safely be retained during trips ashore. The answer is yes: if something cannot be taken stealthily it will not be stolen at all. The grab that takes the ear with the earring simply could not happen in Greece, not so much because it would turn a sentence of six months into one of six years but because it would be wholly out of character. For the same reason you will never be threatened with a knife. Once I was startled to see two officer cadets, one naval and the other air force, in dress uniforms, resort to their ceremonial dirks to determine which was the better service. But that had to do with honour, not crime, and anyway it was a very hot night.

If this is so, you may ask, then why is every bank branch or post office with safety deposit boxes guarded by uniformed police armed with sub-machine guns? The answer is provided by a short but concentrated spate of Chicago-style robberies in the early 1980s. Greek opinion was genuinely shocked, for this was something that had not happened before. Neither has it happened since the guards were assigned.

Police

Until three or four years ago, law enforcement in Greece was shared between the grey-uniformed city police in Athens, Piraeus, Patras and Corfu and the green-uniformed gendarmerie everywhere else. The two forces have now been unified into the blue-uniformed Greek Police (EL-AS for *Elliniki Astonomia*). This obviously makes for greater efficiency and less duplication.

Within the police, there are subdivisions for traffic (white belts and gloves); 'protection of the national currency' (they may check your money when you leave the country); narcotics and the smuggling of antiquities, and 'markets control' (they keep tabs on shops, restaurants and such).

The Aliens Police, to whom you must apply for a residence permit if you are planning more than a holiday in Greece, are a branch of the plain-clothes 'General Security', the detective department. For everyday use, there is the *Ekato* ('One Hundred', named not for its exclusivity but for its telephone number); they make up the flying squad, and are equipped with prowl cars and motorcycles.

Duty officers at the *Ekato* can handle enquiries and requests for assistance in English, and should be dialled if you witness a crime, need an ambulance, accidentally start a fire or are disturbed by noisy neighbours in the 'silence hours' of the night or afternoon siesta. They are polite, patient and seemingly never ruffled, but you should not hold your breath until the car arrives.

There is also a riot squad, equipped with helmets and transparent shields and backed up by water cannon.

Greek police are equipped with pistols and truncheons (known in Greek as 'globs'), but are under strict orders to use the former only if their lives are in imminent danger and the latter with the minimum force required in the circumstances. Most of them, in the cities, also carry two-way radios. A surprising number of policemen now understand enough English to help you if you have lost your way; if they don't, they will usually find someone who does. Instructed since the collapse of the dictatorship to become polite and unfearsome, they now tend to wear their hair proportionately long and bushy.

To avoid unwanted contact with the police, it should be sufficient to observe speed limits, use your seatbelts, never put a child in the front seat of the car, and stay sober. Should the worst happen, remember that his attitude will most probably reflect yours, so stay polite and keep smiling. If you tense up, he will – and then you are halfway towards arrest for the second worst crime a visitor to Greece is ever likely to commit: 'Insulting the Authorities'.

The worst? Just try offering him a bribe!

Drugs

The Greek authorities hope and believe they have succeeded in eliminating any lingering international belief that their country is 'soft' on drugs. But the visitor should bear in mind that, apart possibly from length of sentence, no distinction is made among types of drug, and it is no defence to claim that even a tiny quantity of cannabis was intended solely for personal use.

Although Greece's drugs problem has not attained anything like United States or European dimensions, anxiety over the use of drugs among the young has been made more acute by the AIDS connection. Also, Greece has traditionally been one of the routes along which heroin has reached Europe from the Middle East or Turkey, concealed in cars, trucks, yachts and suitcases.

Two principal weapons are deployed against drug trafficking: close surveillance, including the use of sniffer dogs at airports and land border crossings, and sentences of as much as twenty years if large quantities are involved. Even the shortest sentences are not convertible into fines. In addition, a car in which drugs have been discovered is confiscated.

Purchase of antiquities

If you should decide to purchase an expensive replica of an Ancient Greek statuette or a Byzantine icon, you will be given a certificate that it is a copy. This should be retained in case questions are asked when you leave the country. This rule does not apply to cheaper purchases from handicraft shops.

Greece is concerned to protect its archaeological heritage, a definition covering anything more than a couple of centuries old; sentences for attempted smuggling of antiquities are not much shorter than those for drugs offences. The concern is easily understood: a lucrative market is provided abroad, by private collectors and the less scrupulous museums. The demand is met through finds made by farmers and articles recovered from ancient shipwrecks or stolen from small provincial museums, isolated churches and under-occupied monasteries. While international gangs form the normal link between source and destination, use has occasionally been made of tourists and for this reason the police are watchful.

It should be borne in mind that a pebble picked up at an archaeological site and slipped into the pocket as a souvenir can be regarded as part of the protected heritage. While a guard who sees the action will normally insist only that the pebble or chip of marble be replaced, tourists have been taken to court in Athens for pebble-pocketing at the Acropolis. Though they escape with a fine, they can expect to spend a night in the cells awaiting trial.

It was a 'bad hour'   A last line of defence in a Greek court, one that will secure at least a sympathetic hearing when the situation seems hopeless, is that it was a 'bad hour' (*kaki ora*). This amounts to non-premeditation hung with bells.

In its wider uses, it once kept a British Council teacher out of court. A taverna cat had been importunate, as cats are, and became the subject of a complaint. A waiter, believing in direct action, kicked it out of the door. The teacher walked slowly across to where it had been, and kicked the waiter.

By the time order had been restored, the taverna was abuzz with whispers of *kaki ora*. The teacher apologised, and the waiter agreed not to press charges. Had it gone to court, the outcome would probably have been acquittal or a token fine. For every Greek judge is aware of the narrow line between a threat and its realisation, between a fist brandished and a punch thrown; though few Greeks actually cross that line, those who do have only to say it was a 'bad hour' to be certain they will be listened to with understanding.

Intent is also relevant: 'You surely don't imagine I did it on purpose?' You may expect to hear this from the driver of a car that emerges from a side-street, in defiance of the halt sign, and crashes broadside into your car. You may as well say no more – the 'bad hour' is yours, too.

It does serve to humanise the system.

National and regional characteristics

While Greece is too small and compact a country to have major regional characteristics, the Greeks themselves tend to differentiate among three main groupings: mainland Greeks, island Greeks and 'overseas' Greeks. The last-named are not so much those still living in the communities abroad, who are flattered and supplied with the means of preserving their ethnic identity as if they were indeed a potential fifth column, as those who have repatriated either from choice or by force of circumstances.

**Main-
land
Greeks**
The mainlanders are the ordinary Greeks; those who have become modern in their pursuits and ambitions at the cost of their sense of comradeship, feel themselves oppressed, insult one another with vociferous abandon, and frequently give the impression of regarding any government, even one they voted for, as an occupying power. When you get to know them better, you may find they are not altogether unjustified. It naturally follows that the mainland is particularly disorganised.

**Island
Greeks**
The islanders are reputedly calmer, shrewd rather than crafty, and closer to nature and the sea; their young menfolk are the mainstay of the Greek merchant navy. Until fairly recently, they were only too frequently ambitious to convert themselves into mainlanders; they have now been given less reason to feel isolated, through improved communications, better services, the expansion of the tourist movement and the levelling effect of television. For the most part, they still contrive to live at a more leisurely pace.

Within the islander context, those of the Ionian islands regard themselves as the more cultured – the readiness of considerable numbers of other Greeks to concede this suggests that there might be some truth in it – while inhabitants of the more numerous Aegean islands, from Thassos and Samothrace in the north to the most southerly of the Dodecanese, retort that they at least can keep their women in better order.

Everything is just a little larger than life on Crete, as if the *megalonissos* – the 'big island', and in fact the biggest – were to Greece what Texas is to the United States. The Cretans are a little prouder, a little more generous and hospitable, a little readier to take offence and a little more prepared to die for a cause (consider the novels of Cretan Nikos Kazantzakis and the 1941 Battle of Crete). They provided Greece's greatest modern statesman, Eleftherios Venizelos; the present leader of the opposition is a Cretan, and no prime minister could form a cabinet without at least one Cretan member. In the villages of Crete, national costume is still common and the vendetta is not yet dead; in Athens, any nightclub providing folk dances will include some from Crete. Cretans even tend to write with a larger hand. El Greco was a Cretan, and Zorba 'the Greek' could have come from nowhere else.

**Overseas
Greeks**
Greeks from the communities abroad, for the obvious reasons of education and fluency in languages, are already disproportionately represented in Greece's managerial class; their share is likely to increase still further if governmental hopes of attracting high-technology industries and more international business and services bear fruit. As may be imagined, Greeks from the '*diaspora*' are not particularly well-liked by those who see the plums go into their baskets in the multinationals, the travel industry, foreign and Greek banks and foreign diplomatic missions.

To some extent, they are only living up to their reputations: any Greek will tell you that the Greeks 'do better' abroad than in their own country, work and study harder, are more law-abiding and pay their taxes with greater willingness and honesty. The conclusion drawn is that there must be something wrong with Greece, as state and society; the reaction is a widespread ambition among Greek families of even modest means to send at least their sons abroad for advanced studies and character-building.

Except that Cephalonian names tend to end in *-atos* and Cretan in *-akis* or *-yannis*, inferences of origin cannot safely be drawn from surnames.

Considering all Greeks as one people, some broad generalisations may be hazarded:

● They are such great complainers that they even find fault with the Greek weather. They complain about taxes and the way they are spent, prices and incomes, state services, the bureaucracy and politicians. When all these subjects have been exhausted they will complain about one another and, as a last resort, about themselves.

Karamanlis once made a joke of it, in the days when he was winning one election after another: 'The Greeks', he said, 'swear on the day before that they will never vote for me again, when they go to the polls they re-elect me, and on the morning after they say they will cut off the hand that did it.'

As he almost said, you should beware of taking them too literally. You do not need a particularly close relationship before someone will say to you, 'We are the worst race in the world [*heirotera ratsa tou kosmou*].' A gentle disclaimer is the proper reaction; at most they only half-believe it, in moments of despair.

● They criticise everything Greek, a tendency that leads them to prefer an import, at prices they often cannot afford, to the quite possibly superior and certainly cheaper local equivalent. This explains the profusion of 'boutiques' and the contents of supermarket shelves; it is a characteristic that has resisted years of governmental assault in the form of 'buy Greek' television campaigns based on ridiculing the snobbishness of not doing so.

As a natural corollary, they are outgoing towards foreigners and have a desire to be liked even greater than that of the Americans. They really do have only one word, *xenos*, for both foreigner and guest. Thus they are polite and helpful to the tourist even when inordinately rude to one another.

In this context, hospitality is frequently offered and should be accepted, but with caution. The shared bill is an alien practice to the Greeks. It touches on *philotimo*, literally love of honour but rather closer in meaning to 'face', since an offer to pay half impugns a host's ability to pay all. So accept only what you will be in a position to reciprocate later.

● For a country that invented philosophy, you will find an odd lack of curiosity – except about your personal affairs – and a propensity to view everything in terms of black or white. The idea of fact defined as generally accepted theory does not appeal, and argument, including parliamentary debate, is usually a recital of fixed positions. Very often, a sight not yet seen cannot be worth seeing since otherwise it would have been seen already, and a dish not part of an established household menu cannot be worth tasting for the same reason. Foreign restaurants would die without the foreign community.

● Because there has so often never been quite enough to go round, the Greeks are only now, and reluctantly, learning to wait in line, and given half a chance will still jump a queue. Boarding a bus is a free-for-all, with victory to the sharpest elbows, and you would be unwise to assume a taxi is yours until you are actually inside. A Greek would rather take his custom elsewhere than wait in a queue for service.

● Possibly because of 'the 400 years', the Greeks are curiously reluctant to commit themselves and are not altogether comfortable with a clear situation. 'Protecting one's rear' can often be an excuse for looking only backwards. A civil servant, for example, wants 'the papers' before he will act and 'the papers' generally require at least three signatures because of the safety that numbers provide, so do not expect to complete any business expeditiously. Similarly, you should not assume you can manage anything at all on the telephone; business is transacted face-to-face, across a desk and preferably over coffee.

For similar reasons, a question is likely to be answered with another, leaving to you the responsibility of drawing a conclusion. For example:

You to your hotel porter: 'Will it rain today?'
He: 'Isn't the sun shining?'
You: 'Yes, but will it last?'
He: 'Isn't it August?'

He knows very well it hardly ever does rain in August, but wants to protect himself from the faint possibility that it might.

In a restaurant, you may ask a waiter if there is any roast veal. If he replies, 'Is it on the menu?' instead of 'Certainly!' he probably means there isn't. A Greek takes no pleasure in causing disappointment to a foreigner, so it is for you to judge when his 'tomorrow' should be interpreted as 'never'.

Women travelling alone

Greece is a country where an unaccompanied woman can stroll along a dark street late at night without fear of anything worse than a sprained ankle. The authorities, including those responsible for tourism, take justified pride in the safety of the individual everywhere in Greece.

A woman need not be particularly attractive to anticipate the disguised compliment of a pinch, pat or surreptitious caress in a crowded bus or while waiting to cross a busy street, and she will hear whispered invitations that really amount to no more than the reflex action of young Greeks who consider themselves attractive to all women. A response is not expected, and she will not be pestered.

However, it would be unusual for an entire tourist season to pass without one or two cries of rape. It usually turns out that the rapist had the mistaken impression, in the absence of any other common language, that he was acting on invitation. So beware of any dress or behaviour that could be taken as a come-on. Young Greeks have been known to believe themselves irresistible, and the naïve woman visitor to Rhodes who enquired of a passing Adonis the nearest way to the Colossus should not have been as surprised as she seemed to be when she received the reply, 'But you're looking at me!'

There are occasional outbreaks of bag-snatching in Athens, by youths working in pairs from motorcycles, but increased penalties have made these less frequent in recent years. No woman will be refused service in a restaurant, bar or nightclub because she is unaccompanied.

Homosexuality and unmarried couples

The Greeks like to believe themselves without hypocrisy, which they describe as the 'English vice'; therefore, whatever they may feel about homosexuality in private, in public they behave as if it did not exist.

There are a few 'gay' bars in Athens and the resort islands, and rather more on Myconos. An Athenian woman of sufficient means will enjoy the 'frisson' of being dressed by a homosexual couturier or combed by a homosexual hairdresser, and happily married couples throughout Greece share jokes about homosexual priests and actors. But overt hostility is rare; so too are cross-sector invitations.

These unmalicious attitudes are to some extent threatened by the AIDS virus; there is concern, amounting almost to panic on Myconos, that homosexuality may be about to become bad for tourism and therefore bad for Greece. You should not suggest to a Myconiote, even in jest, that his island may be the future AIDS capital of Europe.

As for unmarried couples, most Greeks really neither know nor care, and would consider it impolite to enquire. They display the normal curiosity over who, in the higher echelons of government and the world of the theatre and cinema, is this week living with whose wife, and are enthusiastic gossips, but ostracism over lack of formal marriage is a rare phenomenon. For a man, the companion of the moment is treated as a wife would be; for a woman, rather greater discretion is required; modern Greece, no matter what the law may say, is still a man's world in spirit. The children of single parents, if not always the parents themselves, now have equal rights in law with those of married couples, and illegitimacy is no longer a social stigma.

Almost every office block offers a 'garconiere' or two – a bed-sitter with kitchenette and bathroom for which the Greeks use the French word, having none of their own; it may be a place of tryst, the establishment of a mistress, the working quarters of a prostitute or the home of a student from the provinces. For those who can afford it, or whose position in society is more sensitive, there are hotel rooms available for indefinite lease. It is almost impossible for a Greek career, even one in politics, to be wrecked by sexual indiscretions.

Arson and terrorism

If you do not wish to contribute towards giving tourism a bad name, you should try to avoid starting fires. Greece is a hot, dry country, with little rain between May and October. It is also intent on preserving the little that remains of its woodland. In July and August in particular, when the *meltemi* wind blows hot from the north, a spark can cause a conflagration; as television spots point out, one tree can make a hundred thousand matches and one match can destroy a hundred thousand trees.

Since the penalties are proportionately high even for accidental arson, care is obviously needed with campfires and cigarette ends; it should also be borne in mind that sunlight focused through a broken bottle can burn down a forest. There are tourists in jail today for forgetting that!

Similarly with terrorism, the Greeks are understandably displeased when visitors who, since they are not resident, are technically tourists, make use of their streets for murdering one another. So you should not take it personally if your bags are searched when you enter Greece.

Gestures

You neither need nor could hope to pick up the deaf-and-dumb language of Greece in the course of a short visit, but there are two gestures which it is advisable to know if you want to avoid misunderstanding. Most Greeks are by now aware that the foreigner's raised right hand to signify 'no, thank you', 'please don't' or 'that's enough' is not to be confused with the almost identical Greek 'sign of the five' that means, in its most polite interpretation, 'damn your eyes!' But in the villages it could still occasion a moment of frigid misapprehension.

If you really do intend to 'give him five', named for the four fingers and thumb that stab in the direction of the face, all you need do is reverse the direction of the gesture for refusal from defensively backward to aggressively forward. You have then administered the worst possible insult that can be offered without use of words; obviously this should be done sparingly, and after due consideration.

The gesture you should not misinterpret is the blown kiss. The head jerks back, the lips open with a sometimes audible pop, and you have been informed that the answer is no, there isn't any, or he's not interested. You have neither been insulted nor made the recipient of an improper proposal.

A few words of Greek

Since the Greek with whom you come into contact has had to struggle hard to learn your language – it would be a mistake to think he picks up a foreign language more easily than the Englishman does, and the only slight advantage he may have is exposure to English through films subtitled in Greek in the cinema and on television – it is only polite to offer him a few words of Greek in exchange. For example, 'thank you' (*efharisto* or, if you prefer, F. Harry Stow), 'good morning' (*kali mera*), 'good evening' (*kali spera*) and 'good night' (*kali nichta*).

Also, you might remember that there is a feminine form for surnames. As a rule of thumb, you convert a man's name ending in *-as* or *-is* into that of his wife or daughter by dropping the final letter (Dimas to Dima, Kapsis to Kapsi); if it ends in *-os*, you convert with an *-ou* and shift the stress one syllable on (Papadopoulos to Papadopoulou). If a man's name ends in *-ou* (for example, Fotiou), obviously his wife's does too. If your guide introduces herself as Miss Papadopoulos, she is simply catering to your assumed ignorance.

A knowledge of Ancient Greek is of little use, except possibly for reading street names and bus destinations.

English is the principal second language, commonly spoken in hotels, restaurants, main post offices and the larger department stores as well as in the upper echelons of the public services. French is the second language mainly of the elderly. Italian is widely understood in the Ionian islands, particularly Corfu, German is spoken by thousands of repatriated migrants, and surprisingly large numbers of Greeks are fluent in Arabic.

An effort should be made to master the alphabet, so that you can find your way around and have a better chance of getting on the right bus.

The alphabet

Alpha	A α	Short as in 'pat'
Beta	B β	Pronounced as V
Gamma	Γ γ	Gutteral G
Delta	Δ δ	Pronounced as soft TH as in 'father'
Epsilon	E ε	Short E
Zita	Z ζ	The English zed
Eta	H η	Long E as in 'heat'
Theta	Θ θ	Pronounced as hard TH as in 'thanks'
Iota	I ι	I as in 'pit'
Kappa	K κ	Simple K
Lambda	Λ λ	Simple L
Mu	M μ	Simple M
Ni	N ν	Simple N
Xi	Ξ ξ	KS as at the end of 'thanks'
Omicron	O o	Short O as in 'hot'
Pi	Π π	Simple P
Rho	P ρ	Simple R
Sigma	Σ σ	Simple S
Taf	T τ	Simple T
Ipsilon	Y υ	Another I as in 'pit', or Y as in 'pity'
Phi	Φ φ	Simple F
Hi	X χ	Simple H
Psi	Ψ ψ	Psee
Omega	Ω ω	Long O as in 'hope'

Note A hard D is written NT, as in Ken Ntontnt (Dodd)
A hard B is written MP, as in Mpomp Hope
OI is pronounced as a long E
AI is pronounced as a short E

The following words and phrases – a vocabulary cut to the bone – should see you through (the second column gives a phonetic transcription, with the stressed syllable underlined):

The courtesies

Good morning	kallymera
Good evening	kallyspera
Goodnight	kallynichta
Goodbye	adio
Hello, goodbye, cheers!	yiasas (yiasou singular or familiar)

Please, don't mention it!	parakalo
Thank you	F. Harry Stow
All right	endaxi
Yes	nai
No	ochi
Maybe	eesos

Basic encounters

Where is . . .?	pou eenai . . .?
How much is . . .?	poso (or poso eenai) . . .?
Too much!	polee
Have you . . .?	ehees?
I want (would like)	thelo

One's bearings

Street	thromos (soft TH)
Avenue	leoforos
Square	plateea

Sustenance (see also 'Eating and Drinking', pp. 89–104)

Food	fagito
Bread	psomee
Water	nero (closer to the late Pandit than the Roman emperor)
Wine	krasi
Beer	beera
Coffee	kafè
Coca Cola	Coca Cola
Waiter	garsonn

Moving about

Restaurant	estiatorio
Hotel	xenotohio (soft TH)
Room	thomati (soft TH)
Post Office	tahithromeeo (soft TH)
Letter	gramma
Stamp	grammatosima
Police	astinomeea
Customs	teloneeo
Passport	diavateerio
Grocery	bakali
Pharmacy	farmakeeon
Doctor	yatros
Dentist	odondoyatros (tooth-doctor)
Entrance	eesothos (soft TH)
Exit	exothos (soft TH)
Car	aftokinito
Bus	leoforeeon
Train	treno

Boat/ship	pleeo
Aeroplane	airoplano (first syllable as in ire for anger)
Garage	garage
Train station	stathmos
Bus station	afetirio
Port	limeen
Airport	airolimeen (first syllable as in ire)
Taxi	taxee
Ticket	eesitirio
What's the time?	tee ora eenai?
Do you speak English?	milatè anglikee
I don't speak Greek	then meelo ellenika
Help!	voeethia!

Counting

One	ena (meea with feminine noun)
Two	thio (soft TH)
Three	treea
Four	tessera
Five	pendè
Six	eksi
Seven	efta
Eight	okto
Nine	ennea
Ten	theka (soft TH)
Eleven	entheka
Twelve	thotheka (initial TH also soft)
Thirteen	thekatria (continue in the same way up to twenty)
Twenty	eekosi
Twenty-one	eekosi-ena (or meea) (continue in the same way up to thirty)
Thirty	trianda
Forty	saranda
Fifty	peneenda
Sixty	exeenda
Seventy	evthomeenda (soft TH)
Eighty	ogthonda (soft TH)
Ninety	eneneenda
Hundred	ekato
Hundred and twenty-one	ekatoeekosiena
Two hundred	thiakosia (soft TH)
Thousand	heeliès
Two thousand	thioheeliathas (both soft TH)
Million	ekatomiria
Billion	thisekatomiria (soft TH)

The Weather and When to Go

Greece is not a large enough country to have major climatic differences between regions. It enjoys a typical Mediterranean climate: a short spring, a long, hot summer and a generally mild winter. The best time of the year to go is between mid-May and the end of September. Rains and cold snaps can be expected from October, but even then they will be interspersed, until around Christmas, with warm, sunny days on which foreigners continue to swim.

January, February and March are likely to be cold and damp everywhere in Greece. The Greeks like winter so little that if they could hibernate they would; when the black arrows on television weather charts denote invasions of 'cold masses' from Russia via the Balkans, the wind strikes far closer to the bone than the actual temperatures would suggest. Any remaining tourists, like the Athenian cats, then find themselves preoccupied with the unhellenic necessities of warmth and shelter.

At the opposite end of the climatic spectrum, July and August lend themselves more to a form of gradual suttee on the beaches than to exploration. If you have to travel in peak season, your objective should be enjoyment of the sea in all its forms – on, in and under the water – with a sunshade to cower beneath during the mad-dog hours.

Increasingly, like everyone else, the Greeks are having to take their own holidays in the heart of summer. In recent years, since a month's holiday became a legal entitlement regardless of length of service, industries have tended to substitute a one-month closure for the previous system of staggered leave. With their regular clients away, many shops and tavernas in Athens and the main cities now follow suit – anyone familiar with a Parisian August will feel at home in Athens.

Greek holiday snobs – senior executives and self-employed professionals – still contrive to make their disappearance in September, not just because the crowds are thinner on the resort islands but out of a desire to saunter comfortably in the sunshine. If you want to move about the country, the ideal months are May, June and September; April can be showery and in October the rains, if they arrive, are likely to be more purposeful.

Average temperatures in Athens and southern Greece range between 12°C/52°F in January–February and 33°C/92°F in July–August. Extremes can be just below freezing point in winter and 40°C/102°F and more in an August heatwave. Hours of sunshine are not officially recorded, but the tourism authorities speak loosely but probably correctly of around 3,000 a year. In Thessaloniki and northern Greece, summer temperatures are about the same as in Athens but winter averages are a couple of degrees centigrade lower.

The edges of mainland Greece and the islands tend to be slightly cooler in summer but also more humid, especially at night.

Rainfall

Over a ten-year period, as reported by the National Statistics Service, Athens averaged 406 mm of rain annually, with 374 mm falling between the beginning of October and the end of May, and only 32 mm in the summer months, largely in the form of thunderstorms. In Thessaloniki, the average was 452 mm: 357 mm from October to May and 95 mm from June to September.

Corfu holds the record for the wettest part of Greece: 1,179 mm in winter and 139 mm in summer for an average annual total of 1,318 mm. It follows that Corfu is also the greenest of the Greek islands.

Still on the ten-year basis, rain fell in Athens on an average of 105 days a year, only 14 of them between May and September. The corresponding figures for Thessaloniki were 112 and 15, and for Corfu 139 and 17, suggesting that in Corfu the summer rain was heavier or of longer duration rather than more frequent.

The meltemi

The summer visitor should be aware in advance of the *meltemi*, which the Greeks both love and hate. For those who would rather have anything instead of savage heat, the *meltemi* is Greece's saving grace. It is a stiff north-westerly wind that sweeps the east coast of mainland Greece (including Athens) and the Aegean islands almost every day from the middle of July until the end of August. The result of pressure differences between North Africa and the Balkans, it springs up at around 8 or 9 a.m. and drops abruptly after sunset.

Undeniably, it does reduce the humidity. On the other hand, not even those who profess to love it could describe it as cooling; at its worst it is suggestive of a blast from an oven with an open door. It can make a beach umbrella unusable anywhere and on Myconos, windiest of the Greek islands, it has been known to carry unopened bottles of beer off street-café tables. It forces cruise passengers to the sheltered sides of the deck and, by the time it reaches Athens, it has picked up enough dust to drive housewives to despair and to make sunglasses essential. The *meltemi* is the unqualified friend only of yachtsmen.

Western Greece, including the west Peloponnese and the Ionian islands, knows nothing of this particular wind. As a result, midsummer there is a stickier season; also, though you escape the sandpapering you may acquire a closer acquaintance with the local wasp and fly populations.

The conclusion is self-evident: if you have the freedom of choice, go to Greece between Easter and the end of June or in September and the first half of October. Should the islands be your objective, you will then reduce the likelihood of suffering from seasickness, either your own or others'. You will also find better service in hotels and restaurants, since they will be less crowded and their staffs more patient, and you will travel in greater comfort whether by land, sea or air.

Swimming

Average sea temperatures are measured, but are virtually meaningless for the swimmer. Whether your dip will be in bracing or tepid water is a matter of the depth of the sea, the strength and direction of wind and current and, to some extent, whether the sea bed is sandy or covered with weeds. Probably the warmest water in all Greece laps on to the long beach at Cavo in the south of Corfu; even there, however, there are chill patches above the clumps of seaweed.

If a warm sea is your weakness and you have a choice of beaches, check with your hotel porter; he will generally be able to tell you which will be warm and which cool, which sheltered and which not, on any particular day.

Final advice

● If you are visiting an island, do not book your return in advance on a ferry that will theoretically get you to Piraeus a couple of hours before you have to be at Athens Airport for your flight home. Apart from the normal unpunctuality, Greece is subject to sudden gales with winds of force 8 or 9 that can keep ferries in harbour for a day or two at a stretch.

It would be a mistake to believe you could then simply tear up your boat ticket and jump on an Olympic Airways flight to Athens. Hundreds of others will have the same idea, including the well connected, and you may find yourself at the end of a very long queue in which promotion depends on influence. Since there is no gale-free season, you need to be a little flexible.

● Even in July and August, you should pack a sweater. The nights can be chilly and, once the *meltemi* has retired to bed, damp also.

Travelling Around

The way to get about mainland Greece in style and with maximum flexibility is to drive your own car or hire one. If you have no wish to drive in an unfamiliar environment and do not need to count your pennies, you can use taxis.

The fastest way is to fly; Olympic Airways provides services to the larger mainland towns, and its affiliate, Olympic Aviation, offers air-taxi facilities, mainly but not only to minor islands.

The cheapest means of travel, and the one preferred by most Greeks, is to go by bus. There is a fairly rudimentary rail network covering eastern and northern Greece, Thrace and parts of the Peloponnese; the speeds are commensurate with single-track operations.

Islands can be visited by coastal ferries, mostly sailing out of Piraeus and the mainland ports of Rafina (Attica), Volos and Kavala for the Aegean, and from Patras and Kylini, in the Peloponnese, for Ionian destinations. If your preference is for greater luxury and you are prepared to accept the limitations of fixed itineraries and brief excursions ashore, there are up to thirty liners waiting to take you on cruises from three days to two weeks in duration.

Best of all, though admittedly costly, is to hire a yacht. You can then take in the islands and, since all the famed archaeological sites are within an easy taxi drive from some mainland port, most of the places you would visit by car also.

Despite their inborn desire to be hospitable, the Greeks do not readily pick up hitchhikers. There are difficulties of communication and, in addition, fears of legal liability in the event of an accident. Also, too many stories have gone round about drunkenness, drug addiction and even assault. If you do insist on trying your luck, you should expect long periods of frustration in the heat and dust of a main road, broken by short lifts as often as not on open farm vehicles.

Motorcycles and mopeds can be hired easily on the islands. Since the summer of 1987 they have been legally rentable on the mainland too, subject to local authority endorsement of proposals made by rental firms to NTOG, but availability is still extremely limited.

You will travel a long way in Greece before you see your first bicycle. With good reason: the Greeks regard them as unsafe in city traffic; elsewhere, cycling is too much like hard labour in a hilly and windy country. If you propose to use a bicycle, you should take your own.

To ride a donkey or a mule, except as a special favour from an amiable farmer, you now have to go the island of Santorini.

Prices

The fares given in this chapter are those of the summer of 1987. With inflation running at around 15 per cent and the government determined to reduce the losses of the mainly state-owned means of transport, this year's prices will probably be between 10 and 20 per cent higher.

By air

Olympic Airways, set up by the late shipping magnate Aristotle Onassis in 1957 and purchased by the Greek state in 1975, has and intends to retain a monopoly on all air transport within Greece. Its principal function is to provide rapid year-round communications at reasonable prices for the Aegean and Ionian islands, as part of the government's effort to deter internal migration. For this reason, the airport construction programme is wholly concentrated on the islands. Nevertheless, Olympic's thirty-two domestic destinations include ten mainland towns: Aktion (for Preveza), Alexandroupolis, Ioannina, Kalamata, Kastoria, Kavala, Komotini, Kozani, Larisa and Thessaloniki. All mainland flights are from and to Athens Airport except for one Thessaloniki–Ioannina service.

In 1985, Olympic carried 5.33 million passengers on its domestic network, the greater part of them to and from the islands, as against 2.12 million on its international flights (it operates to thirty-nine cities in twenty-seven countries).

Olympic and its light aircraft and air taxi affiliate, Olympic Aviation, have exclusive use of the West Terminal at Athens Airport – the Greek capital's original airport at Ellenikon, approached by the coastal road. All other airlines use the newer East Terminal, reached by the inland road. Olympic's headquarters are on Syngrou Avenue, but bookings may also be made from its office in Othonos Street, on the right of Constitution Square looking towards Parliament. The airline is obviously of limited interest to the tourist whose objective is to move about mainland Greece, mainly because of the absence of province-to-province flights.

The following one-way fares are cited with extreme caution, since Olympic is under the greatest pressure to cut its losses. Because competition and regulations keep international fares down, it has no alternative but to make frequent adjustments of its domestic fares.

Athens to:
Aktion   Dr 4,130
Alexandroupolis   Dr 4,880
Ioannina   Dr 4,130

Kalamata   Dr 3,180
Kastoria   Dr 5,050
Kavala   Dr 5,050
Komotini   Dr 5,180
Kozani   Dr 4,650
Larisa   Dr 4,320
Thessaloniki   Dr 5,000
Thessaloniki to Ioannina   Dr 2,880

By train

Greece's rail network is operated by the state-owned Hellenic Railways Organisation (OSE), which is required to give as much emphasis to the movement of exports to European Community markets as to passenger traffic. Housed in unexpectedly palatial headquarters in Karolou Street, behind Omonia Square, with a more conveniently located ticket office at 6 Sina Street in central Athens, OSE exploits a network of 2,571 km of mainly single-track line, of which 758 km is narrow-gauge in the Peloponnese and the rest standard-gauge running up eastern Greece to Thessaloniki; from there, branches run north to the Yugoslav and Bulgarian frontiers and east through Thrace to Turkey.

Because of the two different gauges, Athens has two one-horse railway stations almost side by side, neither of which would do much credit to a far smaller European city. You go to the Larissis station for trains to northern Greece and beyond, and to the Peloponnisos station for trains to the Peloponnese; both stations are reached by trams No 1 and 5 from the top of Constitution Square.

An 'express' train from Athens to Thessaloniki – there are no other kinds – covers the 500 km in the unimpressive time of just under eight hours. The bus is about half an hour quicker, despite meal and coffee stops on the way. Athens to Alexandroupolis, the last main town before the Turkish frontier, takes just over fifteen hours by train for the 850-km trip. Trains are diesel-powered; the railway has not yet been electrified, though it is due to be with European Community help. All seats are bookable, and should definitely be reserved in advance unless you are prepared to risk travelling in the corridor. There are two classes. First-class gives you more elbow room (three a side instead of four) and superior upholstery; the enhanced comfort is obviously worth considering on a long journey – say to Thessaloniki or the three days to Paris. You would take it for a shorter trip if you wished to indulge an aversion to poorer Greeks and backpackers.

Most long-distance trains have restaurants, but OSE is a long way from honourable mention in even the least exacting gastronomic

AIR AND RAIL NETWORK

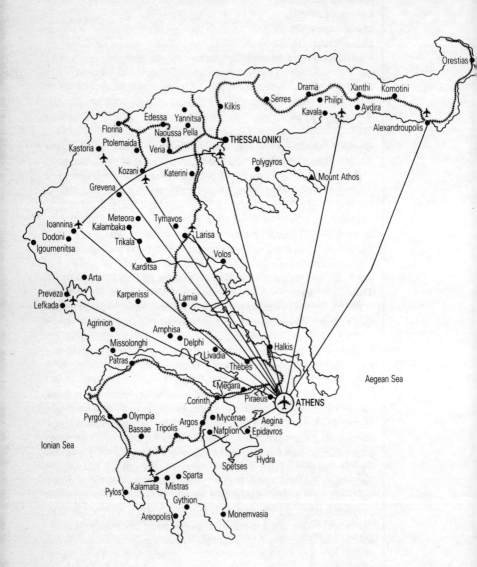

guide to Greece. Passengers in general rely on the frequent offer of sandwiches, soft drinks and coffee, or pack their own meals. Sleepers or couchettes are available on some of the overnight expresses. There are no car-sleeper services in Greece; the cost of transporting a car by rail depends on its type and weight and the distance covered; unaccompanied luggage may be sent by rail, and customs inspection is carried out at the frontiers.

Unless you are heading for Europe or the Balkans, you would probably take a train north only to go to Thessaloniki. However, you could get off at Livadia for a bus or taxi to Delphi, or change at Pharsala for the two-hour trip to Kalambaka (for Meteora), or the one-hour spin to Volos; there is also a branch line to Volos from Larisa. The only other route served north from Athens is the ninety-minute service to Halkis, on the island of Euboia – there are seventeen trains a day.

There are eight trains a day from Athens to Thessaloniki. One-way fares in 1987 were Dr 1,895 first class and Dr 1,265 second class; for a round-trip ticket, double these figures then subtract 20 per cent.

To take a train from Athens to see Thrace would be to invite disappointment as well as discomfort. You would travel for thirteen hours just to reach Serres, pass through the least interesting part of the countryside, and miss Kavala altogether.

The Peloponnese trains, mostly of only two or three coaches, make for a considerably more pleasurable experience but, again, they are markedly slower than buses. Athens to Corinth, where the line branches, takes almost two hours (one and a half by bus); Athens to Patras four and a quarter hours (three and a half by bus) and Athens to the line's end at Kalamata seven hours (five and a half on the bus).

There are twelve trains a day to Corinth, of which seven continue to Patras and three go from there along the coast all the way to Kalamata. One-way tickets cost Dr 410 first class and Dr 275 second class to Corinth; Dr 820 and Dr 545 to Patras and Dr1,320 and Dr 880 to Kalamata. There are no sleepers or couchettes nor any need for them, since only two trains travel overnight. The other five trains go to Kalamata through the interior of the Peloponnese, with stops at or close to Mycenae, Argos (for Nafplion) and Tripolis.

A tourist would be most likely to use a Peloponnesian train in order to catch a ferry at Patras for Italy (the Patras station is on the docks, only a few metres from the customs sheds and embarkation for the ferries), or to get off at Diakofto for the delightful rack-and-pinion railway to Mega Spelion and Kalavryta.

The Athens–Piraeus electric railway, the nucleus of what is one day to become the Athens metro, is run by a separate state-owned company. Departures each way are at approximately five-minute intervals, and the trip takes twenty minutes. The fare is a standard Dr 30 from Omonia Square to Piraeus or intermediate stations, and the same in the other direction to the commuter hill suburb of Kifisia. At Omonia Square the escalators are scarcely ever working and the public conveniences are a disgrace to humanity.

Special OSE arrangements

● A Eurail pass entitles holders to free rail travel within Greece.

● Season tickets and tourist cards allow unlimited travel along a specific route for a specified period. Tourist cards allow unlimited travel on every route within a specified period; they are issued for one to five people for periods of ten, twenty and thirty days.

● Senior Citizen Cards are granted to passengers of sixty and older on presentation of an identity card or passport. Valid for one year, they entitle the holder to five free trips (on restricted dates) and thereafter to a 50 per cent reduction on all routes.

By bus

When it comes to buses, Greece is definitely a bargain country but also a two-nation society, with a kind of Berlin Wall separating those who speak Greek from those who do not. To some extent this is probably inevitable; the tourist, unless particularly budget-conscious, is likely to prefer the greater comfort, companionship of a guide and certainty of a bed at night offered by an organised coach tour to the relative hazards of public transport. But it also has to be admitted that the state has no interest in helping tourists to save money, and in this instance is playing for the same team as the travel agents.

Consider in detail travelling from Athens to Corfu by public bus – a fairly typical long-distance journey. The trip takes eleven hours, a ticket costs Dr 2,310, and there are three scheduled departures a day in each direction.

Almost certainly you will have decided to take the 7 a.m. bus from Athens, preferring a day trip to a night on the road. First, you will probably not get a ticket, at least in the summer, unless you have booked four or five days in advance. To make the booking you have to go to the bus garage at 100 Kifissou Street, which can be reached by the No 51 bus if you can manage to find a little street near Omonia Square called Menandrou. More probably you will take a taxi.

Deposited at the garage, you will be impressed first by the confusion and then by the absence of a single sign in any language but Greek. However, since you would not be there at all unless you had something of the pioneer spirit, you will eventually locate the booking office through a poorly-marked door beside the coffee-shop. You will determine which of the long queues you should join, work your way to the head of it, explain your needs to the patient but probably monolingual ticket clerk, pay, and pocket the handwritten flimsy copy bearing your name as it sounds in Greek, and your seat number. Some time afterwards you will discover the taxi rank, and with a little luck you may be back in your hotel in time for lunch.

Unless you are remarkably fortunate in your travel agent, he will not make the booking for you; he will prefer to explain all the sound reasons why you should take a coach tour instead or, in the case of Corfu, go by air. There is a promise from the Communications Ministry that a booking office will be opened in the area of Constitution Square, and it may possibly have been fulfilled by the time you read these words; however, promises in Greece tend to be slow developers.

Comes the morning of the day. It is better to order your taxi at least an hour before departure time since traffic can be heavy in Athens at 6 a.m. Besides, the taxi has to drop you in the central aisle of the garage, which may be some distance from where the Corfu bus pulls in; there are no porters or luggage trolleys; the bay you are seeking will have the designation *Kerkyra* in Greek without a corresponding 'Corfu' in English; and any luggage other than a handbag has to be checked in, weighed and labelled. Theoretically, should the bus by then have arrived, you can take your seat; however, you would be wiser first to make sure with your own eyes that your suitcase has actually been loaded into the luggage compartment.

The bus will be relatively spacious, probably a 48-seater with plastic-covered adjustable seats. Your share of leg room will depend on whether the passenger in front of you intends to continue his interrupted sleep on a semi-bed. The bus will not be air-conditioned, but at least smoking is forbidden.

Some two and a half hours later, after a pleasant run along the coast and a crossing of the Corinth Canal without a coffee stop, you will disembark from the bus at the dock of the Rio-Andirrion ferry that will carry you from the north Peloponnese to mainland Greece. Here you will find that your bus ticket did not include the Dr 40 ferry charge, so have some loose change ready. You can occupy the twenty-minute crossing by drinking coffee or queueing for the filthiest toilets it is to be hoped you will ever encounter.

Waiting for a ferry, embarkation, crossing, disembarking and finding your bus again will probably take between one and two hours; if it is closer to two you need not fear you will be late in Corfu, since the driver will make the appropriate calculation at the lunch break.

You will then pass outside Missolonghi, outside Agrinion, through Amphilochia and Arta, and somewhere in the Epiros mountains you will stop for a midday meal at a wayside restaurant. Here the cook presides over a display of pans and two boys, possibly his sons, take orders for drinks and present the bills.

This is where you really need a companion. If you are alone, you can find a place at a table while the others are struggling for food but you may then get nothing to eat, or you can join the rush for the kitchen and eat standing up. Though jostled and outshouted, since nothing in Greece releases inhibitions so quickly as hunger, you will finally catch the eye of the cook, who will realise from your silence that you must be foreign and will fill your plate from whatever pan you point out to him that has not already been emptied. Somehow the chicken never seems to run out; if the potatoes have gone, and the rice, he will add a handful (literally!) of cold macaroni. After a morning on the road you will probably find it delicious; you will certainly find it cheap.

Obedient to the clapping of hands, you will return to the bus for the remaining hour's drive to Igoumenitsa, arriving there in the stifling heat of the afternoon. At this point, the born leader emerges. One of your fellow passengers, knowledgeable in the ways of the bus company, will set out in search of the one among the half-dozen agencies selling tickets for the particular ferry that he has somehow discovered the bus will be travelling on. You should not lose sight of him, since you will receive no information from the driver.

You pay your Dr 300, get your second 'supplementary' ticket of the day, find the right ferry and, a couple of hours later, arrive at Corfu for the opening of a new chapter in the book of mysteries.

It is difficult to understand why the 'Athens–Corfu' ticket could not include the fares for the two ferries, but the many virtues of the modern Greeks do not always include common sense. The purpose of this description is not to deter you from taking a public bus; it can be entertaining, and is certainly a way of getting among the people. However, it helps if you are quick-witted, have a slow panic fuse, and are travelling light.

Obviously, a journey is somewhat less complex if it includes no ferries and is sufficiently short not to involve lunch on the road. But even then, the rest of the depiction still applies.

The way of the poor   Given the limited facilities offered by the railway and the high cost of flying, it is obvious that buses are the almost universal means of transport for the poorer and middle-class Greeks. In terms of numbers of routes, they are really very well served by the private KTELs (co-operatives of bus owners, each covering their own area of the country) and by the competing but complementary fleet operated by the Hellenic Railways Organisation (OSE).

For an OSE bus, you go to the Larissis station if travelling northward from Athens and the Peloponnisos station if bound for the Peloponnese. The only real difference from a KTEL bus is that booking is simpler, since you can do it in Sina Street where some of the clerks speak English. However, OSE buses run only on routes that are also served by trains. Tickets cost about the same for each, and are a little more expensive than second class on trains.

The main Athens bus garage is in Kifissou Street, but there is a secondary one at 260 Liossion Street, which can be reached by a No 24 bus from outside the National Gardens in Amalias Avenue.

You go there for buses to Halkis, Delphi and some cities of central and northern Greece.

You can take a bus from Athens to almost every main town in mainland Greece, but you run into difficulties if you wish to travel from town to town in the provinces using local services. It can be done, but is likely to involve considerable waste of time. Since distances are relatively short and taxis still cheap in Greece, you might consider spending a little more for the privilege of leaving when you are ready, going exactly where you want, and enjoying the benefit of the driver's local knowledge. He will probably not speak English but, if the arrangement has been made through your hotel, he will have been briefed on your wishes and the price will have been negotiated.

Naturally, if you stop en route for refreshments you will invite your driver to join you; it would be self-defeating as well as impolite not to.

In Athens and Attica   While in Athens, you should take a bus or a tram at least once; it is an experience you should not miss. The typical Athens bus or tram standard fare is Dr 30 which you drop into a box beside the driver as you enter. The vehicle carries eighteen to twenty-four passengers seated; standing, the number is determined by the driver's patience. Usually there comes a moment when even the most public-spirited driver will decide that the can is full and only perspiration space remains; he will then refrain from opening the door at the next stop. But if the door does open, by all means elbow your way inside; provided you are not shaken off when the bus starts, room will eventually be made for you and at some point the door will close again.

Unless you go to a football match, which is unlikely, you are now in probably the only situation in Greece in which you should keep a hand on your wallet. While you may well be poked and prodded, this should be attributed simply to the overcrowding; also, the laying on of hands is standard procedure in Greece for almost any activity, from simple conversation to the purchase of strawberries. Finally, do not despair if an altercation breaks out between passengers and driver; somehow the driver never actually carries out his threat to walk away and leave the bus and all aboard to stew in the midday sun.

Considering that, if you are travelling simply from your hotel to the centre, a taxi would probably cost you less than Dr 200, you may wonder why you bother. But first you would have to find the taxi, since the Greeks will have asked themselves the same question.

Almost everyone agrees that taxis are ridiculously inexpensive in Greece and ought to be made more of a luxury. But there are political reasons operating against this: the principal beneficiaries of costlier taxis would be conservatives (the better-off passengers, glad to pay more for greater availability, and the drivers who, as self-employed professionals, are generally right-wing), while the main losers would be socialist supporters, including unemployed youths for whom time is money not spent. Conversely, when the conservatives are in power they are unwilling openly to soak the poor. For this reason all hopes are pinned on the Athens metro which, though the first shaft is only now being sunk, is undoubtedly thirty years closer to completion than when the decision to build it was taken.

It makes rather more sense to prefer a bus to a taxi if you are heading out for the bathing beaches or restaurants along the coast between Athens Airport and the Varkiza suburb. The buses will still cost you the standard fare, compared with between Dr 500 and 1,000 for a taxi; although you will probably stand for the forty-minute to one-hour trip, the crowding will be less. For these buses, the terminals are along Olga Avenue, on the edges of the Zappeion across the road from the Olympic Stadium.

You could also use buses, though for these the standard fare does not apply, to go to Sounion and other seaside towns of Attica. To catch an Attica bus, which usually leaves at hourly intervals and on which seats are not bookable, you make your way along Patission Street past the National Archaeological Museum to the junction with Alexandras Avenue.

You might also prefer a bus instead of the electric railway to Piraeus, from terminals at the corner of Constitution Square and Philhellinon Street (green buses) or near Omonia Square in Athenas Street (blue buses). Regardless of colour the fare is the same; only the routes differ.

By coach

Booking an organised coach tour does not necessarily mark you out as timid; there comes a moment when you may enjoy a rest from driving, or feel that you have been making possibly extravagant use of your luck. The coaches themselves, though older and less well appointed than those in use in other European tourist countries, are incomparably more comfortable than the KTEL and OSE buses and will certainly be air-conditioned. Since in Greece the travel profession is extremely competitive, your tour guide will be efficient, knowledgeable and friendly. She (more rarely he) will tell you what you are seeing and what you should look for during your stops, make sure you are comfortable in your hotel room, help out at mealtimes and keep you informed on any available evening entertainment. You will also stay in excellent hotels.

The oldest of the Athens coach tour companies, and the one most frequently booked by travel agents, is CHAT Tours of 4 Stadiou Street, near Constitution Square. It offers seventeen itineraries, ranging from morning and evening sightseeing in Athens to a nine-day 'grand tour of Greece'. This, at a full-board price of $610 per person, gives you two days in the Peloponnese, then takes you through Delphi and Kalambaka (for Meteora) to Thessaloniki for sightseeing in Macedonia and Thrace, with a return to Athens down the east coast.

For a full-board price of $444 per person, you could spend six days touring the Peloponnese: Mycenae and Epidavros on the first day with an overnight stop at Nafplion; Mistras on the second and overnight at Sparta; the Mani on the third with Kalamata overnight; the western Peloponnese to Olympia on the fourth with two nights there to allow a full day for the archaeological site and museums, then back to Athens along the north Peloponnese coast on the final day.

Shorter tours – and these too are typical – include a Sounion half-day; Mycenae and Epidavros in one day or two; Delphi also in one or two days; Mycenae, Olympia and Delphi in four days; the same plus more of the Peloponnese in five; Delphi and Meteora in three days; Meteora and Mount Pelion in three; the north of Greece in six days, and western Greece in five.

Whether you see more on a coach tour than by car depends, of course, on the diligence of your preparations. Allowing for car hire, full rate in hotels and cost of meals, self-driving is unlikely to work out much cheaper. You gain flexibility, but may need more time to cover the same ground. It is really a matter of temperament – but if you are going to do it on your own you really ought to do some advance reading to compensate for the absence of a guide.

The Greeks can make much the same tours far more cheaply, and with a greater variety to choose from, by using companies such as Lagopoulos and Pafsanias in Canningos Square. But then your bus would not be air-conditioned, you would stay in second-class hotels on a half-board basis, you would face a language barrier since the guides would speak only Greek (at least into the microphones), and you might not much appreciate the incessant Greek popular songs and bouzouki music played at full volume over the amplification system.

By car

In Greece you drive on the right, and disbelievingly. At least until a few years ago – possibly it is still done though more discreetly now, since they have been taught the need for an unfamiliarly low profile – American military personnel from the air force base next to Athens Airport were required at the start of their posting to attend a 'defensive driving' course. It included this classic anecdote: the Master Sergeant listens carefully to the admonitions of his instructor, obeys them scrupulously, completes his four-year term without a single accident,

Distance Chart

Cities (diagonal labels, top to bottom): Athens, Agrinion, Amphissa, Alexandroupolis, Argos, Arta, Corinth, Drama, Edessa, Egio, Eratini, Evzoni, Florina, Grevena, Gythion, Itea, Igoumenitsa, Ioannina, Kalamata, Karditsa, Karpenissi, Kastoria, Katerini, Kilkis, Kozani, Komotini, Lamia, Larisa, Livadia, Missolonghi, Nafplion, Niki (Florina), Orestiás, Patras, Preveza, Romanhanis, Pylos, Argos, Rio, Serres, Sparta, Thebes, Thessaloniki, Trikala, Tripolis, Veria, Volos, Xanthi flies back to the States and, when the freighter arrives from Greece, goes to one of the East Coast ports to collect his unscratched car. A block away from the dock gates, he is rammed by a car hurtling out of a side-street through a red traffic light. 'Dear me!', he exclaims (in the printable version), as he walks across to his adversary. 'Would you believe that I have just returned from four years in Greece without even one collision and now, after a couple of minutes back home, see what you have done to me!' The other driver rolls down his window, smiles disarmingly and says, '*Oriste kyrie?*' – roughly translated as 'Was there something, sir?'

Even though traffic fatalities have been reduced considerably since the use of seatbelts was made compulsory, as a ratio of collisions to the number of cars on the road Greece still has one of the worst accident rates in Europe. The explanation lies in a combination of road conditions and national temperament.

On any road, even a motorway, you should be prepared from one moment to the next for the sudden emergence of a heavy truck or farm vehicle. Remember that not even motorways have a central reservation and do not assume that no one would be so foolish as to overtake on the brow of a hill. In the summer, when it rains so rarely, a light shower can turn a road surface instantly into a skating rink. And do not imagine that a tree will be lopped as punishment just because it has grown tall or bushy enough to conceal a traffic light or a road sign.

As for national temperament, the Greeks with some justice pride themselves on the speed of their reactions. Behind the wheel, this leads them to last-minute decisions, compulsive weaving in and out of traffic lanes, and a preference for sudden braking rather than gradual deceleration.

Some twenty years ago, when I had allowed my British driving licence to expire, I decided to obtain a Greek one. This involved me in a refresher and familiarisation course in a car in which the instructor had draped a handkerchief over the rear-view mirror. When I requested its removal I received a magisterial reply: 'We are not interested, sir, in the view behind us!' My subsequent experience has cast doubt on whether this was altogether an eccentric attitude.

I knew an American non-commissioned officer who, having completed his defensive driving course, relieved his own exasperation through development of a peculiarly unfriendly habit. Noting that the driver in front of him would routinely stop just past a traffic light and then rely on him to indicate, with a touch of the horn or a headlight flash, when it was time to move off, he would 'accidentally' give a premature signal. Staring innocently out of the window, or deep in conversation with a passenger, he would quietly enjoy the discomfiture he had caused.

On the whole, however, with the exercise of a little more than usual care, your driving in Greece should be free of mishap. At least you do not have to worry that your car will be broken open and robbed if you leave it in a street overnight.

Traffic rules and regulations

For the following information I am indebted to the Automobile and Touring Club of Greece (ELPA).

Private cars, caravans, trailers and motorcycles are permitted to enter Greece on the strength of a *Carnet de Passage en Douanes* issued by the Automobile Association of the vehicle's country of origin. In the absence of such a document, the vehicle will be admitted temporarily without payment of import duty or tax; a note will be made on the owner's passport, after which a free-use card is issued by the customs. The initial validity of the free-use card is one year. If you wish to leave Greece without your car, you must have the car withdrawn from circulation by a customs authority.

Except for drivers possessing a British, West German, Belgian or Austrian licence, foreign motorists are required to have an international licence. This may be obtained from the Automobile and Touring Club of Greece (ELPA) on the basis of a national driving licence and a passport or identity card.

Third-party insurance is compulsory in Greece. Visitors from Britain and most European countries, but not from the United States, Australia or New Zealand, may use a valid Green Card when driving in Greece. Others can buy local short-term insurance after crossing the borders from Yugoslavia or Bulgaria or at the town nearest to other points of arrival. The Motor Insurance Bureau at 10 Xenofondos Street, Athens (Tel. 3236 733), can help visitors obtain car insurance or put them in touch with the local agents of their own insurance companies.

Cars registered in Greece or imported temporarily must, by law, carry a warning triangle – to be placed 100 metres behind the vehicle in the event of a breakdown – as well as a fire extinguisher and a first-aid kit. The use of seatbelts is compulsory for drivers and front-seat passengers. Children below the age of ten may not be carried in the front seat.

● **Priority at intersections.** Outside towns, traffic moving along a main road has priority at intersections. In towns, vehicles coming from the right have priority. Vehicles approaching and on roundabouts must give way to vehicles coming from the right.

● **Speed limits.** Unless otherwise indicated by signs, speed limits for private cars are as follows: in built-up areas 50 km/h, outside built-up areas 80 km/h, on motorways 100 km/h. For motorcycles the speed limits are 40 km/h in built-up areas and 70 km/h elsewhere.

● **Use of horns.** A horn may be used in towns only in an emergency. Multi-toned horns are strictly prohibited.

● **Overtaking.** You drive on the right and overtake on the left.

● **Parking.** It is prohibited to park within 5 metres of intersections, 15 metres of level crossings, bus or tram stops, 3 metres of a fire hydrant and 5 metres of a stop sign or a traffic light. In some streets, special signs indicate the side of the road where vehicles should be parked. Parking meters operate for between half an hour and two hours, at fees varying from city to city, and the free use of unexpired time is not authorised. In Athens, it is forbidden to park anywhere in the 'green zone' except where parking meters have been installed.

● **Miscellaneous regulations.** In order to lessen air pollution and traffic congestion, a controlled zone has been set up in central Athens, which is forbidden to private cars (not taxis) on alternate working days between 6.30 a.m. and 4 p.m. Cars with registration numbers ending in 1 to 5 are excluded on one day and those with numbers ending in 6 to 0 on the following day. This regulation applies to visiting motorists after they have been in Greece for forty days.

The Greek police are authorised to impose fines for traffic offences but not to collect them on the spot. In handing you the ticket they will tell you where you should pay; if you find a ticket tucked under your windscreen wiper for a parking offence, it will denote where the payment may be made, and by what date.

It is an offence to refuse an alcohol test requested by the police. An alcohol level in the blood of 0.05–0.08 per cent is a misdemeanour; a level above 0.08 per cent is a criminal offence.

The police do not draw up a report when an accident causes material damage only, but motorists are advised to call at the nearest police station to give a description of the incident. If an accident causes bodily injury, a driver who fails to stop, give assistance and call the police is liable to imprisonment for up to three years. An uninsured vehicle is liable to seizure as a guarantee of compensation.

Drivers and passengers of motorcycles must wear crash helmets.

Toll charges

Tolls are levied on some sections of motorways as follows.

	cars	motorcycles
Athens–Corinth	Dr 50	Dr 20
Corinth–Patras	Dr 80	Dr 30
Athens–Lamia	Dr 100	Dr 50
Lamia–Larisa	Dr 80	Dr 30
Larisa–Katerini	Dr 50	Dr 20
Katerini–Evzoni (Yugoslav border)	Dr 80	Dr 30

Purchase of fuel

Fuel is sold by the litre at varying prices that do not differ greatly from elsewhere in Europe. It is generally available as regular (91–92 octane) and super (96–98 octane). As of the summer of 1987, unleaded petrol (95 octane) was available at thirty-five petrol stations, lists of which can be obtained at border crossings and other points of arrival. Diesel oil is available at any petrol station, and sells at just over half the price of regular petrol.

It is forbidden to carry spare fuel in a can in the car.

How to get help

The Automobile and Touring Club of Greece (ELPA), as a member of the Alliance Internationale de Tourisme (AIT) and the Fédération Internationale de l'Automobile (FIA), offers services to members of national automobile associations on production of a valid membership card. These include:

● **Road assistance.** The ELPA road assistance service (OVELPA) covers all main roads and the areas surrounding large cities. If you break down, dial 104. A car will be repaired on the spot if possible or towed to the nearest garage. The service operates on a twenty-four-hour basis in Athens and Thessaloniki and from 7 a.m. to 10 p.m. at Agrinion, Alexandroupolis, Argos, Arta, Veria, Volos, Drama, Thebes, Ioannina, Kavala, Kalamata, Katerini, Komotoni, Lamia, Larisa, Xanthi, Patras, Pyrgos, Seres, Trikala, Tripolis, Florina, Halkis and on the islands of Corfu and Crete.

● **Technical inspection.** Technical inspection stations in Athens and Thessaloniki will carry out free checks of cars to ensure compliance with Greek requirements on exhaust fumes, engine noise and lights.

● **Protection against theft.** On payment of a fee, a car may be registered with ELPA and a special sticker obtained; if it is stolen, ELPA will then launch a search and offer a reward.

● **Legal services.** ELPA will offer free legal advice on all subjects concerning Greek legislation on cars, accidents and insurance. It will supply a lawyer and advance bail on receipt of a telexed guarantee from the mother club. Typical 1987 fine levels were Dr 8,100 for speeding and Dr 4,100 for ignoring a stop sign, improper overtaking, parking offences and failure to use seatbelts.

● **Tourism information.** ELPA offices will supply tourism information and free maps, and will also arrange participation in tours or excursions at special rates.

ELPA headquarters are on the ground floor of: Athens Tower, 2–4 Messogion Street, 115 27 Athens. Tel.: 7791 615 (to 620) and 7797 401 (to 405). Telegraphs: AUTOCLUB ATHENS. Telex: 21 57 63 ELPA GR.

It has branch offices in Agrinion, Ioannina, Kalamata, Kavala, Lamia, Larisa, Patras, Thessaloniki and Volos, frontier offices at Evzoni and Promahonas, and representatives in most other mainland towns.

Hiring a car   Cars may be hired – somewhat expensively, but vehicle taxes are unusually severe in Greece – from about fifty rental firms with offices in the main towns and islands. The widest networks, however, are maintained by Avis and Hertz. Cars are available on time and kilometre or weekly unlimited kilometre rates, which include oil and greasing, road maps and insurance but not local taxes and VAT. Full collision protection is available.

Apart from competitive differences, prices vary according to type of car, season and length of time required. The following examples are indicative:

	daily	weekly
Four-seat economy:	Dr 2,000+ Dr 25 per km (min 100 km daily)	Dr 35,000 (unlimited km)
Five-seat medium:	Dr 2,300+ Dr 28 per km	Dr 39,000
Five-seat executive:	Dr 4,600–5,800+ Dr 42–55 per km	Dr 68,000–85,000
Five-seat luxury:	Dr 7,000–12,000+ Dr 65–120 per km	Dr 100,000– 180,000

By taxi

Greek taxis are yellow, cheap, and for the most part driven by honest men. This said, they do have certain peculiarities. If you anticipate that your taxi will be neither clean nor roomy, and that its driver will be neither sprucely dressed nor clean-shaven, not a linguist and not polite, then you will occasionally have a pleasant surprise.

Taxis are not custom-built in Greece, and may be anything from a Mini to a Mercedes. There are also no special age limits, either upwards for the car or downwards for the driver. You will probably be treated, at no extra charge, to a concert of bouzouki music at deafening volume on the driver's tape-recorder. Legally he has to turn it down or off if you ask him to, but you will then be regarded as unsympathetic towards his need for some relaxation during his arduous hours of work.

How to get one
As you move about Athens you will see dozens of yellow signs for 'Taxi' (the same word in Greek), at queue shelters. These indicate taxi ranks but, except for a couple in Constitution Square, they are the last places at which you should wait. They were erected by the mayor of Athens during his campaign for re-election in 1986, which he lost. They have now been appropriated by motorcyclists.

Your best hope of finding a cruising taxi is to wait outside a hospital and count on accidents and emergencies; maternity hospitals are best of all, since the pregnant and those visiting them with flowers to protect rarely use buses. In the evenings, find a theatre just before the curtain goes up. Elsewhere it is a matter of chance.

Because of the Greek ambition to be self-employed, taxis tend to be driven by their owners during the day and by hired drivers at night. This means that there are fewer taxis on the roads at peak hours, either because their owners are heading home for the midday meal or, in the evening, because the shift is changing. It also explains why the driver of an empty taxi will sometimes ask you where you want to go before deciding whether he will take you; if your route is not his, you are out of luck.

Though a taxi-driver has to pass an advanced driving test, he is not required to have local knowledge; on the contrary, he may be as much a stranger as you are. He will generally know how to find places like the U.S. Embassy, the Grande Bretagne Hotel or the Acropolis, but he may expect to be talked to more esoteric destinations, like an airline pilot descending in fog.

Citizen-band radio is still a grey area in Greek law, but despite this an increasing number of owner-drivers are banding together into 'radio taxi' cooperatives. Your hotel desk will have the telephone numbers of several but they need an hour's notice and generally charge Dr 150 more than is on the clock.

Tariffs   Within Athens, there is a single tariff. For longer trips, at some point on the outskirts of the city the driver will switch his clock to double tariff, which means exactly what it suggests.

The sum on the meter before you start is Dr 30 and minimum fare Dr 130. After 1 a.m. the driver is entitled to a *nichterina*, an extra late-night charge: the price of this, as also for other extras such as suitcases and pick-up at airports and ports, is printed in English on a card that should be displayed near the clock. For three weeks over the Christmas–New Year holidays and for ten days at Easter he collects a 'bonus', the amount of which will also be displayed in English (everyone working in Greece is entitled to bonuses of one month's extra pay at Christmas, two weeks' at Easter and another two weeks' when taking annual leave, so collecting fourteen months' pay in a working year).

For a trip from central Athens to the airport or to Piraeus you should expect to pay about Dr 500 or 600 depending on the state of traffic.

If you flag down a taxi in the street, are without luggage and it is not the middle of the night, you pay exactly what is on the clock, subject to the Dr 130 minimum. Tipping is not customary.

One final caution: unless you enjoy old-fashioned mystery tours, do not get into a taxi that is already occupied. Taxi drivers are permitted to pick up additional passengers along the way; supposedly this has to be authorised by the original client, but the formality is not always observed. If the taxi already has a passenger, you will be taken to your destination after he has been delivered, but the clock will be running all the time and you will be charged what it shows at the end. It can be costly unless you are prepared, and able, to argue.

Despite its hazards, taxi-travel no longer involves much risk of deliberate run-around; there is too much demand for taxis, and the police are too tough, to make the old tricks worth the risk. But this is not to say that it can never happen.

Incidentally, just because the taxi driver lights a cigarette you should not assume that you can do the same. You have to ask if he minds, and he may object!

Long-distance taxis

If your ambition is to discover how much you can spend if you really try, you can travel about Greece by private taxi or deluxe limousine, which you book through travel agencies. A five-day tour for one to three persons is Dr 232,000 in a taxi and Dr 390,000 in a limousine, the latter rising to Dr 440,000 if your family numbers four or five members. To these prices you add your own and your driver's and guide's hotel accommodation and meals (the driver is not permitted to act as a guide), admission charges for archaeological sites and overtime if your tour includes a Sunday or public holiday.

Should you be a five-member family travelling by limousine for a week in peak season, staying in deluxe hotels and eating and drinking in the style that will be expected of you by your temporary staff, you will not go far afterwards on change from a million drachmas. On the other hand, of course, you will have seen how red the carpets can be.

By yacht

Although yachting is generally associated with island-hopping, and no one would charter a yacht without the intention of visiting at least a few islands, you should not forget that Greece is also a country of small mainland ports. None of the famed archaeological sites is more than a fairly short taxi-drive from where a yacht can drop anchor. Of fifty-one officially designated entry and departure points, twenty-five are on the mainland. The latter include Piraeus, Itea (for Delphi), Katakolon (for Olympia), Nafplion (for Mycenae and Epidavros) and Gythion (for Sparta and Mystras).

Yachts of any nationality entering Greek waters and intending to cruise in them have to put in at one of the designated ports first and last, to receive and surrender their transit log. All harbours except the large commercial ports provide anchorage space for yachts. The NTOG network of marinas includes nine on the mainland, in the Athens–Piraeus area, the Peloponnese, Thessaloniki and Halkidiki. Charges depend on the size of the vessel and the length of stay.

Also, not far short of 2,000 sailing boats, motor sailers and luxury motor yachts are available for charter, with or without crew. Prices range from $100 to $4,500 a day, according to type of vessel, numbers carried and season. Obviously you do not charter a yacht on the spur of the moment. If you intend to, you can obtain information and a list of the fifty registered Athens–Piraeus yacht brokers from NTOG, travel agencies, or by writing to: *The Greek Bareboat Yacht Owners' Association*, 56 Vass Pavlou Street, Kastella, Piraeus; *The Hellenic Professional Yacht Owners' Association*, 43 Freattydos Street, Marina Zea, Piraeus; or *The Greek Yacht Brokers' & Consultants' Association*, 36 Alkyonis Street, Old Phaleron, Athens.

Where to stay

Introduction

As an independent traveller moving about in Greece as the whim takes you, without firm plans and therefore without hotel reservations, you need have no fear of spending a night under the stars provided only that you are prepared, if necessary, to do without the normal luxury of a private shower and toilet.

At the end of 1986, Greece as a whole, mainland and islands, had 5,488 hotels, furnished apartments, inns and hostels offering 359,377 beds; with the construction boom continuing, at least in the middle and lower categories, the total is now comfortably above 5,500 hotels and probably approaching 400,000 in number of beds.

Rooms in private houses

To this should be added an unknown number of beds available in private houses. The National Tourist Organisation of Greece (NTOG), which counts only those registered with and inspected by the tourist police, speaks of 20,000; the actual figure is reckoned to be closer to 100,000. These unreported beds, which for obvious reasons cannot be booked in advance, are to be found in almost all parts of the country except the two major cities of Athens and Thessaloniki. On arrival anywhere else, through a port, train station or bus terminal, you will be approached by old women and young children enquiring in broken English whether you have a place to stay. If not, you will be led to perfectly adequate, basic accommodation in a room with at least an old-fashioned washbasin and jug, access to the family toilet, and showers by arrangement. A two-bed room will probably cost you around Dr 1,000 a night, without breakfast but almost certainly with the offer of coffee as a friendly gesture and an invitation to converse. The bill you pay, if in foreign currency, will be exchanged on the unofficial market; in no matter what form, it will remain unknown to the tax authorities.

This so-called 'para hotel' cottage industry is a cause of acute distress to professional hoteliers and to NTOG; the latter, despite evidence to the contrary, likes to maintain that it is gradually being eradicated. It dates from the 1967–74 dictatorship when, to confront a sudden growth in tourism that far outpaced hotel capacity, the Colonels offered low-interest loans to householders to refurbish a room and hold it in readiness for visitors when all the hotels in the area were full – something that then applied through most of the holiday season.

With the hotels now built in generally sufficient numbers, the original justification no longer applies. But it would be a strange businessman, and in particular a strange Greek businessman, who would quietly liquidate a profitable enterprise within the black economy just because the state told him to, at a time when the product – the room – remains in demand for reasons of cost and availability. Price-conscious Greek families and budget tourists use the rooms because they are cheap, not because the hotels are full. Others, planning a stay of only a night or two, prefer to save themselves the trouble of searching for a hotel.

So you may go with confidence anywhere, at any time; even in the most crowded resort on the busiest holiday weekend you will find somewhere to spend the night. In my personal experience, acquired on Spetses one Feast of the Assumption, there will at least be straw in a stable, vacated by a donkey 'bounced' to the shade of a fig tree, and a welcome warmer than you will receive from any hotel employee.

If you arrive in a small town or village by car and therefore unexpectedly, with the result that no one accosts you with a whispered offer of accommodation, the tourist police department, if one exists, or otherwise the ordinary police station will have a list of hotels and registered private rooms and, as a rule, a good idea of where vacancies are likely to exist.

Otherwise, try the coffee-shop or grocery, or enquire at the kiosk selling cigarettes; the boy who fetches the woman who has a room to offer will be well satisfied with a Dr 100 tip.

A word of advice   Do not try to save money on hotels. If you wish to economise, avoid expensive-looking restaurants; you will then eat better anyway.

The 'real' hotels

The following table from NTOG, correct to the end of 1986, tells you something.

Number of hotels in Greece (mainland and islands)

Category	Number of units	Number of beds	Average number of beds per unit
Deluxe	38	7,486	460
1st class	227	72,868	321
2nd class	574	78,999	137
3rd class	1,675	100,146	59
4th class	964	30,006	31
5th class	713	16,289	22
Sub-totals	4,191	315,794	

Category	Number of units	Number of beds	Average number of beds per unit
Bungalow complexes and motels	68	8,507	
Apartments	505	15,750	
Inns, pensions, etc.	724	19,326	
Grand total	5,488	359,377	

Miscellaneous information

NTOG offers an estimate that seven out of every ten hotels in Greece are less than twenty years old, built in response to a steady growth in package tour holidays dating from the early 1960s. On the one hand, this accounts for the unusually high proportion of rooms with private toilets and bath or shower facilities. On the other, it explains why you so often find your accommodation in obvious need of renovation, with scratched and possibly broken furniture, plumbing systems that sometimes dribble and sometimes flood, shutters that refuse to close properly, peeling paint and radios that have long since ceased to convey piped music at the touch of a button.

Hoteliers blame low profit margins, high state and municipal taxes, and an inflation rate – matched by the cost of borrowing money and public utility bills – that for more than a dozen years has ranged between 18 and 25 per cent. They say they simply cannot afford to refurbish as often as they should.

NTOG, responsible for supervision of hotels, acknowledges that this is an unsatisfactory situation, but observes that allowance must be made for the fact that an average 55 per cent of a hotel's turnover goes to meet payroll costs. For this reason, its supervision has to be directed mainly towards honesty of operations, cleanliness and standards of meals, and it is unable to push hard on quality of furnishings and plumbing. You may find your sheet is patched, your pillowcase is discoloured and your towel is frayed, but none of the three is likely to be dirty.

Also, outside the main cities, the vast majority of hotels operate only seasonally, from just before the western Easter to around the end of September or early October. This is reflected in the standard of personnel. A hotelier with jobs to offer for only five months of the year is fortunate, and unusual, if he can secure the services of trained, multilingual waiters and barmen; more commonly, he has to recruit where he can among the local population, taking on whoever happens to be unemployed in that particular season. Obviously, it is easier to find chambermaids than adequate head waiters. Similarly, in the provinces, you should not expect too much from your hall porter; if he is entitled to wear the crossed keys he will not be working in a hotel open for only five months every year.

The concentration of new hotel construction on mainly small units of middle and lower categories, and the diminution of the number of deluxe hotels, reflects two tendencies that the Greeks regret but are powerless to combat. The first is the average hotelier's reliance on package business negotiated with a limited number of European and United States tour operators, whose primary interest is in the final cost of the package, not the quality of services, and who are in a position to impose their demands. The hotelier simply dare not rely on independent travellers. The second is the increasing preference for self-catering holidays (in 1987 peak season, deluxe and first-class hotels throughout the country had empty rooms, second and third class were just about full, and it was almost impossible to obtain a room or bungalow with self-catering facilities).

The independent traveller taking a room in a first- or second-class hotel pays a full rate far higher than the portion of a package that goes to the hotelier from group travel. So he may legitimately be disappointed when he has to queue for a self-service meal that offers a choice between two or three warmed-up dishes to which chips have apparently been assigned by numbers, and canned peas and carrots by the teaspoonful. The hotelier would like to offer him full restaurant service and an à la carte menu, but numerically he is simply not a sufficiently important part of the business to justify the expense.

A new trend, not yet widespread but beginning to be observable, is for hotels to retain their restaurants but close their kitchens. They find it cheaper to buy ready-made dishes from a local caterer and warm them up in a microwave oven. If airline passengers do not mind, why should hotel guests? This explains the basic advice offered in 'Eating and Drinking' (p. 92): if you are not on a half-board arrangement, eat in your hotel only if you are too tired to look for a nearby restaurant or taverna.

A word on categories
In theory, and usually in fact, the classification awarded to a hotel is determined by the size of its rooms and public areas, including the lobby, the décor and furnishing of the rooms, and the services provided. Hotels of deluxe, first and second class (also called L, A and B) have dining facilities on the premises.

With a few notable exceptions in the main cities and islands, most surviving pre-war hotels are now of fourth or fifth class (D or E), do without lift, lobby or lounge, and may have added private showers but still have one toilet per floor. In the cities, they are unlikely to be in the newer and pleasanter suburbs (in Athens they are particularly thick around Omonia Square and the railway stations). They can so easily spoil a holiday and, except for a possible overnight stop in a village, should be regarded as last-resort accommodation. There are some whose most permanent guests are cockroaches.

For more than ten years NTOG has had the intention of switching to the star system, and officials say the changeover may finally be made during 1988. The difficulty, and source of hoteliers' opposition, is that this will require the adoption of international criteria, and will lead to the downgrading of a considerable number of units. Nevertheless, officials are confident that all of Greece's deluxe hotels and at least some in first class will be in a position to claim five stars.

NTOG, concerned to prevent excessive competition at the expense of services, which could bring the entire industry into disrepute, decrees only minimum room rates by hotel category. It leaves the hotelier free to charge whatever higher figure the market will stand, subject to registration of rates with NTOG in advance of each season and their posting in every hotel room.

For this reason, it frequently happens that, say, a third-class hotel may be considerably more expensive than another, even in the same area, of second class. The difference is explained by the age of the hotel, its furnishings, and sometimes its position, and should be eradicated through the star system.

In these circumstances, and bearing in mind also the sharp difference between off- and peak-season rates even in hotels open for only five months each year, and the surcharges imposed at times of local festivals or fairs, it is possible to give only the very roughest guidelines to prices by category. For example, in 1987 peak season a double room in an Athens deluxe hotel could have cost anywhere between Dr 5,000 and 30,000 a night. While the spread was less in first class, a double room still ran at between Dr 5,000 and 8,000 a night. At the other end of the scale, there were any number of fourth-class hotels offering rooms for Dr 1,500 a night, as against Dr 2,000 or more asked by some obviously superior fifth-class units.

In general, outside Athens, you should be able to find a comfortable room in an upper-bracket hotel at between Dr 4,000 and 6,000 a night. A likely third-class price is around Dr 3,000 a night, and a hotel of last resort should leave you change from Dr 2,000.

The cost of a continental breakfast ranged in 1987 from a minimum Dr 200 per person in fourth class to Dr 550 in a deluxe hotel. The average price of a three-course table d'hôte lunch or dinner (soup or pasta, a meat dish with salad and ice-cream or fruit) ranged between Dr 1,100 and 1,500, with beverages, bottled water and coffee extra. A fixed-menu dinner in an Athens deluxe hotel can set you back Dr 4,000, but the ambience will be superior and the range of dishes wider.

Most hotels will offer the independent traveller a rate for the room, with breakfast and lunch or dinner as optional extras. If you are quoted only a half-board rate, you should consider looking elsewhere! You may legally be subjected to a surcharge for a stay of less than three nights.

Avoiding groups

In the main cities and resort islands, it is almost impossible to avoid groups, unless you use the kind of hotel that will make you miserable for more substantial reasons, since even one too small to have business with a European or United States tour operator will probably be linked with a Greek agent for domestic groups. However, Greek groups do not normally arrive or leave in the middle of the night.

Also, some comfort may be derived from the fact that only a handful of deluxe hotels in Athens, Thessaloniki and on the islands of Rhodes and Crete are equipped to go after convention business.

Air conditioning

Although Greece is a hot country, air conditioning in the home and in any but the most modern offices is still regarded as the ultimate luxury. It should not be taken for granted in hotels below second class, or in bungalows of any category.

If you are travelling in the provinces, you can expect to sleep with open windows. You might therefore consider bringing with you your own personal mosquito-killer, or buying one on arrival from a grocer or chemist – preferably electric. The Greeks use them all the time. An appliance plus a two-week supply of poison should not set you back more than Dr 1,000, and should save a lot of scratching.

Traditional settlements

Greece has a large number of villages and buildings that have retained their traditional characteristics. To protect this national heritage, NTOG has pioneered a programme based on conservation of selected settlements or individual houses through their conversion into tourist guest-houses and complexes. Eight settlements have been chosen for the first phase, on the islands of Ṣantorini (Thera), Chios, Cephalonia and Psara and, in mainland Greece, at Makrynitsa and Vizitsa on Mount Pelion, Zagorohoria in Epiros, and Areopoli in the Mani region of the Peloponnese.

At Makrynitsa, three mansions provide twenty-two rooms; at Vizitsa there are sixty-nine beds in the thirty-one rooms of five mansions; at Zagorohoria five houses have been restored providing forty-seven beds in twenty-one rooms; and the Kapetanakos Tower in Areopoli has seventeen beds in six rooms. All the settlements, except that on Psara, are open year-round. In 1987, room prices in peak season were generally between Dr 3,000 and 5,000 a night. Reservations may be made by writing to NTOG at 2 Amerikis Street, Athens.

Accommodation is somewhat basic, usually without a private bath. While there are no restaurant facilities, a degree of self-catering is possible. In strict value terms the rooms may be somewhat overpriced, but they are intended for those prepared to pay a little extra to experience Greece as it used to be.

Youth hostels

To obtain accommodation in any youth hostel in Greece requires a membership card from a national association of youth hostels or an international guest card; the latter may be obtained by application to the youth hostel itself or the Greek Association of Youth Hostels at 4 Dragatsaniou Street, Athens; Tel. 3234 107.

There are four youth hostels in Athens and, on the mainland, one each in Thessaloniki, Delphi, Litochoron (Mount Olympos), Mycenae, Nafplion, Olympia and Patras.

Both Athens and Thessaloniki have YMCA and YWCA hostels.

Tents and caravans

There are organised camp-sites in most parts of Greece, some set up and run by NTOG or the Hellenic Automobile and Touring Club (ELPA) but the majority privately owned. All are enclosed and guarded. Legally, camping is allowed only in these organised grounds. Pitch your tent or park your caravan elsewhere and you will be moved along if the police choose to notice you or if their attention is drawn to your presence by a householder or hotelier.

Ex-officio police action is more certain if you are found in places with a high risk of woodland fires than, for example, at the edge of the sea in a remote cove.

While camping equipment can be purchased in the main towns, there are as yet no shops specialising in camping equipment rentals. However, two-person tents with beds can be hired by the night at some of the sites.

Before going to Greece for a camping or caravan holiday, it is advisable to write to NTOG, or ELPA (Athens Tower B, Athens) for lists of sites and detailed regulations.

Time-sharing

Time-sharing was legalised in Greece only in 1986 and has so far made no impact on the hotel picture. But several international time-share companies are understood to be preparing campaigns, and the situation could change quickly.

Eating and Drinking

Greece offers some delightful surprises to those who still retain a secret affection for the simple things of life. In relation to Greek cuisine, that means charcoal.

The Ancient Greeks taught the barbarian world how to cook – wealthy Romans employed Greeks to tutor their children and prepare their meals – and the barbarian world took it on from there, but at home the Greeks just went on grilling.

They set up their grills in the monasteries of the Byzantine era, including those on Mount Athos, which bequeathed to the modern world not a host of new dishes or rare brandies, but the one thing that no self-respecting chef can do without: his white hat.

'The 400 years' are held responsible for a number of 'Turkish' dishes, most notably sweets, though it is more than likely that many of these had simply been appropriated by the conquerors along with much else that was appreciated in old Constantinople. Throughout the four centuries, the Greeks grilled.

Neither European Community nor medical questioning of the long-term effects of charred food on the health will stop them now. There may be a place for Wiener Schnitzel, Bœuf Bourgignon and fish and chips, but the taverna the Greeks will choose for a family outing will be pungent with blue smoke and the perfume of oregano.

If an Ancient Greek could be resurrected today, with his language intact, he would understand little or nothing of what he heard and at best would be able to communicate only with the occasional professor or more learned bishop. But he would feel completely at home in the corner taverna, and would find much that he recognised. His staple foods in particular would all be there: olive oil and olives, fish, lamb and goat, goats' milk cheese, wine and bread, beans, peas, cabbage, lettuce, lentils and garlic, honey, nuts and, come August, figs.

The taverna

As in any country, what you eat and how much you pay will depend on where you go and whether you are in search of a meal or an evening's entertainment. Tavernas (and, for that matter, restaurants and bars) can be broken down into arbitrary but workable divisions between the traditional, the transitional and the new.

The traditional taverna

This will have its large charcoal grill near the entrance, or in summer just outside, tended by the owner. Close by will be a glass-fronted refrigerator displaying plates of veal and pork chops, lamb and goat in joint or cutlet form, 'village' sausages, and hamburgers the size of squashed tennis balls made up of ground meat mixed with bread.

Another display, not refrigerated, will be of cold appetisers (*mezedes*) and whatever meat dishes the owner's family may have prepared during the day; one member will be seated at a table collating the orders, keeping the tax records and manning the till, and others will be serving. Though in the main cities the taverna may have become large enough to require the employment of staff, it will still be a family operation catering to families that are also friends; children old enough to sit up will be at the tables, and there could well be a couple of babies sleeping in prams.

The tables themselves will probably be covered by white cloths, which will not be changed for the next client; instead, a fresh sheet of paper or plastic will be spread over the cloth. Scraps of food left on the plates at the end of the meal will be emptied on to the table and gathered up inside the 'cover'.

The *tavernaris* would be surprised if you sought to make a reservation; he would obligingly lean reversed chairs against one of the tables, but would be unlikely to hold it if a regular customer turned up before you did and no other table was free.

There is no such thing as a non-smoking corner in a taverna, though a number of restaurants, especially in hotels, are now beginning to introduce them.

The traditional taverna is not, above all, the place for a quick meal. If it is eight o'clock and you have a ticket for folk dancing at nine, either go to a restaurant or eat after the show. Leisurely service is a matter of life-style and economics. The Greek goes to his taverna to spend the evening and the owner, knowing he must count on a limited turnover, has no reason not to economise on waiters, while the waiters themselves rely on the percentages from a relatively small number of bills.

The average Greek family will prefer to 'give a table' at a taverna than to entertain at home. Their apartment is probably small, air conditioning is still a luxury, and at the end of the night the bill for six at a taverna is probably not much higher than the cost of the raw materials of a similarly varied menu prepared in a cramped kitchen.

The taverna offers, therefore, exactly what the customer requires: not an aperitif, since he will have had that at home, but a wide range of starters, and a choice among a small number of familiar main dishes.

It follows that a taverna is a place in which to talk. It is unlikely to have music, except possibly from a tape-recorder, though it might be on the beat of a strolling player or singer who will wander among the tables, collect his tips and leave. If it has a piano, it is definitely a restaurant.

A menu, probably handwritten, may be displayed somewhere near the entrance, but there is unlikely to be one on the table and no need to become anxious if you can neither read the menu brought to you nor make yourself understood by the waiter. You are not simply welcome but expected to point to what you want from the dishes on display or stroll into the kitchen. The Greeks do that themselves: they know very well what a moussaka is, but they want to see what this taverna's moussaka looks like before venturing an order.

Suppose you order half a dozen starters to be followed by grilled steak. The waiter will bring you the *mezedes* and then, unless he acquires the impression that you are in a hurry, he will wait for a reminder before telling the *afentiko*, his boss, to put the steaks over the charcoal. The meat will probably reach you extremely well done; the Greeks prefer it that way. Medium rare is better hazarded in an expensive restaurant or steak house, where the meat will probably be imported and almost certainly will have been hung; the *tavernaris* will only have beaten it with a metal weight.

There is no compulsion in a taverna to order what you do not want. You can sit all night with a glass of wine and a plate of beans if you wish, though you will be regarded as eccentric if you open a book.

The taverna is identifiable by its decor: bright lighting, quite possibly from naked bulbs if the owner is of the older generation and regards it as a sign of extravagance not to obtain the full value of what he has paid for. Walls will be covered with whitewash or plastic paint, the monotony broken by an occasional picture in an unglassed frame or secured with tacks. Somewhere, there will be a line of barrels: wine is part of the meal, but in the taverna it is also definitely part of the decor.

You call the waiter by clapping your hands or tapping a knife against a glass. When you want your bill, you can either use the word *logariasmó* or, having caught the waiter's eye, move the hand rapidly from side to side on a horizontal plane with thumb and forefinger holding an imaginary pencil. The bill will be handwritten, probably indecipherable, and honest; the Greek customer at his regular taverna will at most only check the addition.

In the grey area of the taverna in transition, you can expect a fresh tablecloth without a plastic topping, subdued lighting or even a personal candle, a printed menu in several languages, and no sign of wine other than in bottles. The plates may be warm though the helpings will probably be smaller; the bill will probably be higher but at least will be the legible production of a cash register. Whether this is more romantic depends on your personal views.

**Some
tavernas
are uppity**

The elegant taverna will be found mainly in Athens and the resort islands, occasionally in the larger provincial towns, and rarely in the countryside. Unlike its more humble relatives which tend to be named after their owners, their principal feature, speciality or location, its name will lean towards elegance also. It may boast a small combo with a lady vocalist, but if it has a dance floor and a live orchestra it should be regarded as a nightclub.

At the elegant taverna you will be under greater pressure to sample the whole range of starters. If a waiter brings them to your table without being asked, you can at that point reject anything you may find unattractive in appearance and it will be removed without objection. Main dishes can still be selected during a visit to the kitchen.

At some point during the evening, the musicians will circulate among the tables singing requested numbers. They do not need to be tipped unless you ask for something special – if you put them to the test, you will find their repertoire may well include *Waltzing Matilda*. The tip, a couple of hundred drachmas a song, is slipped into the leader's pocket as your signal that he is released.

But are there no restaurants?

Certainly there are restaurants, and of as many categories as there are types of taverna. If you are staying in a deluxe hotel, you will have direct access to some of the most elegant restaurants in Greece, offering the kind of dishes you are accustomed to when in funds in your own country. You will almost certainly be impressed by your surroundings, and may even eat well.

Since restaurants in hotels are longstanding and unlikely to vary much from year to year, some recommendations may be hazarded: the best in Athens are reputedly La Rotisserie at the InterContinental, Ta Nissia at the Hilton, the Templars' Grill at the Royal Olympic, the GB Corner at the Grande Bretagne and, for the excellence of the view across to the Acropolis and its Elizabethan ambience inside, the Tudor Hall at the King George. If you are in Corfu with deep pockets, you could dine at the Achilleion, once the summer palace of the Empress Elizabeth of Austria and Kaiser Wilhelm of Germany, and now one of Greece's three casinos.

It is rather more probable that you will be staying in a hotel of lower category, on a half-board basis. In that case by all means take the meal you have paid for, but give earnest consideration to doing so at lunch, when you will probably not want to fill up anyway.

Crusades have been fought in Greece, not least by NTOG, to impress on hoteliers that not every visitor is a weight-watcher, and some improvements have resulted. The Commerce Ministry has now decreed minimum rations, by ingredient and weight, plus unlimited bread. But you will certainly not eat as well as you would in an equivalent hotel in Italy, Germany, France, England or Turkey.

To do them justice, hoteliers who live from package tours, which most of them do, have a genuine grievance: their contracts are stipulated a year in advance in drachmas, leaving them to confront inflation without the cover that would otherwise be provided by currency depreciation (when the drachma slides, the profit goes to the tour operator). However, they appear to have been persuaded that economies can better be made on waiters' salaries, through introduction of canteen-style self-service restaurants, than by counting the chips.

Outside hotels, the possibilities are wide and varied. Athens all year round and the resort islands in season are well provided with French, Italian and Chinese restaurants; on the islands there will also be restaurants catering to Scandinavians or offering fish and chips (though not quite in the English manner) to cautious Britons. And everywhere there are steak houses. In Athens at least these establishments depend for survival on year-round business from middle-income Greeks and resident foreigners, so if they are not reliable they soon close.

The Old Contemptibles

More Greek, in style and menu, are the longstanding restaurants whose clientele is divided equally among Greeks, resident foreigners and tourists. They open early for the foreigners, midday for lunch and 7 p.m. for dinner, and stay open late for the Greeks, to 4 p.m. and 1 a.m. They employ mainly elderly waiters by whom it is a pleasure to be served, and offer a wide range of Greek and European dishes at middle-range prices – say Dr 1,200–1,600 a head for a three-course meal with wine.

Four places in Athens that have been serving politicians, businessmen, bankers, shop assistants and priests for at least forty years are the Corfu, Syntrivani, Delphi and Ideal, the first three less than a hundred yards from Constitution Square and the Ideal closer to Omonia. But others are easily recognisable: as a rule of thumb, look for Greeks who have discarded their jackets in hot weather, but probably not their ties.

Mainly around Omonia Square in Athens, and in the area of the White Tower in Thessaloniki, there are restaurants where only grilled meats are served as main dishes. At the entrance or in the display window, serried ranks of chickens will be turning on spits; other grills will be processing sucking-pig or dealing with steaks, and somewhere there should be a doner kebab – veal assembled on spits and grilled vertically, so that every slice as it is carved off is succulently crisp. *Souvlaki*, the same veal on individual skewers, will be cooked to order. Except for *souvlaki*, the meat is usually sold by weight, with side helpings if desired of chips, salad or cold boiled vegetables. Chopped raw onion will be sprinkled on the kebab, and mustard is available. The meat is of reasonably good quality, and the prices are moderate.

Lamb also may be used occasionally for *souvlaki*, but will not turn up in doner form. The reason is availability, price and preference. Greece has no mutton – the pasture is insufficient and the demand is always for lean meat. Even around Easter, when it floods the market, lamb is the most expensive of all meat except fillet steak; from June to November it can be hard to find. There is a fairly recent tendency for *psistaries* to make their doner out of pork, to save a few drachmas; since there is no legal requirement to specify the meat used, the curious among their customers will generally assume they are eating veal.

Further out from the centre are the ordinary restaurants of the working Greeks. There is nothing in particular to recommend them, nor any reason to avoid them if sustenance is your only pursuit.

Making do with a snack

Fast-food outlets have entered Greece in a big way. Their habit of compiling menus consisting wholly of pictures of dishes on offer, numbered for convenience of ordering, with the price stuck on top, may charitably be considered a device to save time rather than an implicit acknowledgement that they expect to cater only to the illiterate.

Light snacks, and not just ice cream and cakes, are usually available at most patisseries: sandwiches, toasted or not; spaghetti with cheese or meat sauce; omelettes plain or filled; 'eyes' (*matia*, the Greek for two fried eggs), and the usual range of cold plates.

If you are stricken with hunger on the streets during the act of tourism, solutions are at hand. Most bakeries offer hot cheese pies and 'croissanteries' are coming in. *Souvlaki* can be smelled out everywhere. Individually wrapped cakes are on sale from barrows and at some kiosks, and in the mornings and late at night the *koulouri* men make their rounds with their trays of crisp bracelets of bread sprinkled with sesame seeds. You can also find roast chestnuts, corn on the cob and nuts – including *passa tempo*, toasted seeds so named because each one has to be painstakingly split between the teeth to extract the edible sliver inside.

Sizing up the opportunities

The time has come for a first foray into real food. You have familiarised yourself with what is available at your hotel, identified some likely-looking alternative in the vicinity, and are ready to lay purse and stomach on a strange table.

The purpose of this section is not to list all the dishes that can be found in Greece – they range from roast beef and Yorkshire pudding to lemon pie. Similarly, regional and seasonal specialities will be touched on only if, like the Corfu *sofrito* or the Easter *mayeritsa* soup, they are on offer also in other parts of the country or at other times of the year. And finally, since this is not a cookery book, it would be purposeless to include dishes, no matter how delicious, that are eaten routinely in the Greek home but are rarely if ever found in restaurants or tavernas – either because of their over-familiarity, the time or labour required to prepare them, or the patent impossibility of charging a high enough price to make them profitable. There is an adequate supply of Greek cookery books in English for those who would like to experiment in making bean soup (*fassolatha*), lentil soup (*fakès*) or chickpea soup (*rovithia*): these are not so much soups as full one-course meatless meals – another good reason for tavernas to avoid them. (And a fortune remains to be made by the enterprising small businessman who parks a barrow between the Cumberland and Mount Royal Hotels in London to serve cups of hot *fassolatha* and *fakès* to Greek tourists.)

Over the next few pages you will find brief descriptions of the dishes you can expect to come across throughout Greece in the middle of the summer. The intention is to provide a rough guide to their composition, with a view to preventing unpleasant surprises, disappointment or waste.

'Killing the appetite'

Mezedes

The Greeks are dedicated nibblers, to whom *mezedes* are the essential prelude to every meal, and may indeed become the whole meal in the middle of the day. At its simplest, the *mezè* (one *mezè*, two *mezedes*) can be no more than a plate containing a slice of cucumber, a few pickles, olives, a piece of cheese and a quarter of a hard-boiled egg. But usually something a little more elaborate is preferred.

This could take the form of a dip: *Rossiki* (Russian) salad, *taramousalata* (a pink paste of fish roe and potato), *hatziki* (thick yoghurt blended with cucumber and garlic), *melitzano salata* (a similar preparation based on aubergines) or, mainly but not necessarily as an accompaniment to fish, *skordalia* (from *skorda*, the Greek for garlic), a purée of potato or bread with garlic, oil and lemon.

Self-caterers will find all these dips ready-made in supermarket refrigerators. The Greeks eat them spread on slices of bread, but they can also be used to improve strips of raw or salad vegetables.

Obviously, *skordalia* has to be a group activity, unless you propose to go into a twenty-four hour retreat. Two highly prized properties are ascribed to garlic: it is said to combat blood pressure and induce sleep. The strings of garlic hanging from rafters or festooning taverna walls have nothing to do with vampires, which in Greece drink only from wallets, but are intended to convey a promise of healthy eating. However, a virgin stomach may appreciate an alka seltzer after the first encounter, and, though raw parsley helps, there is really not much you can do about your breath.

The cold dip negotiated, you are ready for the hot *mezè*: *tyropita* or *spanakopita* (cheese or spinach in hot flaky pastry), or a combination of the two in the form of *spanakotiropita*, or a plate of *kolokithia* or *melitzana tiganitès* (fried eggplant or aubergine). *Patatès tiganitès* (French fries; ask for 'tsips' in Greece and you get a packet of crisps) are the most common *mezè* in the vegetable category. Cheese will be feta.

As an accompaniment to the hot *mezè*, which in many tavernas may also include *keftèdes* (meatballs), you have a choice of whatever *horta* (boiled vegetable, served cold with olive oil) the taverna has prepared that day. In the traditional taverna you may also expect *kokoretsi* in the evening, though not for lunch. This is a highly spiced preparation consisting of the offal of lamb threaded on a spit and wrapped round and round with intestine. A cut from the spit makes a helping, and it really does taste better than a description of its components might suggest.

In a fish taverna or restaurant, the *mezedes* will probably include *marides* (whitebait) and *kalamarakia* (squid). The *marides* – up to two dozen a helping – will be larger than the whitebait commonly encountered in other countries, but are still eaten head and all. For the squeamish, the taverna cat can come in useful. The *marithes* will always be fresh, since they are never frozen and do not keep. The same does not apply to *kalamarakia* and even less to *garithes* (shrimps), though legally if they are not fresh they should be identified on the menu as *katapsigmeno* (deep-frozen).

At their tastiest, *kalamarakia* are small enough to be fried whole after a simple washing; you pull out the semi-transparent bone and eat them guts, ink and all. In the more expensive restaurants they will have been filleted and sliced into rings and strips, losing much of their flavour but posing less danger to clothing from flying ink and also, it must be admitted, less danger of mild poisoning or allergic reaction. That is the real problem with *kalamarakia*: you have to try it once to be sure you can take it.

Soup

Soup, if served at all, is more likely to follow than precede the *mezedes*. Outside the deluxe hotel, the choice is limited: *kotosoupa* (chicken soup, usually thickened with egg and flavoured with lemon), *hortosoupa* (vegetable soup) and *psarosoupa* (fish soup, but definitely not a bouillabaisse). At Easter everywhere, but at some restaurants throughout the year, *mayeritsa* is also on offer. This so-called 'Easter' soup represents an alternative use of the lamb offal and intestines that more commonly go to make a *kokoretsi*; enjoyment is aided by not dwelling too much upon the contents.

Picking and choosing

In the traditional taverna, the main dish will be a choice among *brizoles* (steaks) of *moushari* (veal) or *hirino* (pork), *païdaki* (lamb cutlets) or *biftekaki* (hamburgers). Sometimes the taverna, and certainly the restaurant, will also offer what in Greece are known as 'cooked' dishes, prepared in the *tapsi* (pan) earlier in the day and kept warm.

These include veal, pork and chicken *sto fourno* ('in the oven', i.e. roast), garnished with a couple of chips or potatoes also *sto fourno*. The same meat slices or chickens quartered will turn up with spaghetti or a small heap of rice. In general, partly because of the previous *mezedes* and also to keep prices low, vegetables have to be ordered separately as side dishes.

There are three other delicious pre-prepared dishes found everywhere in Greece: *moussaka* (which has and needs no translation), *pastitsio* (much the same as moussaka but with the aubergine or potato replaced by pasta) and *stiffado* (meat stewed with onions and garlic). *Sofrito*, the national dish of Corfu, also turns up in Corfiote restaurants around the country; it is a fillet steak stewed in a garlic sauce and served with mashed potato.

Common though less ubiquitous are *youvetsaki* (meat stewed with tomato and served with pasta), veal *stamnas* (much the same, with vegetables instead of pasta) and lamb, kid or rabbit *lathorigani* (stewed in olive oil and flavoured with oregano). Variations are played on all these themes, so it is a good idea to visit the kitchen before you decide.

And finally a word on *dolmadakia*, meat and rice wrapped in vine leaves and served with a thick egg-and-lemon sauce. These can be eaten either as an appetiser or a main course. They bear no resemblance to those you can buy in cans in Greek supermarkets, which contain no meat, have no sauce, are swimming in olive oil, and are eaten only cold.

The finny drove   Fish is much more expensive than meat, whether ordered in a restaurant or bought from a fishmonger. Around Athens, fish restaurants are mainly to be found, as might be expected, in Piraeus, the nearby yacht marina of Mikrolimano and along the coast to and beyond Athens Airport. In the provinces, they will be sitting on beaches, and on the lesser islands you will find them close to the harbour. In the resort islands you may have to search. You can expect to pay at least Dr 2,000 a head if you have substantial appetites to satisfy.

Here again, except for slices of *synagrida* or similar white fish (any translation is open to dispute and could be misleading), you will select the fish you want from the restaurant icebox and it will be grilled or fried to order and served head and all. If grilled, it will be accompanied by an oil and lemon sauce. A scrap of paper on the dish will give weight and price: keep this so that you can check the bill.

Barbounia and *glossa* (these are indisputably red mullet and sole respectively) will usually be dusted in flour and fried. *Bakalarakia* (cod, either fresh, frozen or imported dried from Iceland or the Soviet Union) will also be fried, though in batter, and probably accompanied by *skordalia*; not a highly-regarded fish in Greece, this is relatively cheap.

You should consider yourself fortunate if you find *lithrini*, *fangri*, *sargos*, *spathari* or *melanouria*: order them grilled and do not torment yourself about what they may be called in English since no two experts agree.

Apart from *marides* and *kalamarakia* as a *mezè*, you may also be offered *ktopodi* (octopus, grilled or stewed) or *garithes* (shrimps, grilled or fried with tomato sauce). If in funds you could also go for a lobster, boiled or grilled, though unless it twitches when you shake hands you should assume it is frozen. Greeks eat them only after winning a lottery.

Winding up on the way home

With the possible exception of an ice or a cream caramel, you will not find dessert or coffee on the menu of the traditional taverna and middle-ranking restaurant. The Greeks end their meal with fruit, then go to a patisserie if they want more.

Cakes are either recognisably international or *sto tapsi* ('in the pan'); the latter may once have been Turkish, but should certainly not now be described as such. Essentially, they comprise the *baklava*, *kataifi* and *galaktobouriko*. The first is the nut-filled and honey-flavoured pastry now familiar around the world, the second is much the same but in the form of a 'shredded wheat', and the third is a custard pie. The Greeks will prefer them for safety if they are in any doubt about the reliability or freshness of the cream-and-chocolate confections, and you might well do the same for these and two additional reasons: they are more 'Greek' and less likely to cause an upset stomach.

On the subject of coffee

You may still, if you wish, order a *turkiko* but it would be more polite to your hosts if you requested an *elliniko*. A few years ago, what is now 'Greek' coffee began to disappear from patisseries, though not from the working-class coffee-shops. This was because its prices were, and indeed still are, set by the Commerce Ministry under regulations covering 'products of wider popular consumption' while those of 'French', 'American' – espresso, cappuccino and the rest – were not. But responding to protests, the Ministry eventually made it illegal for any kind of coffee to be served unless 'Greek' coffee was also available.

You are over the first hurdle when you request Greek and not Turkish coffee, but to earn the respect of the waiter and therefore a better result you should be familiar with at least the three basic subdivisions: *variglyko* (heavy and sweet), *glykivrasto* (sweet and boiled) and *metreo* (medium sweet). Order one of these and the coffee should reach you hot, accompanied by a glass of iced water; use only the generic term and you may get instant tepid in a small cup.

All too often, your hotel will expect you to brew your own, at least at breakfast and after meals, from the cup of lukewarm water and the packet of Nescafé in the saucer. If a patisserie does the same, go somewhere else next time.

Bread and water

About the one place where the Greeks are prepared to wait for service is a bakery. This is natural enough, since bread is their staple food and its perfume when fresh from the oven makes a bakery a most pleasant place to be. A glance at the rubbish bags left outside apartment blocks in the evenings would suggest that the Greeks are champions not only in eating bread but also in discarding it. This is not simply because it is cheap – its prices are more strictly controlled than those of any other product – but because even families for whom nothing is inexpensive insist that the bread must be fresh (they will make their economies elsewhere).

It follows that there is little demand for wrapped and even less for sliced loaves, though both are on display in supermarkets for the occasional family that puts toast or sandwiches on the table. If you do buy packaged bread for your self-catering requirements, check the expiry date carefully and still look for mildew.

Some twenty years ago, a young Greek who had made a fortune from sliced bread in Melbourne lost it in Greece when he set up what was then this country's first 'bread factory', equipped with the latest machinery and a fleet of delivery vans. Once the novelty wore off, sales slumped; towards the end he was giving away to hospitals and army barracks as much as he sold to a potential market of three million consumers in which he had no competition. He failed partly because his ovens were inhospitably remote: he simply could not cook the family meal that is the main function of the neighbourhood bakery once the day's bread is sold.

The insistence on freshness governs the size and nature of the loaf: relatively small, crisp and usually white. Brown bread, which in Greek is *mavro* (black), has never been very highly regarded since it suggested poverty; after the Chernobyl disaster it became practically unobtainable because of the caesium concentration in the husk of the wheat. But the so-called *horiatiko* (village) bread has retained its popularity; every baker will produce some and a few bake nothing else. This is grey, fairly flat and looks unappetising, but it has a tastiness that more refined flours do not provide and retains its freshness for the few hours demanded by its purchasers.

The bakery will also offer a range of biscuit-type products sometimes containing sultanas but more usually sprinkled with sesame seeds. Try the dark brown *moustalevria*, which has a suggestion of ginger but is actually flavoured with the must of wine. In the early morning you may find a bakery with the rings of *koulouria* bread, which should definitely be eaten while still warm. More ambitious bakeries have encroached on bar and patisserie territory with the offer of *pitsa*, the boat-shaped *penirly* rich in butter and egg, spinach or cheese pies and cakes of non-cream varieties. You can also go to a bakery for a *tsoureki*, a kind of overgrown tea-cake which at Easter has a red hard-boiled egg protruding from the top. Few bakers, however, have yet succeeded in making respectable croissants, and these are best purchased from a supermarket or a specialist shop.

In a taverna or restaurant, bread in thick slices will be placed on your table with the knives and forks before your order is taken, to keep you going until the other starters arrive. It will not be accompanied by butter, which the Greeks eat only at home. In a taverna it may already have rested for a moment over the charcoal grill; if not, the word 'toast' (pronounced 'tossed') will launch it on its journey provided there is still room on the grill.

A carafe of iced water will normally be put on your table along with the bread; if not, you ask for *neró*. Is it safe to drink? You will observe that the Greeks consume it by the gallon, and normally regard bottled water as the ultimate extravagance. But since there are sharp regional differences in water content and quality, even the Greeks will sometimes order a bottle when away from their home town. You might wisely do the same, since it would be a pity to lose a day's wellbeing for so little reason.

You can buy water in one-and-a-half litre disposable plastic bottles from a *kava* (wine and spirit merchant), grocery or supermarket: you will find Ivi, which comes from springs at Loutraki near Corinth, in most parts of the country, but there is no agreement among the Greeks themselves on which is better and which not so good. All bottled water is 'natural', never aerated.

The ubiquitous olive

Olive oil is something you simply have to come to terms with. It will be in almost all cooked food – the Greeks never use butter and rarely margarine – and on the salad or boiled vegetables; fish, chips and eggs will have been cooked in it and, mixed with lemon juice, it will have basted the grilled fish.

There is no tree so highly prized in Greece as the olive, unique as a provider of food, and once of heat and light too, without damaging itself, as well as the finest of all shades for hedonising under. Until the dowry was abolished, a small grove could be the precipitant of marriage. The plumpest olives and finest oil are supposed to come from Kalamata in the Peloponnese and Amphisa in the general area of Delphi, but most Greek families have their own secret sources and share the knowledge only with their closest friends. They buy it in the winter in 17-kg cans, delivered to their homes, preferring first-pressed virgin oil if they can afford it. 'Refined' may be bought from a grocery for salads, but the demand is secondary. When the Greeks speak of *lathi* (oil), they mean olive oil; tankers from the Middle East carry *petrelaio*.

Drunkenness is said to be a rare phenomenon in Greece because the Greeks never drink without eating. But a more precise explanation may be that what they eat always includes olive oil, which delays alcohol absorption. You could venture a half-glass drunk neat before a night on the tiles as a hangover preventive.

The olive itself is more easily avoided. While a few may be scattered on your salad, its relative expense dictates that it should be served mainly as a separate dish. Olives may be large or small, black, brown or green, preserved in oil or brine, firm-fleshed or mushy. A 'village salad' (*horiatiko salata*) has olives and feta cheese mixed into it. Feta, made from the milk of sheep or goat, is the cheese with which most Greeks will end a meal. It is rather an acquired taste, but since it costs so little you should try it. About the only other cheeses on offer outside the supermarkets are soft yellow *kasseri* and the rather harder *gravieras*. These are safe, but unexciting.

The Greek equivalent of a ploughman's lunch is a slice of feta scattered with oregano, surrounded with olives and doused in oil, accompanied by thick slices of bread and a glass of wine or ouzo. At a wayside table shaded by vines on a hot afternoon this can be a royal feast. When you too polish the plate with the last of your bread, you will have solved all your eating problems in Greece. You will also be enjoying the same meal on which Greek soldiers traditionally go into battle.

Drinks before, during and after

If you are to stay with the local product, Greece offers ouzo as an aperitif, wine or beer with the meal, and brandy afterwards. Ouzo is the aniseed-flavoured national drink that has now been joined in the Greek home, though rarely superseded, by imported Campari and even the occasional gin and tonic. Distilled from grape, it is colourless in the bottle but turns cloudy when water is added. The Greeks prefer it on ice with water, at most half-and-half. With an alcohol content of 42 per cent vol it is not particularly potent but nevertheless it is always accompanied by something to nibble, even if only a biscuit and a piece of cheese. In quantity and without food, it has the un-Greek habit of attacking the stranger on two fronts, but at least the condition of your stomach then helps to distract your attention from the state of your head. Try it, but with caution!

More than 90 per cent of all wine consumed in Greece is white, and the Greeks prefer it *heema* ('loose') from the barrel, not just because it is cheaper but because they believe it is less likely to have chemical additives. With comparatively rare exceptions, if it's from a barrel it's resinated. Most Greeks will tell you retsina got that way because the barrels had to be caulked with pine resin, but even earlier, resin was applied to the inside of earthenware wine jars to guard against seepage. Now, it is simply the preferred flavouring. The first sip may suggest turpentine but a taste for retsina is not hard to acquire. However, for the faint-hearted, tavernas keep a few bottles of drinkable non-resinated white wine in the ice-box. Restaurants will offer a choice between resinated and non-resinated carafe wine, or will not offer *heema* wine of any kind. Restaurant retsina is likely to be of reliable quality, neither so excellent nor so atrocious as that supplied in some tavernas. As a rule of thumb, be wary of retsina that is cloudy, and of any kind of 'loose' red wine.

Bottled wines

Though no accurate count exists, there are said to be close on 500 wines now available in bottles; the number is increasing annually as an effect of European Community membership, which has created new markets abroad, and the growth of cooperative production and bottling. Also, standardisation procedures are being improved, though there is still no real conception of vintage. Similarly, there are no little vineyards to which the passing stranger will be invited for the trampling. The closest approximation is the summer wine festival at Daphni, on the outskirts of Athens, where the price of admission gives the right of unlimited tippling. But if one goes there at all it is for quantity, not quality.

Among the bottled whites, those you will find on sale everywhere in Greece include Kambas (retsina or unresinated Hymettus), Santa Helena, Cellar and Boutari's Lac de Roches and, at the more expensive end of the spectrum, Porto Carras. Boutari also markets the most popular of the reds, under the name Naoussa, closely pursued again by Porto Carras. There are also a few dessert wines, heavy and sweet. The best of these are probably Samos, which Byron implored the Greeks to 'dash down', and the darker Mavrodafni that inspired Henry Miller in *The Colossus of Maroussi* to prose even purpler than the wine itself, bemusing some Greeks and amusing others. Sweet wines are simply not drunk except by tourists.

Three wine industries, Cair of Rhodes, Achaia Klaus of Patras and Zitsa of central Greece, now market sparkling dry and medium-sweet wines that are acceptable approximations to champagne at far more reasonable prices, but these too have not really caught on and are more likely to be found in supermarkets than in restaurants. However, if you are treating yourself to a lobster . . . .

Probably the best wine you will ever drink in Greece, if you are lucky enough to be offered a small glass, will accompany a couple of olives and a piece of cheese in the refectory of a monastery. But for that you not only have to go to the monastery but to arrive on a day and at a time when the monks are receiving. You will then get an idea of what wine used to be like when its production was still a cottage industry and it didn't matter whether it travelled or not since it wasn't going anywhere.

You will find the better-known international beers on sale in Greece, but only in pale or lager form, in cans or bottles. You might come across a supermarket with cans of Guinness.

There is no reason to fear Greek brandies, provided you go for the five-star, seven-star or VSOP: Metaxas and Votrys are the most ubiquitous.

A word on bars and pubs

Except in hotels or nightclubs, Greek bars bear no relation to bars in other countries, and even less to pubs. You go to one if you want to sit down with beer, wine or ouzo and eat a fairly substantial meal but without a main course. Typical orders might be chips, baked beans, meat balls, cheese in slices or fried in flour, fried eggs, omelette, Russian salad, olives, or a cold plate of ham and salami. Many bars are open only during shopping hours, which gives an idea of the reason for their existence, while there is usually a small one, also serving coffee, on the mezzanine floor of an office block. This explains why eating at his desk need not be a particular hardship for a businessman, and there is no such thing as a packed lunch. The oldest surviving bar in central Athens, in an arcade in Panepistimiou Street opposite Zonars, is Apotsos, where the decoration consists of framed Victorian advertisements for Pears soap and such immortals.

The pub in Greece is really a myth. Certainly there are places that call themselves pubs, sometimes whole clusters of them in areas of concentrated British tourism, such as the Glyfada suburb of Athens and Benitses or Cavo in Corfu. They will have a polished bar and bar stools, and possibly even a rail for the feet, along with a barman in some kind of uniform, a selection of whiskies, gins and brandies, and beer in bottles or possibly even drawn from small metal barrels and presented as 'draught'. The music will be piped or provided by a pianist, and the lighting will be equally subdued.

These pubs have been opened, sometimes by British or Irish immigrants, to offer a home-from-home to the British tourist and to persuade him to leave some of his money in the hands of his compatriots; occasionally they will employ a couple of barmaid–waitresses recruited from among the British girls who arrive with the swallows with the intention of financing a protracted summer holiday through part-time work. What should not be anticipated is a recognisable pub atmosphere. Like the acoustics in some concert halls, this is a problem that has so far eluded solution. There are too many barriers to its creation.

One is the climate. Between May and October, which is when the pubs must cover their costs for the year and is the only time many of them are even open, the idea of a pub as a place of shelter and warmth is untenable. It has to remove its windows, and may well spill on to the pavement. So there is no cosiness.

Another is the Greek lack of interest at best, and antipathy at worst. The Greeks do not drink standing up, do not drink at all without eating, and do not like to be served by women except in quality cafés. Not being drunks themselves, they have a natural nervousness at the prospect of confronting a possibly drunken foreigner. Greek men, though kings in their castles, rarely go out at night without their wives, and would be hard put to persuade a woman to enter a place so inherently unsympathetic as a pub with all the connotations of immorality inherited from its predecessor, the 'girly bar' that survives mainly in the docklands and the vicinity of American military bases.

Greeks can occasionally be found in pubs and may genuinely have been attracted there by a liking for foreign ways acquired during studies, work or holidays in England; but it is equally likely that their objectives will be business or a pick-up. You need not boycott them; simply do not expect too much.

There are no licensing hours in Greece for the sale of alcoholic beverages. All places of entertainment are required to close at 1 a.m. except on holidays, but under legislation governing staff working hours and for the sake of economising on electricity, not because the Greeks cannot be trusted to decide for themselves when they have had enough.

Entertainment

Entertainment in Greece falls into two broad categories: eating while talking, and watching while eating. Culture, on the other hand, at its most pure, is when you cannot even get a bag of crisps. On that definition, the cultural highlights of the Greek tourist season are certainly the Athens and Epidavros Festivals. Theatre runs them pretty close, since cakes and sandwiches are available only at the intervals. At the cinema, by contrast, you can slip into the bar for a hot or cold snack at any time, and some of the open-air summer cinemas provide waiter service while the film is running.

Unless you attend a performance of folk dancing by the Dora Stratou company in Athens, you will be exposed to this most picturesque form of callisthenics at the luxury tavernas where, of course, you have to eat. At nightclubs and bouzouki tavernas you will be offered food, but would probably be wiser only to drink. You will probably enjoy the Sound and Light spectacles in Athens, Rhodes, Crete and Corfu: to these, since Greeks rarely go unless accompanying foreigners, you have to take your own sandwiches.

Festival season

The Athens Festival runs from the middle of June to the second half of September and is staged, with performances on most nights, at the open-air Herod Atticus Theatre on the slopes of the Acropolis. Built in AD 161 by the Roman emperor whose name it bears in memory of his wife Regilla, it can accommodate 5,000 at a squeeze. The acoustics are good even in the cheap seats, 'the gods', but if that is all you can obtain or afford you will really need a pair of opera glasses. You sit on marble tiers, with your personal space delineated by the width of the plastic cushions; you also sit with a straight back, unless the person behind you has no objection to offering you the use of his knees as your shoulder supports. You may also bear in mind that only the rows, not the cushions, are numbered: if your tickets are for sections 'A' or 'E', at the edges, you should arrive at least half an hour early so as to obtain space with a view of the whole of the stage.

With the illuminated Parthenon behind you and the original Roman proscenium in front and, if you are particularly lucky, a full moon overhead, if you don't feel a shiver run along your spine you should probably not be there at all. Sometimes the performance can be almost a superfluity and the setting alone is enough, which is why you may well enjoy an Ancient Greek play of which you have never heard in a language, modern Greek, of which you have no knowledge at all. On a 'big night', with not a cat's space of unoccupied seating and the atmosphere electric with anticipation, it is magical.

For reasons obvious from its date of construction, the Herod Atticus is not the theatre at which the plays of Aeschylus, Sophocles, Euripides and Aristophanes had their first performances; they were staged at the nearby theatre of Dionysos, larger but unrestored and now unusable, of which you will catch a glimpse during your visit to the Acropolis.

The festival programme follows a pattern that varies little from one year to another, comprising performances on about sixty-five evenings, slightly more than half by foreign companies and the rest by Greek. The Greek nights will provide ancient drama, symphonic and choral music, and singing: the Greek singer Nana Mouskouri has given a September concert which promises to become a regular item. Foreign visitors may include national symphony orchestras, ballet, opera and theatre companies, and individual performers giving recitals and concerts.

The problem for the tourist, apparently insoluble so long as the festival retains its reputation for quality, is that tickets for the performances you would most like to attend will probably have been snapped up within hours of going on sale by Athenians prepared to queue all night. However, it is just possible that your hotel can manage something.

In terms of music and dance, Athens is unfortunately a deprived city. It has one symphony orchestra, which is forced to give its winter concerts in a barn-like cinema with deplorable acoustics; for this, among other reasons, it cannot attract the following that would give it a sense of mission and destiny. The single opera company faces comparable obstacles, and there is no ballet at all.

The concrete shell of what is to become Greece's first custom-built concert hall, alongside the United States Embassy, has for a decade now provided silent testimony to the good intentions of successive governments, but at best it will not be completed until sometime in the 1990s. Until then, resident music-lovers have to continue to make do with the Athens Festival, hence their passionate pursuit of tickets.

If you cannot find a ticket for the Herod Atticus, you might try for the open-air theatre near the top of Mount Lycabettus. This is used for musical performances considered insufficiently august for inclusion in the festival programme, such as concerts by Mikis Theodorakis and his disciples or by jazz ensembles.

The Epidavros Festival, which dates from 1954, offers Friday and Saturday performances from the middle of June until early September, almost exclusively of Ancient Greek plays. Usually there is one exception: in 1987 it was to have been a weekend of Shakespeare's *Antony and Cleopatra* by the British National Theatre, under the direction of Peter Hall and with Anthony Hopkins as his near-namesake. Finally, the performances were cancelled, for reasons not stated by the Culture Ministry.

The Epidavros theatre, capacity 16,000, was built in the third century BC and is properly renowned for its acoustics. Tickets are easy enough to come by for these performances; the problem is the 154-km journey each way from Athens. However, you might combine a night at Epidavros with a weekend coach excursion, or even consider going by boat.

The mainstay of both festivals is the National Theatre of Greece, which in winter performs a wider repertoire in ramshackle quarters near Omonia Square.

Greek folk dancing

Folk dance in Greece in its purest form, which is not what you see in tavernas and nightclubs, owes much to Dora Stratou. Some years ago, in an interview with me spread over two days, she told of how she came to form her Society of Greek Folk Dancing and Songs, which throughout the summer performs nightly at a theatre on Philopapus Hill across the road from the Herod Atticus, and of what the spectator should look for:

'I was always very fond of the folk gatherings, the folk festivals that used to take place – and are still taking place – around the country on saints' days. The people there have a religious festival; sometimes they spend the night around the cloister or the church and they follow the ritual of the church, but then they have a great festivity and dance and sing all night probably. It lasts one or two days. . . . You can understand much more about what is called a nation if you get together with the people while they are having a festivity. And, of course, the first expression of the human person is the music, the dance, something that is practically inarticulate.'

The historic continuity of the Greek race, Miss Stratou explained, can be found not only in the works of art and writings of the Ancient Greeks and Byzantines, but comes alive in the dances, songs, customs, superstitions and festivals of the people. As an example she offered the simple circle, a characteristic of most Greek folk dances. 'The circle means most probably the closing up of the people so as to throw out evil, a kind of defence against evil. It has most certainly to do with the seasons – for instance, to have a good season or to avoid the rain.'

One of the principal difficulties facing the Society in its early days was to find the dances and the performers. 'When I started, everything was dying out with that excitement of the Greeks to go forward and to progress. After we became a nation, after centuries of occupation, it was quite natural that the Greeks should want to throw away everything that reminded them of slavery. It was the same with Greek folk dancing. But the Greeks were forgetting that what they had been doing all these years was keeping their characteristics and the historical traces of the Greek ways.'

Miss Stratou sought out the dances, located the instrumentalists, recruited the dancers and rescued the costumes. The Society considers that its 'moment of recognition, when the people accepted their heritage', came in 1961 at the first of its annual panhellenic folk dance and song competitions.

'The Cretans danced their proud, eagle-like dances, the men of Naoussa came with chests ablaze with coins, the people of Pontus showed their Homeric war dances, the tender girls of Cephalonia sang their lively melodies, timidly the women of Macedonia punctuated with their rhythmical steps a tragic lament. The costumes, the work of love and wonderful taste, shone like jewels, and the art and talent of the dancers enthralled the audience.'

Greek folk dances are basically divided into two types, the *syrtos* or drag-dances and the *pedektos* or hop-dances. Almost always, the men have the more important role and the more intricate steps. By tradition, the women are modest, with downcast eyes; this, and the weight of their costumes, explains why most of the women's dances are of the quiet *syrtos* type.

The *syrtos* itself is believed to be the oldest of the Greek folk dances; it is the round dance depicted on many ancient vases and Byzantine frescoes, with the leading dancer twirling a handkerchief. The *kalamatianos*, a panhellenic dance, and the *tsakonikos*, are variations of the *syrtos*. In the *tsakonikos* the dancers hold tightly to one another's arms, as if striving not to lose each other on their way out of a maze. Plutarch describes a similar dance peformed by Theseus and his Athenian companions when, during their return voyage to Athens from Crete after the slaying of the Minotaur, they anchored at the island of Delos to sacrifice to the gods.

The *sousta*, best known of the hop-dances, is performed mainly in Crete and the Dodecanese islands, with differentiations peculiar to each island. In the villages around Pella, birthplace of Alexander the Great, a ceremonial dance is performed by women wearing headdresses vaguely reminiscent of an Ancient Greek helmet. According to legend, Alexander bestowed this privilege because of their prowess on the battlefield; he was about to be defeated when the women seized arms, rushed on to the field, and turned the tide.

No programme of Greek folk music is complete without some of the dances of Pontus, brought back to Greece by the refugees from Asia Minor. One of them, the *serra*, is the nearest surviving equivalent of the Ancient Greek Pyrrhic dance, and even now ends with two warriors duelling with swords.

Folk music is usually performed by a small orchestra consisting of a clarinet (which has replaced the shepherd's pipe), violin, lute and santouri, sometimes enriched with a drum or tambourine or both. The lyre is still widely in use on Crete, and the bagpipe can be heard in parts of Macedonia.

It would be a pity, while in Athens, not to go one evening to Philopapus.

Ari, Zorba and the bouzouki

To the regret of many Greeks, who profess to find it unbearable, bouzouki music was made respectable by Zorba 'the Greek', with a little help from Alan Bates and Aristotle Onassis. In the film, Anthony Quinn created his *syrtaki* to the music of Mikis Theodorakis and finally got his young English friend doing it too. Onassis, who for all of twenty years set many paces in Greece, helped to take the bouzouki out of the waterfront dives in which it had languished and on to the dance floors of hotel ballrooms and luxury liners. But you can still find establishments where plates are smashed to cries of '*Spasta!*', though it is rare now for the more exuberant to burn a banknote or a jacket.

Broadly speaking, bouzouki defines an instrument, a club, a dance and a form of entertainment; more strictly speaking, it is an instrument like a mandolin, but with a harder tone and an elongated stem. It has three pairs of strings each tuned in unison, the first pair to A, the second to D and the third to A flat, and is played with a tortoise-shell or feather plectrum. As a form of music, bouzouki is of disputed origin; some claim it is an offshoot of Greek folk music while others dismiss it contemptuously as 'refugee' music, assert that it was brought to Greece after the Asia Minor disaster, and blame it on the Turks.

At a bouzouki taverna, the orchestra and singers sit in a straight line along a narrow stage, with ferocious amplification, and sing of the pathos of life, disappointments in love and the faithlessness of women: misery is rampant. Never at any moment does a true bouzouki instrumentalist or singer stand up, and never is there a moment of pianissimo. The floor show is provided by the customers, usually men, moved to dance by themselves and for themselves the intricate steps of the *zeimbekiko*, *tsifteteli* or *hassapiko*. Piles of plates are kept in readiness for audience participation, which can be expensive.

Though you may at times believe you are listening to Radio Cairo, you have no hope of seeing belly-dancing.

Deluxe tavernas and nightclubs

To qualify for either of these titles a place of entertainment requires a live orchestra, but the resemblance ends there.

The taverna may be open-air; if it has no garden, it will often transfer to its roof in the summer. The orchestra will mix Greek with foreign songs, the latter of the *Moscow Nights*, *J'Attendrai* and *Fascination* generations, and the floor show will at least include, and probably comprise, Greek vocalists, a bouzouki soloist and folk dancing in which you may be invited to join. The food will be international with some Greek dishes, and relatively expensive. You should go soon after 9 p.m., expect to stay about three hours, and budget possibly 3,000 drachmas per person.

The nightclub will be indoors, and you go there an hour or two later. The floor show will emphasise bouzouki and sex, including striptease, as well as acrobats, jugglers and magicians, but as a rule you will not see folk dancing there. A single male will find 'hostesses' available, but only as table companions. Whether you eat (choosing from an extremely limited menu) or content yourself with a couple of drinks the bill will be about the same, and considerably higher than for the far superior taverna fare. The Greeks do not much care for nightclubs.

There is, of course, the usual host of discos, where you might be anywhere in the world. The *boites* are a little more unusual – bars opened by guitarists or singers to give them a place to entertain their friends, and strangers too, for the price of a drink. But they tend to be excessively Greek and peculiarly uncomfortable. In the open-air variety theatres in the Zappeion and Pedion tou Areos parks in Athens, you will find bowdlerised nightclub entertainment; the cost of admission is an ice cream, cake or drink.

Theatres and cinemas

The theatre is very much alive in Athens, with an average of thirty-six companies performing at any one time. But in the straight theatre, even if you understood the language, you might find the acting styles somewhat histrionic. At the revue theatre, which depends on a mix of satire and sex, you would need to be informed on current politics and scandals to appreciate the jokes, while the chorus lines could only with great charity be described as limber. A safer bet, if you want to go to the theatre, would be a musical.

Foreign films are never dubbed in the cinemas and, except for the occasional children's film, never on television either, so there you would face no language problem. In the summer you go to an open-air cinema, where performances begin at 9 and 11 p.m., children play during the intervals and sometimes during the film, and the soundtrack may be almost inaudible because of complaints from nearby apartment blocks. But this is the place to go if you want to smoke – something you may not do in the indoor cinemas or theatres. The nicest and most accessible Athens summer cinema is the Agli, in the Zappeion, where you can enjoy your refreshments at small tables in the coolest part of the city. With rare exceptions, the only indoor cinemas that stay open during the summer are those showing pornographic films.

As a footnote

If the chance comes your way, do take in a performance of *karagiozi*. This is a Greek shadow theatre with more 'bite' than Punch and Judy; the children love it, and it also has its weekly spot on television. You will obviously miss a lot if you cannot follow in detail the misfortunes of the 'little man', but the fun is always contagious.

Sport

Many of the newer hotels and some of the NTOG beaches provide tennis courts, usually asphalt or cement, where balls can be knocked about without the need to book in advance. Tennis clubs, however, are for members only, and many of them have waiting lists. It is much the same with golf. There are only four courses in Greece (Athens, Halkidiki, Corfu and Rhodes) and the visitor, unless well connected, will have to content himself with the occasional hotel mini-golf installations.

For obvious reasons, you are best served on the beaches, where you will find opportunities everywhere for water-skiing and, increasingly, for wind-surfing. Underwater fishing is prohibited at organised beaches, but elsewhere permitted subject to two restrictions: divers under the age of eighteen may not use harpoons, and a harpoon may not be used to catch a fish weighing less than 150g. But this must be without the use of breathing apparatus, defined as anything that enables the diver to stay underwater beyond his natural capabilities. Such apparatus is forbidden in all Greek waters (seas, lakes and rivers) to protect the cultural heritage. The reason is the number of ancient shipwrecks found but not yet explored, and presumably the many more not yet located, at fairly shallow depths.

By special exemption, breathing apparatus is permitted at designated areas of Halkidiki and some islands where the Department of Antiquities has guaranteed that nothing remains to be discovered. Even there, however, the use of metal detectors or sonic equipment is strictly prohibited. Deep sea divers observed plunging from yachts can expect a quick and unfriendly visit from the coast guards.

If, despite the odds, you find something old on the sea bed, you acquire the legal obligation to inform the nearest police station immediately. Provided you have neither photographed the object nor attempted to move it, you will receive thanks for your public-spiritedness.

If you want to ski, climb a mountain, make a jump by parachute or use your holiday to learn how to sail or ride a horse, NTOG will provide you with lists of telephone numbers.

Shopping

If you came to Greece for the shopping, which would imply a certain eccentricity, your best buys would probably be gold jewellery and silverware, fur coats and antiques. Converted back into your own currency, you would find the prices of these reasonable. Also, with the exception of the fur, they could be regarded as minor diversifications in an otherwise humdrum investment portfolio. Since Greece in effect went off the gold standard in 1965, when restrictions were placed on the purchase and sale of gold sovereigns that made them unattractive to the hoarder, the Greeks have collected their favourite metal in the form of rings, bracelets and chains.

But if your interest lies in souvenirs, you will have a wide choice of quality work ranging from ceramics, woodcarving and metalwork to rugs, embroidery and articles of marble, alabaster and onyx.

Clothes   But first, a few things to bear in mind: Greece is not and probably will never be a serious contestant in the world of *haute couture* or a major producer of high-quality ready-to-wear clothes. Certainly you can buy women's dresses off the peg in wide varieties, but as a rule the patterns are either undistinguished or so excessively Greek that the dresses are more likely to serve as a conversation piece than to create an impression of tasteful elegance. Except for the wealthy who patronise specific designers, Greek women buy from boutiques, which in turn do their shopping in Italy, or from department stores that are stocked by such as Marks & Spencer; what might seem a bargain to them would scarcely seem so to you.

Leather   Similarly, Greece is no rival to Italy or France in the production of quality leather goods, or even to Turkey in that of hard-wearing leather coats and jackets. Your best buy in this area would probably be a pair of sandals or leather slippers, to be found especially in Athens and Rhodes.

Imports   Finally, Greece is not the place to buy anything at all not actually made there. Though Community membership has played havoc with tariffs, Greece is still an expensive country for imported goods because of the cost of transport, the small market and high taxes and mark-ups. The sole exception is whisky on Rhodes: because of special tariff dispensations harking back to the incorporation of the Dodecanese after the Second World War, hard liquor is cheaper there than in many duty-free stores.

These remarks, of course, assume that you are visiting Greece from a western democracy. Yugoslavs pour into Thessaloniki on shopping

113

expeditions and to them, as to the occasional group allowed out from the Soviet Union and eastern Europe as a whole, the most startling feature of a Greek department store is that it can be entered without lamp or password. Before Community membership, the Greeks had the same impression of Harrods.

Serious shopping

This can best be done in Athens, Thessaloniki, Rhodes and Myconos. The two co-capitals have the concentrated shopping areas, to which products are brought from all parts of Greece. And Rhodes and Myconos are the indispensable ports of call for almost every liner on a Mediterranean cruise; they have reciprocated with a determination that no passenger on a shore excursion should experience difficulty in supporting the local economy.

Gold and silver

People on cruises do seem to go for gold. When, as in 1986 and to a lesser extent in 1987, the Americans failed to arrive, the cruise companies fought back with special rates for Greek passengers but still the goldsmiths languished.

As little as twenty-five years ago, a mention of Greek jewellery would bring to mind the silver filigree work of Rhodes and Ioannina, a kind of embroidery with silver wire, and gold bracelets of 18 and 22 carats worked in a similar way and known locally as Smyrneika. Since the early 1960s, Greek goldsmiths have learned to visit the museums for their inspiration. The result has been a new flowering of a 4,000-year-old art, to be seen in rings and earrings, necklaces and bracelets, and articles for use and display – bowls, chalices and plates. They are of guaranteed quality and, considering their workmanship, not particularly expensive. It is unlikely that this would have happened to such an extent without tourism, in particular cruising, and the withdrawal of the gold sovereign from circulation.

Fur

Fur – essentially mink, chinchilla and stone marten – may seem a curious specialisation for a hot country, but it is indisputably one of the better buys. If you intend to pick up a coat, jacket, stole or hat, you will probably make the purchase in Athens or Thessaloniki. Why this is so is a story that belongs to Kastoria (see Gazetteer, p. 247).

Antiques

A degree of caution is required in buying antiques and antiquities; above all, it is necessary to know the difference between the two. As a rule of thumb, anything pre-dating the 1821 War of Independence is likely to be classified as an antiquity, and to require an export licence. In practice, difficulties arise most frequently over Byzantine icons.

If a traveller is found with antiquities in his luggage without a covering export permit, the articles will be confiscated and he will become liable to prosecution. So buy only from a reputable dealer, who will provide you with the necessary documentation and tell you where to go if confirmatory signatures are needed. You should have nothing to do with an 'Alexander the Great coin' or a 'Cycladic statuette' offered surreptitiously; in the improbable event that it turns out not to be a fake you could find yourself wishing it had been.

There are some excellent and reputable antique shops in Amalias Avenue and the neighbourhood of Voukourestiou Street in central Athens and, more particularly, in the Monastiraki area. Also, the National Archaeological and Benaki Museums in Athens sell freely exportable replicas of some of their exhibits.

The casual buy

Rugs If weight is no problem, you could do much worse than pick up a *flokati*. These luxuriously soft, shaggy rugs are one of the few indigenous products that the Greeks themselves prize highly; in the past they were routinely included among the contents of a dowry chest. You will hear from dealers that they are both uniquely Greek and the direct descendants of the rugs that covered the walls and floors of Agamemnon's palace at Mycenae and the bed of Helen of Troy.

The best *flokati* are still made by women in their homes. They twist the yarn on special spindles to give it a fluffy texture, then weave it on looms to produce a rug with a matted base and a surface of long wool strands. The completed rug is immersed in running water for several days, to soften the wool and shrink the pile to a length of about four inches. It is then dyed, traditionally in flaming red or soft shades of brown or blue, or left in its natural cream colour.

Cottage production is concentrated in the mountain villages of central and north-west Greece, where the *flokati* tradition was kept alive during 'the 400 years' and into the first century of the present Greek state by families whose only concern was warmth and who learned subsequently, often with astonishment, that they were also artists. Factory *flokati* are lighter and less closely packed than those made by hand, and therefore cheaper. Both can be used on beds as well as floors, or hung on walls.

These and the *arachovas*, wool carpets with brilliant patterns named after the village near Delphi that used to be the centre of production, can be found in particular in Monastiraki. *Arachovas* are mostly tacked to walls, often above a divan, but strips of them can be sewn together to make larger rugs. Most dealers can arrange shipment of the purchases home, for those travelling by air.

Carpet shops also offer *tagari* bags, which hang from one shoulder by a thick cord. While not very practical for general shopping, they make a bright accessory for the young and slim and a highly-regarded, inexpensive present. With the shoulder cords removed, they can be used as cushion covers.

Pottery

While Athens and Rhodes are the twin centres of Greek ceramics, many of the regions have their own specialities and you could usefully set aside an hour for browsing wherever you spend the night.

The main outlets are the general handicraft and souvenir shops. But before leaving Athens, consider a 500-drachma taxi trip to the suburb of Maroussi, where there is a permanent display of local and regional pottery. You can also find attractive modernistic articles among the traditional ware, some baked in kilns and hand-glazed on the premises. On Rhodes you will be invited to the Ikaros factory, where you can watch the girls painting the intricate designs and make your purchases from the display rooms.

Other crafts

For the little trinket, you can go almost everywhere: you won't find a bargain, since the souvenir shops are aimed at tourists only, but neither will you be seriously cheated. A degree of gentle haggling is permissible and may, for larger purchases, result in a 5 or 10 per cent discount on the total bill. The shops themselves are closely supervised by government departments that are well aware of their importance to Greece's tourism image.

To give you an idea of the range available, the National Organisation of Greek Handicrafts and Small Industries has a permanent display at 9 Mitropoleos Street, around the corner from Constitution Square in Athens. It does not sell, but it tells you where to find.

General Basics

Banking and shopping hours

Banks work a five-day week, from 7.40 a.m. to 1.30 p.m. Some in central areas stay open in the evenings and at weekends for currency exchange only.

Shopping hours vary slightly according to category and season. In general, shops are open by 9 a.m. and close between 1.30 and 2.30 p.m. On Tuesdays, Thursdays and Fridays they reopen for three hours in the afternoon, from around five to around eight.

However, in the autumn of 1987 there were moves afoot to separate the opening hours of department stores and supermarkets from staff working hours. If and when this happens (corner groceries were mounting bitter opposition), this category of shop will be open throughout the day, probably from 9 a.m. to 7 p.m., with personnel working a forty-hour week.

Restrictions on shopping hours already do not apply to folk art and souvenir shops nor, in practice, to groceries in tourist resorts. Newspaper and cigarette kiosks can also work the hours they wish, and some in central Athens never close.

Barbers and hairdressers broadly follow the same hours as shops, but may stay open later on Saturdays. Men can expect to pay Dr 500–1,000 for a haircut, and women Dr 2,000–4,000 for a trim, shampoo and set; tipping is optional but expected.

For pharmacies see 'Health', p. 122.

Cinemas

Almost the only Greek indoor cinemas that stay open during the summer, between the end of May and middle of September, are those showing pornographic films; others found even air-conditioning insufficient to attract clients.

So, for most of the tourist season, the legitimate cinemas are open-air, with two performances a night. The first starts as soon as it becomes dark enough, and the second a couple of hours later. A ticket costs between Dr 150–220, depending on the location of the cinema.

Winter cinemas are slightly more expensive, with a start-up at 5 or 7 p.m. and three or four performances a night. Imported films are subtitled in Greek, never dubbed.

In all cinemas, films are shown in two parts, with a twenty-minute intermission in the middle for refreshments.

You do not tip an usherette and, in any case, will not be shown to a seat. Instead, you are expected to buy a 'programme', offering Dr 10 or 20, when your ticket is torn.

Clothing suggestions

Carry lightweight, easily washable clothing, with a shawl, jacket or sweater for the evenings. You will need a jacket and tie or a cocktail dress only if you are planning to go on a cruise or lose money at one of Greece's three casinos on the outskirts of Athens (in the Mount Parnes Hotel), on Corfu and on Rhodes.

Swimming costumes may not be worn at archaeological sites. To enter a monastery or church, men should wear long trousers (not shorts) and shirts, and women a dress or full-length skirt (not mini) and a top with sleeves. Shawls can often be borrowed at the entrance. Heads need not be covered.

Cultural organisations in Athens

British Council (and library): 17 Kolonaki Square.
Hellenic American Union (and library): 22 Massalias Street.
Goethe Institute: 12–14 Omirou Street.
L'Institut Français: 29 Sina Street.
Instituto Italiano: 47 Patission Street.
Australians have to make do with the Qantas office at 45 Nikis Street, near Constitution Square.

Currency and currency regulations

Greek currency

The Greek currency is the drachma (Dr). While the drachma for purposes of commercial calculation is divided into 100 lepta, inflation has overtaken the old lepta coins and they are no longer in circulation. Coins in actual circulation are of 1, 2, 5, 10, 20 and 50 drachma.

Banknotes are in denominations of Dr 50 (now being phased out and replaced by the Dr 50 coin), 100, 500, 1,000 and 5,000.

Restrictions

As of 1988, under Bank of Greece regulations revised at the end of the 1987 tourist season, visitors are permitted to enter Greece with up to Dr 25,000 in Greek currency, in banknotes of up to Dr 1,000, but they may not export more than Dr 10,000 in Greek currency.

There are no restrictions on the amount of foreign exchange, including gold in coin or bullion, which may be brought into Greece. However, sums in excess of US $1,000, in any form other than travellers' cheques made out in the name of the bearer should be declared on entry since otherwise re-export will not be permitted. This is logical, since the Greek authorities are delighted to see money enter the country but loathe to see it leave; for that reason, you should not neglect to make a currency declaration if you calculate that you may still be carrying more than $1,000 at the end of your trip. While it is mostly Greeks who are subjected to body-searches by currency control officers, Greek legislation makes no distinction as regards nationality.

Entry

In this connection, beware of the transit trap at Athens Airport if you happen to be making only a stop-over. Faced by a wait of a few hours for a connecting flight, you may think you have time for a quick trip to the Acropolis; this involves formal entry to Greece, and on your return to the airport you will be treated like any departing tourist. If you are found with more than $1,000 that you did not declare on leaving the airport, you will become liable to arrest, trial, jail or fine, and confiscation of the money.

Plastic money

All major credit cards are accepted in hotels, top restaurants and many shops, and money can be drawn against them through cooperating banks, but they are not yet extensively recognised in the provinces. Most useful are American Express, Diners, Visa, Access and MasterCard. Travellers' cheques and Eurocheques can be exchanged at banks and used in most hotels; elsewhere, a polite refusal should be expected.

Exchange rates

For currency exchange, banks usually offer a slightly better rate than hotels; their rates for the day will be posted prominently near the main door. It is not worth shopping around among banks unless large sums are involved. You will note the unusually wide spread between the buying and selling rates (as much as Dr 6 on the dollar and Dr 10 on sterling); in buying drachma, of course, you get the lower figure. In resort areas, currency can also be exchanged in shops displaying Bank of Greece authorisation; these may not always keep their rates up to date, especially when the drachma is on one of its slides.

Foreign currency

You can pay in foreign exchange at most souvenir shops (though the rate may be poor), but other shops, restaurants, bars and taxi-drivers are becoming less willing to accept dollars or pounds. For reasons not entirely clear, Greece's once flourishing currency black market appears to be in the doldrums. One explanation offered for the drop in demand is that the black economy is now surfeited; another is that there are now fewer drachma seeking means of flight, because there is less money about, because the serious money has already gone, or because safer means of smuggling have been developed. Where a few years ago you could expect to make up to 25 per cent on an illicit sale, now you will be lucky to get much more than 5 per cent, so it is hardly worth the effort even if there is no risk.

On a small scale, currency regulations are an example of legislation which the ordinary Greek feels fully justified in breaking; he has the obvious dislike of being told what he can do with his own money, and a conviction that everyone else is breaking the rules too. Though the foreign exchange allowance for travel to an EC country has reached the comparatively reasonable level of 800 ECU a year (possibly higher by now), for travel elsewhere it had been pegged at the equivalent of US $250 for a decade and only from 1988 has been raised to $600. One asks why, and sees no justifiable reason.

Suppose you are Greek, and are crossing by coach into Yugoslavia, Bulgaria or Turkey for a ten-day tour. The coach will be boarded by a policeman who will advise the passengers that, in their own interests, they should confess at once rather than await the results of his inspection of wallets, handbags and suitcases. You know very well that the inspection is most unlikely to be made, and that after a decent interval of silence he will leave the bus and you will leave the country.

On your return, loaded with shopping, you will pass through customs. If there are duties to pay, settlement will be accepted in drachma that should legally never have left the country at all or in dollars of astonishing elasticity. You may even choose to declare almost as much foreign exchange on returning as you supposedly possessed on leaving, in order to have the legal right to keep it and use it as an addition to your currency entitlement for the following year.

It is just another instance of the Greek talent for adaptation to unenforceable legislation.

Documents needed to enter Greece

Nationals of European Community countries, the United States, Canada, Australia and New Zealand require only a valid passport for a stay of up to three months.

For a longer stay, you need a temporary residence permit from the Aliens Police (in Athens, this service is a department of the Security Police in Alexandras Avenue). In practice, first and second extensions are normally granted without much formality.

The holders of passports bearing a visa, stamp or other indication of a visit or intention to visit the Turkish-held part of northern Cyprus are liable to be refused entry to Greece (see 'National Issues', pp. 28–30).

Electrical current

Greek current is standard 220 volts A/C, and therefore transformers are not required for European appliances. However, you will need a plug adaptor if your appliance has a plug with square, not round, pins.

Embassies and consulates

● **Britain:** 1 Ploutarchou Street, 106–75 Athens; tel. 7236.211–219. The beautiful white house behind it, possibly the finest remaining example of a neo-Classical home in Athens, is the British Ambassador's residence.

● **United States:** 91 Vassilissis Sophias (Queen Sophia) Avenue, 115–21 Athens; tel. 7212.951–959. Once a kind of modern Parthenon crowning a grassy knoll and symbolising the open society, it has now been surrounded by high steel fencing and concrete tank-barriers disguised as flower pots and has become part of fortress America. This is not only a matter of terrorism; it was costing too much to scrape away the paint after Greece's routine anti-American demonstrations. It is on the left past the Hilton Hotel and adjacent to the permanently uncompleted concert hall; expect to be searched if you want to get in.

● **Canada:** 4, I. Gennadiou Street, 115–21 Athens; tel. 7239.511; suitably modest premises in a residential street.

● **Australia:** 15 Messoghion Street, 115–26 Athens; tel. 7757.650–654. Turn right at the Athens Tower and it's on your left.

● **New Zealand:** 15–17 An. Tsoha Street, 115–21 Athens; tel. 6410.311–315. Hard to find, but not much looked for; you will need a taxi.

Health

Vaccination or inoculation certificates are not required for entry to Greece from the European Community, United States, Canada, Australia and New Zealand. The prohibition of import of narcotics and drugs does not extend to internationally recognised medications in small quantities which are clearly intended for personal use.

First aid There are no endemic dangerous diseases in Greece, nor any dangerous insects or wildlife. However, it is advisable to ensure that anti-tetanus injections are up to date. Mosquitoes and gnats can be an irritant, and a first-aid bag might include a repellant and ointment, in addition to a laxative and a medication for diarrhoea. Because of the danger of allergic reactions (for example, to fish or seafood, or unfamiliar dust or pollen) an anti-histamine might well be considered. At some point you can expect to need an elastic bandage (if the pavements don't get you, the archaeological sites probably will).

Sun oils and creams can be bought everywhere in Greece, but are expensive. Beware of over-exposure to the sun at the beginning of a holiday.

If you are dependent on glasses, carry a spare pair or at least your prescription.

Pharmacies

Pharmacies are open normal shopping hours, but closed on Saturdays as well as Sundays. In every city, one or several will provide an all-night and weekend service, on a roster system: the lists are published in the Greek daily press and displayed, also in Greek, in pharmacy windows. Hotels should be able to provide the information in English.

Most of the larger pharmacies have one or two English-speaking staff, who will advise on simple remedies for minor indispositions. Prescriptions are not required for the milder antibiotics and anti-histamines. You can also go to a pharmacy if you need an injection.

Aspirin can be bought at any newspaper and cigarette kiosk.

Doctors and dentists

In the event of illness, your hotel will be able to call a doctor; embassies and consulates (including vice- and honorary consulates outside Athens) can supply lists of English-speaking doctors. You can expect to pay Dr 3,000–5,000 for a consultation.

It is definitely advisable to stay away from the Greek National Health Service, which is still in its formative stage. The Greeks resort to it only if their first concern is over the cost of the treatment.

Consult your hotel if you suddenly need a dentist. A simple extraction or replacement filling ought not to cost more than Dr 5,000.

The best advice on hospitals is to try to avoid accidents or major illnesses! The treatment will probably be adequate, since Greece is well supplied with doctors, but you will not enjoy the overcrowding nor be impressed by the standards of cleanliness. Preliminary examination may well be carried out in a corridor. However, most large hospitals now have intensive care units for victims of heart attacks.

Risky foods

How to avoid the nuisance of an upset stomach? Play safe and drink bottled water; be careful of milk and milk products, including ice-cream and soft white cheeses (start with a sip or nibble on your first encounter); show a similar respect for cooked seafood (particularly *kalamarakia* (squid) and boiled shrimps), and decline all uncooked seafood no matter how tempting. You should be all right with salads but, in any case, you could hardly avoid eating them in Greece. You have to assume the grapes have been properly washed, but you should peel other fruit.

Flies you have to learn to live with.

Laundry and dry-cleaning

This is generally quick and efficient, though somewhat expensive, in the hotels that provide the service and on cruise liners; you will be told in advance how much it will cost, and how long it will take. Dry-cleaning shops generally need at least forty-eight hours, and do not expect to serve tourists. You are unlikely to find a launderette.

The wise tourist washes what can be washed in a hotel bathroom, and leaves the rest for later.

Newspaper, radio and television

Athens in mid-1987 had no fewer than fifteen daily 'political' newspapers, in addition to three financial dailies, several sports papers and a dozen or more weekly news, women's and special interest magazines, satirical newspapers and party mouthpieces. Though the Athens dailies are Greece's closest approximation to national newspapers, a circulation of 200,000 is regarded as triumphant and several stagger along with less than 10,000. Nevertheless, they are taken with pedantic seriousness by all governments. For reasons of survival, none claims to be apolitical.

English-language papers Greece's only English-language daily is the *Athens News*, now some forty years old. It is useful for its summaries of world and Greek news, but relies more on its classified advertising (from rent or purchase of property to the addresses of massage parlours) and its exclusive provision in English of theatre, cinema, radio and television listings. Its former rival, the *Athens Daily Post*, went out of business four or five years ago.

There is a quality monthly magazine in English, *The Athenian*, as well as a fluctuating number of weekly or monthly give-aways in which the restaurants that you will be advised to patronise tend to be those that advertise; you will find these in your hotel.

The Athens News Agency issues a daily bulletin of Greek and world news, including main European and United States stock exchange closings, in English and French; this is not on sale on the kiosks, but copies are purchased by the larger hotels as a service to clients. The bulletin makes no claim to be exciting or comprehensive in its coverage of Greek and international affairs.

The main European newspapers, plus the *International Herald Tribune* and international edition of *The Wall Street Journal*, reach the kiosks in the early evening of the day of publication, at about double the cover price.

While the press is as free in Greece as in most democracies, television is not, and the shackles on radio are only slowly being loosened. The state-controlled Greek Radio–Television (ERT) broadcasts three national radio programmes (First Programme, supposedly informative; Second Programme, mainly light entertainment; Third Programme, basically classical and light-classical music).

Under liberalisation rules introduced in mid-1987, Athens Municipality launched its own radio programme (popularly known as EV–ERT, a pun on the name of Athens Mayor Miltiades Evert and the state media). This has given the Athenians their first taste of live uncensored political discussion on radio.

The two Greek television channels, ERT I and ERT II, are closely supervised by the government's general secretariat of press and information; as a result, their news bulletins are of almost unbelievable monotony.

Although all Greeks pay a radio and television subscription regardless of whether they have either (it is added as a surcharge to every electricity bill, even those for eternal lights on graves), both channels also carry advertising. ERT I starts up in mid-afternoon with educational broadcasts, and ERT II at around tea-time with programmes for children. Both close at or soon after midnight.

Apart from advertising and up to two hours of 'news', their mainstays are Greek serials and old films, friendly interviews lasting on occasion up to three hours with government officials, and documentaries. Foreign serials, mainly American and British, are carried subtitled in Greek, as are films from America, Britain, France, Italy, the USSR, China, Japan, Hungary, Poland, Czechoslovakia, West and East Germany, Yugoslavia, Rumania, Brazil, Nicaragua and Cuba; from 1988, Albanian films are to be added. They are always in their original languages. A saving grace of television is that the advertising, no matter how much, always precedes and never interrupts a film or serial.

With rare exceptions, mainly basketball, only domestic sport is covered. The finals of the Wimbledon and French Open tennis championships used to be carried, but were quietly dropped after some lengthy matches had encroached on 'news' time. However, if you happen to be in Athens in May you can watch the British FA Cup Final live.

Similarly, every New Year's Day ERT I broadcasts a concert – the one from Vienna.

ERT radio, First Programme, carries news in English, French and German every morning between seven forty and eight. The only other source of radio news in English, in the Athens area, is the American Forces Radio Service, broadcasting from the US base at Ellenikon (1594 khz). For reasons of safety, or delicacy, the AFRS prefers to ignore Greek news.

ERT II television has dropped the five minutes of news in English that it used to provide before the 6 p.m. Greek bulletin.

You can easily appreciate why hotels have not found it necessary to put a television set in every room, even in the unlikely event that you would be interested in watching television while on holiday in Greece.

Pets

Entry | Dogs can be brought into Greece on presentation of a certificate, not more than one year old, of injection against rabies. Cats require a similarly current certificate of general good health. There is no quarantine system in Greece.

Public transport | Unfortunately, dogs cannot be taken on any form of public transport in Greece, nor cats unless in baskets. This is a situation that burdens my conscience. Many years ago, without really wanting to, I chanced to acquire a toy poodle puppy just before a scheduled holiday on Corfu. Since there were then no kennels in Greece, and the creature was in any case only a few months old, my wife and I decided to take it with us. It accompanied us to the island by boat from Piraeus (at that time the main means of transport), no questions asked. Our return, however, was to be made by bus.

We went to the Corfu bus garage to buy tickets, and enquired whether our poodle would be a problem. The clerk, after some deliberation, said he guessed not but, to be safe, why not buy it a child's half-ticket? This was done; the ticket was made out with the handwritten notation that 'this passenger is a small dog, not entitled to a seat.'

On the morning of departure, toy poodle took seat on lap, and uproar began. At the end of the ferry crossing to Igoumenitsa, my wife, the poodle and I were briefly arrested and the bus was escorted to police headquarters for further enquiries. There, an officer perused the half-ticket and, after the poodle had contributed by licking his hand, announced his decision. If an offence *had* been committed, it was by the Corfu bus garage, and the dog was entitled to complete its contracted journey inside the bus, I having rejected a compromise proposal that space should be cleared for it among the suitcases in the luggage compartment.

Though a Greek student on holiday from a German university strode boldly into the fray, insisting that 'abroad, dogs go everywhere' and venturing an opinion that 'the poodle is probably the cleanest passenger on the bus', the majority feeling was that lives were in danger, and that honour and dignity were under assault through the admission of livestock. Several weeks later, presumably after study of the Igoumenitsa police report and possibly letters from offended passengers, the Public Order and Communications Ministries jointly determined that no dogs could henceforth be carried in buses, trains, trams, boats or taxis.

I bow to the ground, and pour dust over my head, at the thought of the pleasure of which I have deprived generations of tourist dogs which otherwise might have gone where mine went and seen what it saw, if only the issue had been deferred until Greece had begun its tortuous journey into Europe. But I categorically disavow any responsibility for a later Health Ministry order that no dog may swim in the sea – a prohibition that obviously applies only to dogs accompanied by their masters since it is the dog's attendant, not the dog itself, that is subject to arrest and fine. As for my poodle, even the sight of the weekly bath induced symptoms of hydrophobia.

Photography

Photography with a small, portable film camera, without flash or video, is unrestricted and free of charge in museums and archaeological sites. A complex scale of fees, obtainable from NTOG, applies for photography with tripod and lighting, or which involves the use of power supplies or requires the assistance of personnel.

In moving about Greece, you will sometimes encounter signs in Greek and English warning that it is not permitted to take photographs. This means there must be military installations somewhere in the vicinity, even if you cannot see them, and the prohibition should be obeyed scrupulously. A useful precaution is never to photograph anything that looks like a landing strip, even if there are no warning signs.

The Greek authorities are suspected of being philosophical about resident agents of intelligence services; they are said to find it simpler to watch those they know than to expel them and then have to identify their successors. However, this tolerance does not extend to amateur or freelance spies.

If you are arrested for photographing what is not permitted to be photographed, you can expect to be lodged in jail on a holding charge of espionage until the film has been developed and scrutinised by experts at the National Defence Ministry. This can take several days.

Post offices

Most post offices (in Greek, *tachydromion*) work a five-day week, as do postmen, closing around 2.30 or 3 p.m. Main cities usually have one that stays open in the evenings and on Saturdays – in Athens it is the one in Constitution Square.

Letters can be sent ordinary airmail, express (the same word in Greek) or registered (*systimeno*); they all need to be weighed, and letters sent by registered mail have to be presented open for inspection.

You should expect a long queue, since post offices also accept payment of public utility bills. If you are mailing numerous letters or postcards, it is advisable to check both the addition and the change. Parcels have to be mailed from special offices (in Athens, the most central is in an arcade off Voukourestiou Street, close to where it runs into Constitution Square). If you know your letter weighs less than 20 g, you can buy postage stamps (*grammatosima*) from most cigarette and newspaper kiosks, at a small surcharge.

Letters may be mailed in any of the yellow boxes along main roads and in squares; some of the larger have two slots, one for domestic (*esoteriko*) mail and the other for foreign (*exoteriko*). Express letters should be put into the red boxes.

Religious services

You can, of course, attend a Sunday morning service at a Greek Orthodox church, if your interest lies in chant without accompaniment. If you happen on a wedding, you will be offered on leaving the same handful of sugared almonds wrapped in tulle as the invited guests.

In Athens there are five main non-Greek Orthodox churches:
● Roman Catholic: St Denis (Dionysios) at the corner of Panepistimiou and Omirou Streets.
● Protestant: St Andrew (American inter-denominational) and the Christos Kirche (German evangelical) at the top of Sina Street.
● Anglican: St Paul at 29 Philhellinon Street.
● Russian Orthodox: St Nikodimos, one block closer to Constitution Square.
See also 'Religion and the Church', pp. 37–39.

Shoeshine

The shoeshine industry is just about dead, killed by inflation, new shoe fabrics and declining standards of dress. A dozen years ago there were still lines of shoeshine men in the main streets and squares of

Athens; others had secured more sheltered 'posts' in open-fronted shops reminiscent of old New York. The shops are long gone, and the itinerant operator has become an extreme rarity.

Similarly, you are unlikely to be pestered any longer by little shoeshine boys while eating in a taverna; they, like those with even less capital who used to offer combs or matches, have either found jobs or are continuing their education and are no longer in need of a dignified alternative to begging. Probably the last survivors of the class of breadwinning ten-year-olds are the girls who hawk gardenias among the tables of open-air restaurants at night.

If you do happen on a shoeshiner, the offer of Dr 100 ought still to be satisfactory.

Shoeshine boxes, with their rows of brass-topped polish bottles, frequently turn up for sale in the Athens 'flea market'.

Siesta

The siesta is part of the Greek way of life; European Community membership is clearly not going to change it. Outside the main resort areas, Greece is a quieter country from three to five in the afternoon than in the middle of the night. Police can be called to deal with noisy neighbours during the period of 'afternoon quiet', and one of the worst examples of ill manners would be to make a telephone call to a household when it is presumed to be sleeping.

The siesta governs and is governed by Greek working hours. Though these have been staggered to some extent to reduce traffic congestion, by 8 a.m. most offices are hard at work and the banks are open; shops follow at around 8.30 a.m. Office workers and bank clerks are away for the day by 3 p.m., and shops also take a siesta.

The only real exception to the general picture is the nine-to-five day introduced by foreign businesses and branches of multinationals and, in particular, shipping and shipping-related offices in Piraeus. If you smile at the siesta, you will be reminded – all Greeks know this – that 'Churchill won the war while sleeping in the afternoon'.

Smoking

Greek governments, for sound economic and social reasons, are ambivalent in their attitude towards smoking. In deference to medical opinion, they do not permit cigarette advertising on radio and television, and smoking is officially prohibited in public buildings and public transport except taxis. At the same time they are not uncon-

In public buildings

scious of the thousands of provincial families living from tobacco production and cigarette manufacturing, nor of the foreign exchange receipts from tobacco exports and revenues from cigarette tax.

So you may not smoke in an indoor cinema or theatre (except in the foyer or a special *kapnisterion*, smoking room), in a bus or train (except in the corridor of the latter), or in a department store. But feel quite free to light up in a bank or post office; if there isn't an ashtray beneath the no-smoking sign you may use the floor. The first no-smoking sections are just beginning to appear in restaurants, but so far it is the abstainers who are assigned the out-of-the-way tables. The Greeks are fond of the story of the American woman in a restaurant who asked the party at the next table if they objected to her eating while they smoked. Their reply: not at all, provided they could still hear the conversation.

In restaurants

Greek cigarettes made of local oriental leaf sell at around Dr 60–80 for a packet of twenty, between a third and half the price of imported brands. There is a popular theory that Greek cigarettes are less hazardous to the health because Greece, as a hot country, has no need to lace its tobacco with combustibles; if you place a lighted Greek cigarette to your ear you will hear no crackle, and if you lay it in an ashtray it will go out.

Price of cigarettes

For tax reasons, you cannot roll your own cigarettes in Greece; the prohibition is applied indirectly through a ban on the sale of cigarette paper. Pipes and cigars are not a Greek weakness; if they are yours, you can obtain your supplies at any kiosk.

Telephoning home

International telephone calls can be made far more cheaply from any office of the Hellenic Telecommunications Organisation (*Organismos Telepikoinonion Ellados*, or OTE) than from a hotel, which will add a surcharge.

Country codes include:

- **United Kingdom and Northern Ireland:** 0044.
- **United States and Canada:** 001.
- **Australia:** 0061.
- **New Zealand:** 0064.

Cost per minute or part of a minute for calls placed through OTE:

- **United Kingdom and Northern Ireland:** Dr 152.
- **United States and Canada:** Dr 400.
- **Australia and New Zealand:** Dr 505.

You should also go to an OTE office to send a telegram or a telex.

Time differences

Standard Greek time is two hours ahead of Greenwich Mean Time; between the last Sunday of March and the last Sunday of September, it is three hours ahead. Thus, except for possible jagged edges caused by different changeover dates, when it is midday in Greece it is 10 a.m. in London.

To calculate the time in the United States, subtract seven hours (eastern standard), eight hours (central), nine hours (Mountain) or ten hours (Pacific).

Australia and New Zealand are ahead of the Greek clock. For Australia, add eight hours (Melbourne and Sydney), seven hours (Canberra, Brisbane and Hobart), six and a half hours (Adelaide and Darwin) or five and a half hours (Perth).

For New Zealand, add nine hours.

Tipping

The tipping situation is not the only disorderly mess in Greece, but simply the one to which the tourist is most regularly exposed. The main thing is to avoid doubling the tip by adding 15 per cent to a bill that already incorporates a 15 per cent service charge.

You will find two prices beside each item on a menu; the higher is the lower one plus 15 per cent, and is the one you pay. Nevertheless, the waiter still expects a tip. Current Greek practice is to leave him the loose change on the plate in an ordinary taverna, restaurant or patisserie, and perhaps Dr 50 for each member of the party at a more expensive establishment. Don't add 15 or 20 per cent to the total bill unless you have received exceptionally good service – you'll ruin the market. The waiter picks up what is on the plate; some additional coins or a small note may be left on the table for the boy who lays the table and serves the water, bread and wine.

Your hotel bill will include service, and anything else is a matter of choice. The barman expects something, the doorman hopes for Dr 100 when he finds you a taxi, and chambermaids like to be remembered on the last day.

On cruises, where you sign for everything, you definitely do not tip as you go along. Your final bill from the purser's office will be accompanied by an envelope and a printed suggestion of a fair tip per person per day.

Tour guides may be tipped on the basis of Dr 100 per person per day, on the assumption that you have received only routine service. Give more if it has been better.

Porters may show you a rate card, and you pay accordingly; if they do not, you should allow Dr 100 per suitcase.

At a cinema, you do not tip the usherette but buy a perfectly useless 'programme' on entering for, say, Dr 10 or 20. At a theatre or concert, where you will be shown to a numbered seat, the usherette will be happy with Dr 50 for a couple.

You may add 10 per cent to a barber's or hairdresser's bill as a fair tip.

Greeks definitely do not tip taxi drivers; at most, they may decline the change if only a few coins are involved. But if you happen on one who speaks your language or, in the countryside, takes you to a taverna that he can recommend, he hopes to be rewarded.

You are not expected to tip a shop assistant, and should never offer a tip in a bank or post office.

Toilets

The best advice, though it is not always practicable, is to use only your own; this alone would justify insistence on a hotel room with private facilities.

In Athens, there are public toilets in Constitution Square (built into the wall in the top right hand corner as you face Parliament), Omonia Square (in one of the corridor entrances to the underground) and Kolonaki Square; Piraeus has one at the electric railway station (beside the bookstall on the right as you emerge from the trains).

The Grande Bretagne is the last of the hotels in central Athens offering the hospitality of toilets easily accessible to non-residents (down the stairs beside the lifts).

If your courage matches your need, and you are not dressed too obviously as a tourist, you might try the third floor of the Bank of Greece (take one of the lifts on the right of the revolving doors and remember to look as if you know where you are going). In Piraeus, the customs and police services housed in the Port of Piraeus Authority (OLP) exhibition centre are well provided; climb the stationary escalator on the right and look for the WC sign.

The customary marking in Greece is WC, though sometimes the word *apohoritirion* is used. Usually there is a single entrance for men and women; sex separation, if any, takes place inside.

In the larger cafés, you may find an old woman seated at a table at the entrance to the toilet. Her responsibility is cleanliness and replenishment of paper, and Dr 5 or 10 should be dropped into her plate. This is not, however, as in some Balkan countries, an admission fee!

Public toilets tend to be relatively clean, at least in comparison with some of those compulsorily provided even by the smallest restaurant, coffee-shop and bar. In the provinces especially, but also in the older Athens buildings, you will occasionally happen on a survivor of the once ubiquitous 'Turkish toilets'. These are holes in the floor, flanked by guidance in one form or another as to where the feet should be placed. To the extent that they are more easily swilled, they may inspire greater confidence than those with bowl and seat. The trick is to retain your balance.

Museums and most archaeological sites have toilets, as an inducement to the acquisition of culture. Those at cinemas can be expensive if you have no intention of seeing the film. At a restaurant or café, whether you order first depends on how brash you are: you could sit at a table, ask for the menu, ask for the toilet, then quietly leave.

Carry some toilet paper in your bag, and you are one strike up before the game begins.

Wildlife

Greece has none that is dangerous, unless you are allergic to bee and wasp stings or put flies in that category. Village dogs are nature's bullies; accustomed to regular beatings, they require resolute confrontation. Should you actually be bitten, you may take comfort from the thought that there is no rabies.

Occupants of bungalows may anticipate inspection by families of newts; these should be left in peace, since they are said to discourage mosquitoes.

In areas of particularly high mosquito concentration, many open-air tavernas have installed an electrical appliance that looks like an inefficient blue light but massacres what otherwise would make you itch. At peak immolation periods, the noise can be distracting – but every 'crack' means one enemy less. It may put you in mind of a gnatcracker suite for muted kettledrums.

Gazetteer

Introduction

For the purposes of this section, the following assumptions are made:
- that you have at least three weeks at your disposal for exploring mainland Greece, either in one visit or over the course of several;
- that although you did not come to Greece just to sit on a beach, you still as a general rule prefer the shore to the mountains, and the opportunity of a quick dip in the sea rather than a distant view of sheep grazing;
- and that, although you did not come for the archaeological sites alone, you will wish to see at least the main ones: Olympia, Mycenae, Epidavros and Delphi.

Within this context, and for the sake of convenience in terms of distances and times, five journeys are proposed in this gazetteer.
- Around Attica while you are based in Athens, with side-trips to one or several of the offshore Argosaronic islands: these are worth seeing but would never, by themselves, justify a holiday in Greece.
- The Peloponnese in one swing, around its edges. This could be split into two separate excursions if you do not have enough time for the whole tour during a single visit, by bisecting the circle with a drive along the mountainous diameter.
- Central and western Greece because, having got as far as Delphi, you should continue to Nafpaktos, from where the whole west coast awaits you. And if you reach Ioannina, the only way to avoid retracing your route would be to cut across the middle of the country.
- Eastern Greece: a way of converting a straight journey to Thessaloniki into an enjoyable exploration of Greece's two finest mountains, Olympos and Pelion.
- Finally, northern Greece, both east and west from Thessaloniki, to take in Macedonia and Thrace and the mountain ranges adjoining

Yugoslavia and Albania. This could well be subdivided into two journeys, since the directions are opposite, but it is presented here as one
because of the relatively short distances involved; also, Thessaloniki,
Greece's other capital, is the obvious starting point for both.

Physical, geographical, temperamental and climatic differences
really do not arise when you are touring mainland Greece. The only
real distinction that could be drawn would be between the mainland
and the islands.

With the experience obtained from thirty years of business and
holiday travel in Greece, I have listed fourteen towns as most suitable
for overnight stays outside Athens: Patras, Olympia, Sparta and
Nafplion in the Peloponnese; Delphi, Nafpaktos, Parga, Ioannina and
Kalambaka in central and western Greece; Volos in eastern Greece
and Thessaloniki, Kavala, the Halkidiki peninsula and Kastoria in the
north.

A further thirteen should not be missed, but need only two or three
hours: Corinth/Loutraki, Pyrgos, Tripolis, Kalamata and Monemvasia during a tour of the Peloponnese; Livadia, Missolonghi, Arta
and Metsovon on a journey through the centre and west, and
Komotini, Alexandroupolis and Edessa in the north.

These lists omit some of Greece's main provincial cities north of
Athens, such as Agrinion, Larisa, Lamia, Xanthi, Drama and Veria.
With apologies to their inhabitants, although they may be of great
importance to the Greek economy, they do not offer much to the
holidaymaker. There is no particular need to avoid them, but more
attractive alternative routes are usually available.

For convenience of presentation and because this is the way things
usually are, the journeys are arranged for the motorist. While they
are feasible by public transport, subject to certain reservations (see
'Travelling Around', pp. 63–73), it is still comparatively rare to see a
tourist on a long-distance bus.

Patterns of town and travel

With the exception of Athens and possibly Thessaloniki, there is no
town on mainland Greece where you are likely to spend a second night
unless you need to use it as a base for a trip to an island or an excursion
in the vicinity. In mainland Greece at least, very much of the pleasure
of a journey lies in the travel, rather than the arrival: in the sudden,
breathtaking views you will encounter on the way, and not in the
places where you will bed down for the night.

Consider a typical Greek provincial city, one with a population of
between 20,000 and 40,000. It will have been reconstructed after its
liberation from the Turks, sometime between 1821 and 1912, and

largely rebuilt again after the Second World War and the Civil War. With its concrete-and-glass municipal buildings and banks, and its apartment blocks, it is now a city for the inhabitants to take pride in, but not for the visitor to take much pleasure from.

If the city is also a port, its centre will be its waterfront, where you will find the best hotels and restaurants. If it is not by the sea, there will be a central square for national day parades and a cathedral church (but not, in any European sense, a cathedral) as its auxiliary heart. The bus terminals and streets for parking will be on or near the quay or central square, as will the railway station if there is one. Exploration should not take more than an hour or so.

Ioannina is an exception to these points for special reasons (late liberation in particular), but even Thessaloniki is not; for the visitor, Greece's second largest city is the long seaside promenade and the immediately parallel streets. And the Akti Miaoulis *is* Piraeus.

If there is a pattern to mainland towns, so too there is a pattern to mainland tourism. If you have not opted for a resort hotel, you will be spending your days on the road and at night asking only food and shelter – the function of an inn throughout the ages. You should not expect, since its inhabitants do not, that the city can offer you sports facilities beyond a beach to swim from or a wood to walk through. If you want music, you will either listen for a taverna with guitars or settle for a discotheque.

You will almost certainly be staying in one of two kinds of hotel, each equally functional. If it dates from before the war, it is likely to be of fourth or fifth class. A corridor will lead from the street to the porter's desk at the foot of the stairs; there will be no lift, lounge or bar, let alone a restaurant; there will be a washbasin in your room, but only one shower or toilet to each floor. This is the sort of hotel where no amount of scrubbing can dissipate the atmosphere of squalor or eliminate the suspicion of beetles! If, as is more likely, your hotel is less than thirty years old, you will enjoy your private bath and toilet and at least a continental breakfast. You will be reasonably comfortable, but not particularly impressed.

For your evening meal you should look for a restaurant or taverna within easy walking distance of your hotel, because that is where most of the better ones will be. Even if one were recommended in the back streets, you would have no real incentive to seek it out. It is probably significant that no organisation in Greece – not the National Tourist Organisation, not the Hotel Chamber, not the travel agencies, not even the Automobile and Touring Club – has either assembled a catalogue of provincial restaurants or is prepared to recommend individual restaurants to its clients or members. In Athens and Thessaloniki you will find such lists, in publications distributed free in hotels; you need not distrust them, but you should bear in mind that indirect advertising is probably involved.

Athens and Attica

Marathon

Drossia
Ekali ● ● Dionyssos
Kifisia ● ● Nea Makri
▲ ● A. Andreas
Mt Pendeli ● Rafina
PIRAEUS ● ATHENS
Spata ● Loutsa
▲ Peania ● Vravrona
SALAMIS Mt Hymettus
● Glyfada Markopoulo
Voula ●
● Vouliagmeni
AEGINA ● Aphaia
Aegina ● ● Aghia Marina
Angistri ● ● Moni
P. Fokea ● ● Lavri
Saronic Gulf ● Sounio

POROS

Argolikos Gulf

HYDRA
SPETSES

Athens and Attica

Athens

Introduction and recent history

Athens is a village that outgrew itself, inhabited by refugees. When it became the capital of modern Greece in 1834 it had an estimated population of around 20,000, considerably less than the present resident foreign community or the number of hotel beds; within the borders assigned to Greece at that time by the Protecting Powers, the total population was about three-quarters of a million.

The ten-year census taken in 1981 found that Greater Athens – Athens, Piraeus and the suburbs of both cities – was home to just over three million inhabitants, close on a third of the total Greek population. The promise, or threat, is of four million by the end of the century. This population growth resulted not from industriousness after sunset but from a movement to the city throughout the century-and-a-half of provincials seeking a better standard of life and, after the lost war with Turkey in 1922, of refugees from Asia Minor.

This is the essential explanation of the village-like concept of the modern capital. It grew outwards from the original settlement at the foot of the Acropolis without incorporating any small towns with an existing history and tradition of their own. The result is that even today Athens has only one real shopping centre, within the triangle cornered on Constitution, Omonia and Monastiraki Squares. The housewife living in Kallithea, Old Phaleron, Psychico, Halandri or Patissia – all populous suburbs by any comparisons – can buy her groceries close to home but must travel to central Athens for less routine shopping. She, and her husband, must do the same for almost any requirement involving state services, other than paying money to them. So the first thing that will strike you in Athens is the traffic congestion.

Main areas and getting about

Geographically, Athens lies in the Attica Basin and is bounded by four mountains: Parnis where the casino is (1,413 m), Pendeli where the marble comes from (1,109 m), Hymettus of the once-purple sunsets which you land alongside at Athens Airport (1,026 m) and Aegaleos which has no claim to fame (465 m). It is studded more centrally with a number of humps and hillocks, of which Lycabettus (277 m) and the Acropolis (156 m) are the most prominent. Acquiring a sense of direction is simple since at least one of these two is visible from almost everywhere.

There is a main street, Panepistimiou, leading from Constitution (Syntagma) Square to Omonia Square, on which the city's three glories of neo-Classical architecture stand side by side: the Academy, the University and the National Library. Hold these in your mind as landmarks. Facing them, and occupying a whole block, is the sand-stone-coloured Bank of Greece; there, if overtaken by fatigue or heat, you can relax in comfortable armchairs without fear that anyone will ask you your business.

Parallel to Panepistimiou, but with traffic flows in the opposite direction, are Akademias above (with nothing to show except the back of the Academy, the University and the Library) and Stadiou below. The Hellenic Telecommunications Organisation (OTE) office at 15 Stadiou Street is the handiest place for you to send a telegram or telephone home if you wish to avoid the higher prices legitimately charged by your hotel.

Halfway along Stadiou, Klafthmonos (Weeping) Square offers coffee-shops beneath trees as a kind of oasis for the shopper; the stores flanking it specialise in television sets, video cassette recorders, washing machines, refrigerators, cookers and saucepans at probably the highest prices in western Europe – look, and feel pity! There are two theories for the name of Weeping Square: the former proximity of a labour exchange and the permanent proximity of the university. If the name was new, it would be an obvious reference to the prices.

Running parallel out of Constitution Square are Ermou Street, the capital's principal shopping street for clothing, and Metropoleos Street on which the Cathedral (Metropolis) occupies a square of its own. Both lead into Monastiraki Square, heart of the flea market.

Turn right at Monastiraki, with your back to the Acropolis, and you walk along Athenas Street to Omonia Square. You have now circum-scribed the triangle in which you can:

● do all the shopping you are likely to want to do;

● change money at any of several dozen banks (the National Bank of Greece at the corner of Constitution Square and Stadiou Street stays open in the evenings and at weekends and also offers tourist information);

● post letters from one of three post offices: at the corner of Metropoleos Street and Constitution Square, at the corner of Stadiou and Patission Streets and inside the Omonia Square underground station;

● eat at the kind of restaurants you are likely to select for lunch (a wider and better choice is available for dinner).

Take Aghiou Constantinou (St Constantine) Street out of Omonia Square and, following the blue indicator signs, you will reach the capital's two railway stations: the two bus stations are definitely not within walking distance (see 'Travelling Around', p. 68).

PLACES OF INTEREST
1 Tourist Office
2 Academy
3 University
4 National Library
5 Cathedral (Metropolis)
6 Acropolis
7 Parliament
8 Presidential Palace
9 National Gardens
10 Zappeion Park
11 Parthenon
12 Theatre of Dionysos
13 Theatre of Herod Atticus
14 Areopagos
15 Pnyx
16 Philopappou

17 Hadrian's Arch
18 Temple of Olympian Zeus
19 Agora
20 Temple of Thesseion
21 Roman Market
22 Kerameikos

MUSEUMS
23 Acropolis
24 National Archaeological
25 Byzantine
26 Benaki
27 Goulandris Museum of Cycladic Art
28 National Gallery
29 War Museum

BYZANTINE CHURCHES
30 Kapnikarea
31 Aghii Theodori
32 Aghios Eleftherios

OTHER CHURCHES
33 St Paul's Anglican
34 St Andrew's
35 St Denis
36 Synagogue

ATHENS
STREET MAP

Getting out

Though this may seem premature, your enjoyment of Athens is likely to be enhanced if you are familiar early on with the escape routes, of which there are several. To reach the National Road (the so-called motorway) that leads along the east coast to northern Greece, you take Vassilissis Sophias (Queen Sophia) Avenue out of Constitution Square, keeping Parliament on your right. After about half an hour's driving in a straight line – which will take you past (in order) the Hilton Hotel, the US Embassy, the Athens Tower skyscraper and the new Olympic Stadium – you will reach the agreeable hill suburb of Kifisia. There, prominent signposts direct you to Greece's main motorway. It can also be reached from Omonia Square, along 3rd September Street, but this route is less pleasant and more congested.

To get to the motorway to Corinth and the Peloponnese, you take Aghiou Constantinou Street from Omonia Square and follow the signposts – and the bulk of the traffic.

For a tour of Attica, you have a choice between the coastal route and a crossing of the central Messoghion plain. For the former, you turn right at Constitution Square (Parliament and the monument to the Unknown Soldier is then on your left), pass the National Gardens, Zappeion Park and Temple of Olympian Zeus, and continue the length of Syngrou Avenue until you reach the sea. There the road forks, right for Piraeus and left for the Olympic Airways terminal at Athens Airport, the seaside suburbs and eventually Sounion. If you prefer the inland route, you set out as if for Kifisia but branch right along Messoghion Avenue on reaching the Athens Tower, the first 'skyscraper' you will see and the only one you will reach.

Vouliagmenis Avenue, for tourist purposes, leads only to the international terminal of Athens Airport, and for that reason is more likely to be seen through the windows of an airline coach or taxi than from behind the wheel of a car.

Central Athens on foot

Constitution Square

The centre not only of Athens but of its modern history, Constitution Square acquired its name from protest: it was the scene of a riot in 1843 when the Athenians gathered to demand a constitution (*syntagma*) and refused to disperse until King Othon (Otto) not only agreed to their demands but, when they still refused to go home, had a charter drawn up and signed it on the spot.

Just 101 years later, a skirmish in Constitution Square marked the 'first round' of the Communist Rebellion, known popularly as the 'Dekembriana' (December Days). For several weeks, the square and the streets abutting it formed practically the whole of the Kingdom of Greece, with the government operating out of the Grande Bretagne Hotel. Some of the older Athens buildings still bear the bullet scars.

In 1954 the square was the scene of the first 'enosis' (union) demonstration at the beginning of the campaign for the independence of Cyprus from British rule and the incorporation of the island into Greece; only the former aim eventually proved attainable.

Today, wind-up campaign meetings are held there during the week before general elections: they had to be moved from Klafthmonos after construction of an underground car park made the traditional meeting place unsafe for crowds of 100,000 and more, let alone the million that parties claim they gather.

Since the building of which the post office occupies a ground-floor corner is the National Economy Ministry, marches to protest about wages, prices, taxes, unemployment, the educational system and the health service almost invariably end in Constitution Square. All too rarely, a bandstand is set up for a concert; most of the time you sip your coffee and eat your ice cream and cake with only the traffic to listen to.

Parliaments and palaces

The squat yellowish building across the top of Constitution Square is the present Parliament of Greece, which is attributed, believe it or not, to a piece of meat. According to the story, when Othon moved his capital to Athens from Nafplion in the Peloponnese he was faced with a housing problem: he might not be king of much, but he still needed a palace. Fortunately for the modern tourist movement, a suggestion that site-clearance on the Acropolis could make room for a structure with suitably regal views was turned down. However, with a stream flowing down what is now Stadiou Street, much of what was available elsewhere was swampy and the breeding ground of malarial mosquitoes. At this point one of the King's Bavarian entourage with enlightened views on public health hit on the idea of hanging pieces of meat at intervals between the Acropolis and Lycabettus. The palace was built where the maggot count was lowest.

Subsequently a second royal palace, now the Presidential Palace, was built in Herod Atticus Street. Parliament, until then housed in the building in Stadiou Street (behind the equestrian statue of the Independence Revolution hero Theodore Kolokotronis) that is now the Historical and Ethnological Museum, moved into the vacated first palace.

The decorated wall beneath Parliament, guarded by two *evzones*, is frequently described as the 'tomb' of the unknown soldier; in fact, it is boneless. Wreaths are laid there on national occasions and by official visitors, to the accompaniment of martial music and traffic jams.

The *evzones* wear uniforms based on those of the *klefts* who took up arms against the Turks in 1821; their elaborate slow-motion drill has been compared, unkindly, to the mating ritual of an exotic bird. Except during the full changing-of-the-guard ceremony on Sunday mornings, the *evzones* are perfectly willing to pose for photographs with tourists, eyes stoically to the front and never a hint of a smile. Allowances should be made for the whiff of embrocation, since the square is draughty and the skirts are short.

The other opportunity to be photographed with an *evzone* is at the Presidential Palace in Herod Atticus Street, which was the royal palace between the time George I surrendered Parliament and the abolition of the monarchy in 1974. The adjacent and more attractive white building is supposedly a guest house for visiting heads of state and government but since 1981 it has been occupied by the Prime Minister's personal advisors – a kind of White House without bedrooms. Herod Atticus and the side-streets comprise Greece's most expensive residential area, home to industrialists, film stars, composers, the conservative New Democracy Party, the Turkish Embassy and the Athens Fire Brigade.

The central hostelries

The Grande Bretagne Hotel, the 'GB', is a showplace in its own right, as well as an Athenian landmark. Built in 1862 as a sixty-room mansion to accommodate official visitors, it was converted ten years later into an eighty-bed hotel with two bathrooms. Enlarged and renovated several times since then, it now offers 668 beds (naturally, every room has a bath) and has been included among Greece's protected historic monuments.

If the routine check of the sewers had not uncovered a cache of explosives there at Christmas 1944, Winston Churchill might never have seen the end of the Second World War. The hotel's last brush with destiny was in 1974 when, with the collapse of the dictatorship, Premier Constantine Karamanlis set up his headquarters there until the threat of a new coup had been eliminated.

Though superseded by larger, more modern and certainly less romantic hotels as a venue for conventions, the 'GB' is still the first choice for governmental and business cocktail parties. The non-resident is welcome to buy a drink at the bar or lunch at the 'GB Corner' restaurant, probably the best and most expensive of those that do serve lunches; provided you look foreign, no one will stop you using the toilets, down the stairs beside the lifts, for a free wash-and-brush-up.

Next to the Grande Bretagne is the King George, where the toilets are less hospitable but the view from the Tudor Hall restaurant is magnificent. Next to that is the N.J.V. Meridien; the initials are those of shipping magnate Nikos J. Vardinoyannis who started the construction but never lived to see the completion. Across the road from the Grande Bretagne and Parliament, at the corner of Panepistimiou and Vassilissis Sophias, is the Athens Astir Palace, part of the chain owned by the National Bank of Greece. Neither it nor the Meridien are much frequented by non-residents.

The other ten Athens deluxe hotels, some of them more deluxe than others, are some distance out of the centre. Only two of them, the Hilton and the Athenaeum Inter-Continental, attract moneyed Athenians to their restaurants and bars.

Parks and gardens

Turn right in front of Parliament, along Amalias Avenue, and you come to the former Royal, now National, Gardens and the adjoining Zappeion Park. Together they form the capital's only considerable patch of greenery: the small Pedion tou Areos (Park of Mars) on Alexandras Avenue is scarcely more than an exercise ground for toy poodles.

The National Gardens were laid out by a German landscape gardener for Othon's wife, Queen Amalia, whose style of dress, 'the Amalia', became the national costume for women who could not or did not wish to claim a regional Greek origin and were prepared to dress in the same material with which they covered their sofas. The gardens close at sunset, but by day, with their shaded walks and placid duck-ponds, they are several degrees cooler than anywhere else in Athens. Generations of well-to-do Greeks have passed their infancies there, picking up French and German and occasionally English from their nannies; fortunately for English girls with cultivated accents and clean noses, the profession is not yet completely dead.

The Zappeion is more formal, not at all romantic, and never closed. Its benches, among the marble busts of forgotten dignitaries insulted by birds and ignored by humanity, are preferred by old men passing the long mornings of retirement without benefit of coffee-shop. The park contains a restaurant and an open-air cinema in the summer and a year-round café which, in the hot weather, becomes an open-air variety theatre at which the price of admission is a drink, an ice-cream or a cake (all three are called the *Aigli*). Until a few years ago, children and others without money could enjoy the variety show free, in roped-off enclosures beyond the spread of tables; now their view is blocked by canvas screens, and they can only listen.

The Zappeion is named after a wealthy Greek–Romanian benefactor, Constantine Zappas (1812–91), who provided the money for the construction of many Athens public buildings and also commissioned schools in Constantinople, Adrianople and Epiros. The centrepiece of the park is the Zappeion Hall, a semi-circular edifice with a Corinthian portico constructed with Zappas' money as the 'Olympic Building'. It was begun in 1873 under the direction of a Viennese architect, opened in 1883, and used until the 1970s mainly as an exhibition centre. Then, when Greece became an EEC member and had to face the problem of housing Community services and the wind-up summit during its six-month tenure of the presidency, the hall acquired its present interior arrangements. Its main non-Community use is for governmental press conferences. In its time, it has served also as a cinema and theatre, military hospital and store, and studios of the Greek radio and television services.

Even though the Community has now become the great benefactor, the tradition of Zappas and many others is still maintained. Since the Second World War Athens has acquired a planetarium and conference centre (the Evghenidion on Syngrou Avenue) from a shipowner legacy, and Thessaloniki a modern hospital from Greek–American donations; while a heart hospital is under construction in the capital with funding provided through the will of Aristotle Onassis. Latest entry into this somehow nineteenth-century activity is a still youthful shipping magnate, Minos Kyriakou; much is expected from his newly created Aegean Foundation.

Leaving the Zappeion by the broad avenue facing the hall, you reach the terminus for bus services to the nearer coastal suburbs on the way to Sounion – Old Phaleron, Kalamaki, Ellenikon, Glyfada, Voula, Vouliagmeni and Varkiza. For a bus to Sounion itself you go to the Pedion tou Areos.

That pointed hill

How to get there

An Athens walking tour should certainly take in Lycabettus, for its view, its two churches, its restaurant at the top, two cafés half-way up, a little courting or just the exercise.

Walk towards it and eventually you cannot help but reach the *periferiakos* (ring road). Turn either way along that, take the first footpath entrance you come across, and keep climbing. It should take about 45 minutes from Constitution Square to the summit.

There are also two roads leading to a car-park outside the open-air theatre below the summit. The theatre, a demonstration in tubular steel and planks of the Greek axiom that nothing is more permanent than a temporary situation, is used as a kind of 'second stage' for Athens Festival performances when the main Herod Atticus theatre at the Acropolis is occupied. Though usually reserved for concerts of modern and popular music, the English actor Derek Jacobi gave his much-appreciated Hamlet there some years ago. From the car-park, to which you can take a taxi for about Dr 200, you reach the top by the only obvious footpath.

The easy way to the summit is by funicular from Kleomenous Street: a No. 23 bus (be careful, not a No. 22!) from Kolonaki Square will drop you off at the station.

The view is not simply the finest in Athens but the only one that extends in all directions, taking in the four mountains that form the sides of the 'basin' plus the islands of Salamis and Aegina and the laid-up tankers on the approaches to Piraeus port. The Acropolis in mid-distance, pink in the morning or evening sun, floats above the blue haze of traffic exhaust without which the Athens *nephos*, or pollution cloud, would lose its bite; the whole city is laid out before you.

The little white church at the top, with the big Greek flag, is dedicated to St George and is almost always open. Unfortunately, the rather more interesting grotto church near the car-park, shared by Saints Gherasimos and Isidoros, can be visited only during Sunday morning services.

A few steps below the Church of St George, at the upper funicular station, the Dionysos restaurant exchanges a magnificent view for an expensive meal. Greeks as a rule prefer one of the two cafés half-way up, for a drink or a snack. Take the stone steps down from St George and you cannot miss the western bar, fine for sunsets but rather hot in the middle of the day. Take the cement ramp from the church in the opposite direction, then follow the road downhill, and you will come to the eastern bar: set among trees, this is more shaded and is delightful in the moonlight.

It must be emphasised that Lycabettus is 'safe' in the small hours also, even if you venture along the footpaths; on a hot night, you might politely avert your gaze when passing the occupied benches.

The Plaka and the Flea Market

Plaka

The Plaka, much more than just a place to eat dinner, contains almost all that is left of nineteenth-century Athens. Huddled along the lower northern slopes of the Acropolis, Plaka (its name is believed to derive from 'flat place' to distinguish it from the cliffs above) is a district in its own right but is generally lumped in with Anafiotika and a part of Monastiraki, where the flea market flourishes and the electric train from Omonia Square makes a stop on its way to Piraeus.

It is reached easily on foot from Constitution Square: walk along Philhellinon Street and turn right at Peta Street or take Metropoleos Street and turn left at Mnisikleos Street. By taxi you should not exceed the minimum fare.

The houses, many of which have been converted into tavernas, bars, souvenir shops and small art galleries, date mainly from the half-century that followed the transfer of the capital to Athens. They co-exist with remains of earlier periods: Ancient Greek and Roman ruins, Byzantine churches and mosques from Turkish times.

Often, the two- and three-storey houses are grouped in threes around a vine-shaded courtyard, entered through a gate or door. One such complex is at 15 School Street (Odos Scholeiou), where no one is likely to object if you enter by the door beneath the fig tree and stand in the flagged courtyard roofed by vines and bounded by whitewashed houses; the ground floors give on to the court, and those above on to a narrow balcony. There was a time when they took in lodgers: one of them was Lord Byron, who is said to have written *Maid of Athens* there before heading for Missolonghi and Greek immortality.

Anafiotika, which you enter imperceptibly from Plaka, takes its name from the masons of the Aegean island of Anafi who were shipped to Athens to build Othon's capital. With the lower slopes of the Acropolis, subsequently Plaka, reserved for more expensive houses – including the first Athens university – the masons built their own homes further up. Anafiotika today consists of three or four parallel streets linked by flights of crumbling stone steps and bearing such revelatory names as Klepsydras – he who steals water. You go there for the walk and the views, and possibly a drink in a *boite*. You eat in Plaka itself.

Curiously, in view of the damage done to the environment by hotels elsewhere in Greece, Plaka might no longer exist but for the post-war growth of tourism. Despite its designation as an archaeological site to protect it from the six-storey apartment blocks that were changing the face of Athens, in the late 1950s the Communications Ministry came up with a plan for a new road through Plaka to relieve traffic congestion in the city centre. The plan was fought, in the end successfully, by the then Mayor of Athens, George Plytas (who had the cockney distinction of having been born in Plaka), and by the Department of Archaeology. One of the arguments that carried particular weight was that Athens, with so little to offer tourists apart from its ruins, could not afford to destroy its more recent past.

Plaka nevertheless fell on hard times. It became garish with neon and unbearable as a place of residence because of the amplification systems of rival tavernas and nightclubs, the proliferation of bars, the entry of narcotics and the roar of motorcycles. The inhabitants moved out and the houses, with no money spent on their upkeep, began to crumble.

Since 1974 the clock has been turned back, in Greece's single most successful demonstration of environmental protection. Many of the streets have become pedestrian precincts, the bars have been ousted along with the neon, amplification and drugs, and the residents have moved back. Even the Greeks have resumed eating there, in family groups and not only when entertaining guests from abroad. It is a quiet pleasure to lunch there, at open-air tables; at night, when the music begins, the food is only part of the entertainment.

Flea Market

The nearby Flea Market, based on Pandrossou and Yfaestou Streets, comes into its own on Sundays but is only relatively less crowded on weekdays. You can buy almost anything there: swords, daggers and muskets, cooking pots and christening fonts, scales, cauldrons, candlesticks and oil lamps, old books, old clothes and old shoes (not necessarily in pairs), guitars, bouzoukia, accordions and second-hand gramophone records, cameras, binoculars and ancient telephones, chess and *tavli* (backgammon) sets of marble, metal and onyx, furniture, carpets, wrought-iron chairs and tables, stuffed birds and sometimes even a horse too old to work.

Apart from the routine souvenirs – ashtrays, plates, vases, busts of the philosophers and playwrights, Athenian 'owls' for use as paperweights and replicas of Ancient Greek works that the moderns consider indecent – more practical buys include small *souvlaki* skewers, copper wine jugs of the kind used in traditional tavernas, and hand-made sandals.

However little it costs, you are expected to haggle.

The archaeological sites

For those who want a stone-by-stone introduction to the Parthenon, Ancient Agora, Stoa of Attalos, Roman Market or Temple of Olympian Zeus, are concerned to know who built what and when, under what circumstances and what it looked like originally, and feel they should be able to distinguish at a glance an Ionic from a Doric column and both from a Corinthian, learned guides to the monuments are available by the score in Athens book-shops. Potted versions are contained in NTOG pamphlets handed out free at airports and border crossings and distributed through hotels and travel agents.

There are guides at the Acropolis who will lead you step by step around its flat top (dimensions 270 by 156 m), and if you want to get from the Acropolis to the Roman Market and Tower of the Winds it is better to take a taxi or to book a city tour in a comfortable coach that will pick you up from your hotel and have you back in time for lunch. Just walking around the sites is tiring enough; there is no need to walk to them as well.

The Acropolis   At the Acropolis, in particular (the same applies also to Knossos in Crete), there are now so many of you traipsing around that you have had to be restricted to roped-off walkways. A few years ago you could wander anywhere you chose and, if you were lucky enough to be in Athens at the right time, enjoy the unforgettable experience of the Parthenon in the light of a full moon; unfortunately, but understandably, that is no longer possible.

Millions of feet wearing away the stones, and of stiletto heels (even at the Acropolis!) chipping at them like tiny mason's hammers, were among the three most recent threats to the monuments and the easiest to deal with by use of wood and rope. Air pollution was another, and the third was well-intentioned, but misguided, restoration.

In 1977, after frightening reports had been submitted to the government on the condition of the marble, action was taken in several directions, including an international appeal for funds through UNESCO. The nub of the reports was that the 'static equilibrium' of the temples was 'at its limits'; translated into more graphic language, the marble was diagnosed to be 'clinically dead' and collapse was not excluded.

The principal villain was identified as Athens pollution. Though this had not caused particular concern when it was thought to affect only the inhabitants, the discovery that it was also threatening the touristic future of the country led to drastic action. Restrictions were placed on industry, traffic and central heating. That the Athenians now breathe more easily is thanks in large part to Pericles.

On the Acropolis itself, the rescue effort centred on the replacement of rusted metal pins and tenons used in restoration work carried out between the two world wars, and the removal of some of the statuary to the controlled atmosphere of the Acropolis Museum. The need to do this, and the superior condition of the so-called Elgin Marbles (once the Parthenon frieze) now housed in the British Museum in London to those his lordship was unable to sequester have strengthened the British case in their continuing argument with the Greek government over whether the marbles should be returned. If they have to be in a museum anyway, say the British, they may as well be in one in London.

Even before Lord Elgin, the Acropolis had had a rough passage through time. The Parthenon became a brothel in the Roman era, and

147

its interior was gutted by fire. The early Christians made it a church, while the 12-m statue of Athena by Phidias, covered in gold and ivory, was taken to Constantinople and there lost in one of the city's many conflagrations. The Turks naturally made the Parthenon a mosque. They also stored gunpowder in the Acropolis; when a lucky shot struck the magazine during a late seventeenth-century siege by the Venetians the Parthenon was converted instantly into its present condition. Though Lord Elgin has had a bad press ever since Lord Byron compared him unfavourably with Alaric ('Arms gave the first his right, the last had none, But basely stole what less barbarians won'), he should be seen in the perspective of what had preceded him.

Whatever the morality and motives of his action, and regardless of whether the firman he acquired from the Turkish Sultan as British Ambassador to the Porte actually gave him the right to remove the statues, Elgin could well have believed that he was taking them to a place where he had every reason to assume they would be better protected.

A statement in a semi-official Greek publication in the context of the campaign for their return – 'The name of this English aristocrat has become a byword for the theft and sale of works of art' and 'his visit to the Acropolis . . . must be numbered among the blackest pages in its long and troubled history' – would seem a trifle extreme.

Regardless of whether the Greeks seriously expect to get the marbles back, they are certainly pressing hard through UNESCO and other international organisations, and directly in London. At one point they seemed to have, or believed they had, the backing of British Labour Party leader Neil Kinnock; from that aspect, the 1987 British general elections went the wrong way for Greece.

The opening hours are 7.30 a.m. to 6 p.m. on weekdays and 8 a.m. to 5 p.m. on Sundays. The entrance fee, Dr 500, includes admission to the museum. There are four principal monuments on the rock:

● **The Parthenon** itself, built in the Doric style by Iktinos, with Pheidias responsible for the decorations, and dedicated to the goddess Athena; it was more or less completed in 438 BC.

● **The Propylaea**, the entrance to the Acropolis, designed by Mnisikles immediately after the Parthenon but never completed because of the outbreak of the Peloponnesian War.

● **The Temple of Athena Niki**, also known as the Temple of the Winged Victory, built of monolithic Ionic columns to commemorate the victory of the Greeks over the Persians at Plataea in 479 BC.

● **The Erechtheion**, with the porch of the Caryatids, completed in about 394 BC. The present Caryatids are copies; of the original six, one is in the British Museum and the rest have been removed to the Acropolis Museum.

On your way to or from the Acropolis you should take a look at:

● **The Theatre of Dionysos**, the oldest of the Greek theatres, dating in its present form mainly from the fourth century BC, at which the works of the Ancient Greek dramatists were first performed.

● **The Theatre of Herod Atticus**, the restored Roman theatre now used for Athens Festival performances.

Across the road from the Acropolis you will find:

● **The Areopagos**, a rock with a levelled top, south-west of the Acropolis, which was used for meetings of the senate of Ancient Athens and for criminal trials (its name survives today as the Areos Pagos, the Greek Supreme Court). St Paul addressed the Athenians there in AD 54: one of his instant converts was subsequently canonised as St Dionysios the Areopagite and declared the patron saint of Athens.

● **The Pnyx**, the hill on the west side of the Acropolis now used for sound-and-light performances. In ancient times it was the Athenian meeting place; a rectangular block is identified as the tribune from which the ancient orators – among them Solon, Themistocles, Pericles, Aristides and Demosthenes – addressed the national assemblies.

● **Philopappou**, known also as the Hill of the Muses, crowned by a monument to a second-century AD Roman benefactor of Athens, Gaius Julius Antiochus Philopappus. It offers almost as good a view of Athens as that from the Acropolis itself. A cave is believed to have been the prison in which Socrates drank hemlock.

Returning to central Athens along Dionysios Areopagitos Street, you will come upon:

● **Hadrian's Arch**, built in AD 132 by the Roman Emperor Hadrian to mark the boundary between 'the city of Theseus' and 'the city of Hadrian', and now the official gateway to the city of Athens. Dignitaries honoured with the freedom of the city receive their gold key there if the weather permits an open-air ceremony.

● **The Temple of Olympian Zeus**, lying immediately behind Hadrian's Arch. It was begun in 530 BC and completed by Hadrian. Only fourteen of the original 104 columns are still standing.

To complete your tour of Ancient Athens you could take a look at:

● **The Agora**, open 9 a.m. to 3 p.m. on weekdays, 9 a.m. to 2 p.m. on Sundays, entrance fee Dr 300, including admission to the Stoa of Attalos Museum. The commercial and public centre of Ancient Athens, spread out at the foot of the Acropolis, the Agora now has to offer only the foundations of buildings among a litter of stone and marble slabs. Inside are:

● **The Thesseion**, the best preserved of the Ancient Greek temples, in Doric style and dating from the fifth century BC. It is believed to have been dedicated to Hephaestos, god of artisans and blacksmiths. Though often used as a trick photograph on Greek television quiz shows (people mistake it for the Parthenon), it is unspectacular in that there is no point at which it can be observed from below.

- **The Stoa of Attalos**, the only one of several arcades to have been fully restored. It is today a museum housing finds from the Agora excavations.
- **The Roman Market**, open from 9 a.m. to 3 p.m., entrance fee Dr 200. Begun at the time of Julius Caesar and completed in the reigns of Hadrian and Trojan, it consists of a rectangular commercial arcade surrounded by an outer courtyard. It is entered from Aeolou Street.
- **Kerameikos**, open from 9 a.m. to 3 p.m., closed Thursdays, entrance fee Dr 200 including the museum. The area contains sections of the ancient city walls and cemetery. It is entered from Ermou Street.
- **The 'Tower of the Winds'**, made for the first century BC hydraulic clock of Andronikos Kyrrestos. It stands at the western entrance to the Roman Market. Its popular name derives from the reliefs representing the prevailing winds on each of its eight sides.

The Athens museums

Time should definitely be found for two museums: the Acropolis Museum itself, and the National Archaeological Museum in Patission Street. What else you see will depend on your more specialised interests.

- **The Acropolis Museum**, opening hours the same as for the Acropolis, entry fee included in the Acropolis admission; closed on Tuesdays. Built inconspicuously in the south-eastern corner of the Acropolis, the museum's few galleries contain sculptures found on the Acropolis itself, votive offerings to Athena and adornments for the temples.

The Culture Ministry is planning a new and larger Acropolis museum in a former police barracks between the Acropolis and the Temple of Olympian Zeus. It is intended that it should be ready by 1996, when Greece hopes to stage the Olympic Games on the 100th anniversary of the first modern Olympiad, held at the all-marble stadium across the road from the Zappeion park. (It is also hoped that pride of place in the new museum will be taken by the Elgin Marbles, if the British have been persuaded by then to give them up.)

- **The National Archaeological Museum**, open from 8 a.m. to 6 p.m.; Sundays and holidays from 9 a.m. to 4 p.m.; closed Mondays; admission Dr 400. One hundred years old in 1974, this museum in Patission Street houses a staggering number of sculptures in its galleries and is reputed to have almost as many spare in its basements. It can justifiably claim to be the only museum in the world in which so many masterpieces of ancient art have been assembled in an unbroken sequence from the Neolithic age to the last years of the Roman Empire.

Those to pause before include: the Minoan frescoes removed from Thera (Santorini); the treasures found in the royal tombs of Mycenae by Heinrich Schliemann, among them the so-called death mask of Agamemnon; the Piraeus Apollo (earliest bronze statue in Greek sculpture); the Poseidon of Artemision; the Antikythera bronze; the Boy of Marathon; the Aphrodite with Pan found at Delos, and the incomparable boy jockey on a galloping horse. Most visitors find it preferable to ignore the show-cases, except for those containing the Mycenae treasures, and keep their eyes on the statuary; to look at everything in detail would take several days.

Unlike that at the Acropolis, the Archaeological Museum has a pleasant, tree-shaded café near its main entrance. Once one of the capital's better nightclubs, it has given generations of tourists the strength and courage for a second assault on the museum. Souvenirs can be purchased from an exhibition of copies and castings taken from objects in museums throughout Greece.

● **The Byzantine Museum**, 22 Vassilissis Sophias Avenue, open from 9 a.m. to 3 p.m., closed Mondays, admission Dr 300. This contains sculptures, wall paintings, mosaics, icons, manuscripts and liturgical objects representative of Byzantine art from the early days of Christianity to the late eighteenth century. The reproductions on sale make excellent Christmas cards.

● **The Benaki Museum**, 1 Koumbari Street and Vassilissis Sophias Avenue, open from 8.30 a.m. to 2 p.m., closed Tuesdays, admission Dr 150. The exhibits are representative of all aspects of Greek folk art and handicrafts, from prehistoric times to the modern age, and include gold Byzantine and post-Byzantine jewellery, silverware, ceramics and embroideries.

● **The Goulandris Museum of Cycladic Art**, 4 Neofytou Douka Street, Kolonaki, open from 10 a.m. to 3 p.m., closed Tuesdays and Sundays, admission Dr 150. This is Greece's newest museum and, as the name suggests, specialises in works from Delos and the other Cyclades islands.

● **The National Gallery**, 60 Vas Konstantinou Street, open from 9 a.m. to 3 p.m., (Sundays from 10 a.m. to 4 p.m.), closed Mondays, admission free. Across the road from the Hilton Hotel, in an ultramodern building, this mainly displays paintings, sculptures and engravings by Greek artists from the early nineteenth century to the present day. One gallery contains European works from the Renaissance onwards, among them works of El Greco, Rubens, Delacroix, Picasso and Modigliani.

● **The War Museum**, corner of Vassilissis Sophias Avenue and Rizari Street, open from 9 a.m. to 2 p.m., closed Mondays, admission free. Definitely only for those interested in the martial arts: weapons, uniforms, regimental flags, medals and decorations, and models of ships and aircraft. The museum itself was built during the 1967–74 dictatorship and is regarded as an architectural eyesore. Unlike its counterpart in Istanbul, it does not offer afternoon band concerts.

Byzantine churches

Although Athens is not the best place to see Byzantine churches – Thessaloniki has much more to offer on the mainland – there are three that are both centrally located and well worth a look, all dating from the eleventh and twelfth centuries.

Kapnikarea stands on what is virtually a traffic island in the middle of Ermou Street, Aghii Theodori (the two Theodores) is in a corner of Klafthmonos Square, and Aghios Eleftherios is tucked away behind the ugly nineteenth-century cathedral. Known popularly as the 'Old' or 'Little' Cathedral, Aghios Eleftherios is sometimes used for the lying-in-state of dignitaries not quite exalted enough to merit post-mortem exhibition in the cathedral itself. In juxtaposition to the cathedral, it has been described as an object lesson in the decline of church architecture over a period of six centuries.

If you find yourself at a loose end for a couple of hours, you could take a taxi to Kessariani Monastery, on the slopes of Mount Hymettus about 7 km from Constitution Square. Built in the eleventh century close to the ruins of a temple of Aphrodite, this is one of the oldest and most important monasteries of Attica. You can visit the church, refectory, mill, bakery and bath-house, and drink water from a spring in the courtyard.

The three main Athens churches that are neither Byzantine nor Orthodox are St Paul's Anglican in Philhellinon Street, St Andrew's interdenominational in Sina Street and the Roman Catholic St Denis in Panepistimiou Street. There is also a synagogue in Meldoni Street.

Where to stay The 1987 directory published by the Hotel Chamber of Greece lists 376 hotels in central Athens alone and another 129 in the nearby coastal or hill suburbs. Of the central Athens hotels, fourteen are deluxe, twenty-four first class and eighty-one second class. Anything below second class should be regarded with caution, as should the travel agent who recommended it, unless economy is more important than neighbourhood.

Since only minimum rates are decreed by the Commerce Ministry, prices quoted for 1987 vary widely even within the same category and, according to season and size and quality of room, within the same hotel. In the deluxe category alone, double-room prices quoted for high season run from less than Dr 7,000 a day to more than Dr 30,000, with suites priced as high as Dr 45,000 a day. Also, such is the nature of the business, there is no hotel in Athens that would reject a tour group if it could get one; if it cannot hope for foreigners, it will settle for provincial Greeks. In these circumstances, you are wise to make your reservations before leaving for Greece, if visiting in high season.

However, there are a few comfortable and relatively central hotels in which I would not hesitate to book my friends if requested; all of them happen to be first class, quoting rates for a double room in 1987 in the Dr 6,000–8,000 a day range, excluding breakfast.

They include:

Amalia, 10 Amalias Avenue;

Astor, 16 Karageorgi Servias Street;

Attica Palace, 6 Karageorgi Servias Street;
Elektra, 5 Ermou Street;
Elektra Palace, 18 Nicodimou Street;
Esperia Palace, 22 Stadiou Street;
Olympic Palace, 16 Philhellinon Street.

If you are in trouble – in Athens in peak season without a bed – there are two hotels that, because of their size, usually have a room empty:

The President, 43 Kifissias Avenue, tel. 692.4600, first class with 912 beds – a long way out on a noisy street and full of groups, but bearable; Dr 5,500 in 1987;

The Titania, 52 Panepistimiou Street, tel. 360.9611, second class with 754 beds; the same remarks apply and it is about the same price.

Where to eat

Since the Greeks like to dine out there are literally hundreds of restaurants and tavernas to choose from in Athens and its surroundings. And since the Greeks are demanding patrons, if the place that catches your eye has at least half-a-dozen tables occupied by obvious Athenians it may be considered reliable.

If for some reason you want a change of cuisine, you may also choose among French, Italian, Korean, Mexican, Lebanese/Arabic, Cypriot, Indian, Indonesian, Spanish, Czechoslovakian, Austrian, German, Chinese, Japanese and vegetarian restaurants.

The most inclusive lists of places to eat are published in two English-language monthly magazines: *The Athenian* (Dr 250) and *This Week in Athens* (distributed free through hotels). For expensive dining in an international atmosphere, you could try any of the fourteen deluxe hotels and expect to pay roughly what you would pay in any European capital.

The following list includes only favourite places of the Greeks that have been in existence for at least twenty years. Telephone numbers are given only if booking is necessary.

Constitution Square area

For lunch or dinner in this area, try:

Corfu, 6 Kriezotou Street, specialises in fish but offers a full range of meat dishes, including the Corfiote *sofrito*.

Delphi, 13 Nikis Street, is usually crowded – a quick-service, general-purpose restaurant.

Ideal, 46 Panepistimiou Street, on the right just past the University/Academy/Library as you head for Omonia Square. It looks like a small shop, but is quite spacious inside.

Kentrikon, 3 Kolokotroni Street, in an arcade beside the (closed) Athenee Palace Hotel in Stadiou Street, near the equestrian statue. The tables are moved outside in the hot weather.

Sintrivani, 5 Philhellinon Street, down a passage and into a garden with a fountain (*sintrivani*) that gives it its name. Favoured by shop assistants and the occasional priest from the cathedral. The menu tends to become sparse by 10 p.m. but is extensive at lunch.

Gerofinikas, 10 Pindarou Street, tel. 362.2719. Reputedly the best place in Athens for Turkish dishes and sweets, but does tend to be expensive. Booking recommended.

Near the Acropolis

Dionysos, across the road from the Herod Atticus Theatre for lunch or dinner. A pastry-shop as well as a restaurant, it lives on tourists but treats them well.

Plaka

Xinos, 4 Aghiou Geronda Street, tel. 322.1065. The first place Greeks think of for dinner when they have a foreigner to entertain. In the summer it moves into its garden. Old Athenian music is provided by a songs-to-the-guitar trio.

Four tavernas that offer a live orchestra, folk and bouzouki dancing, vocalists and a small dance floor for clients, patronised mainly by tourists but in no way to be considered tourist traps, are:

Vrachos, 101 Adrianou Street, tel. 324.7575;

Kalokerinos, 10 Kekropos Street, tel. 323.2054;

Mostrou, 22 Mnisikleous Street, tel. 322.5337;

Paliakritikou (Old Cretan), 24 Mnisikleous Street, tel. 322.2809.

Also in Plaka, you can eat fish and chips at the Bakalarakia (Cod), 41 Kydathinaion Street. The fish is salted cod imported from Iceland or the Soviet Union, once the luxury of the poor but now becoming one for the middle class also. It comes with *skordalia* (garlic sauce).

Near Omonia Square

For lunch or dinner, simply wander in the side-streets and look for any of the grill restaurants: chickens and doner kebab on one grill, steaks and hamburger on another, and probably a lamb or sucking pig turning on a spit. In these you do not even enquire about fish.

Athens as a base

For the individual travelling outside the package system and determined to see as much of the countryside as possible, Athens is almost the only possible base. That is why it is so well provided with quality hotels; changing fashions in tourism explain why, despite the disappearance of several in the past five years, many of those that remain are in the 'distressed gentlefolk' category.

Until about a decade ago there was a recognisable, balanced and apparently inevitable pattern to the growth of tourism in Greece. No matter how many times you had seen the Acropolis before, you had to go to Athens to take your boat or flight to the island on which you intended to spend the greater part of your holiday. In this atmosphere of contented certitude, plans were laid and agreements signed that added the InterContinental, Marriot, Meridien, Chandris and Athens Astir Palace to a luxury hotel class previously dominated by the Grande Bretagne, King George, Hilton, Royal Olympic, Kings' Palace, Athenee Palace and Ambassadeurs.

The three last-named no longer exist as hotels; they and a larger number of lower classification hotels have fallen victim to a programme of airport construction and extension that has made it possible to fly directly, in charter aircraft of economical size, to all the resort islands and many of their smaller satellites. The future of tourism in Athens is now seen as lying in the attraction of 'quality' tourists, who by definition are unpackaged. In particular, there is intense pursuit of business conventions, for which a new convention centre is to be built on the coast between Athens and Piraeus, and of incentive travel.

It is also beginning to be appreciated that if a tourist is to be brought back again and again to a city that has become easier to avoid, two things are needed,

● The visitor's appetite for travel in the mainland, for which Athens is indispensable, must be whetted by improvement of the means of communication and transport and of facilities in provincial cities, which is being done.

● There must be more varied opportunities for passing leisure time in Athens, something on which only slow progress is being made.

So if you ask what you can do in Athens after the shops and archaeological sites have closed, on a night when you have no ticket for the festival, there is only one real answer: eat!

Piraeus: a port that needs a purpose

Piraeus, with a population of about half a million, is the principal Mediterranean port east of Italy, the centre for Greece's seaborne export–import and transit trade, home for Greece's merchant navy and at the same time one of the largest ports in the world in terms of passenger movement. It neither has nor needs a single deluxe or first class hotel, since Athens is only 10 km away.

Museums

The Piraeus Archaeological Museum, 31 Harilaou Trikoupi Street, open from 8 a.m. to 5 p.m., closed Tuesdays, admission Dr 200. Exhibits include finds of the Classical, Hellenistic and Roman periods.

The Piraeus Maritime Museum, Themistokleous Quay, Zea-Freattys, open from 9 a.m. to 12.30 p.m., closed Mondays, admission Dr 50. Exhibits include ship models, busts and uniforms of naval heroes of the Independence Revolution, and paintings of naval engagements.

With so little remaining from its ancient glory, and even that requiring a search comparable to the one mounted by Diogenes for an honest man, there are really only two reasons why you should go to Piraeus: to catch a boat and to eat fish.

The former will take you to the Akti Miaoulis (Miaoulis Quay, named after a seadog hero of the 1821 Revolution and pronounced Mee-ow-ou-lees with the stress on the final syllable). If you have arrived by the underground train from Omonia Square – the parking problem in Piraeus is so horrendous and the distances are so short that it would be foolish to drive there – turn left at the waterfront on leaving the station. (The other direction would take you only to the container terminals, oil reception facilities and a succession of slums.)

Opposite the station you will see Akti Posidonos (Poseidon, or Neptune, Quay), from where you take most of the ferries for the Aegean islands and Crete. The Cretan ferries make the journey overnight: they leave Piraeus or Heraklion/Chanea around sunset, salute one another as they pass in the night somewhere off the east coast of the Peloponnese, and spend the day in port. Ships for the Dodecanese, Cyclades and North Aegean islands prefer morning departures, which means that between 7 and 9 a.m. is the best time to be in Piraeus if you find romance in watching ships coming and going. On Fridays the cruise liners start entering in stately procession soon after 6 a.m., at the end of their one-week or four-day itineraries. On summer nights the grassy Karaiskakis Square at the entrance to Akti Posidonos acquires a strange, multi-coloured carpet, formed by the sleeping bags of backpacking tourists awaiting a morning ferry.

Where the Akti Posidonos makes its gentle turn into the Akti Miaoulis, you find the smaller ferries for the Saronic islands – Aegina, Poros, Hydra and Spetses – and the even smaller boats, virtually river craft, for Salamis. Departures on these lines are at roughly two-hourly intervals during the morning, so there is no need to despair if the first sailing is missed nor, indeed, to set out from Athens at dawn.

Though you can generally buy tickets for any of the ferries from tables at the bottom of the gangplank, it is safer to pick one up a day or two in advance from a travel agent except for ships to the Saronic islands. For the Cretan ferries in particular, advance reservations are essential if you want a cabin; an overnight deck passage is definitely only for the young and hardy. Information in English, though not tickets, is available from a Coast Guard quayside booth.

Along the Akti Miaoulis   The Akti Miaoulis starts at the 'modern Byzantine' Piraeus Cathedral of the Holy Trinity and runs past the old Customs House and new exhibition centre of the Port of Piraeus Authority to the succession of protuberances dedicated to cruise liners. The first part, from the Cathedral to the Customs House, provides overspill docking for Cretan and Aegean ferries. If you have taken a taxi to the Akti Posidonos you should not pay off the driver until you have located the ship you want, just in case it has been relegated to the Akti Miaoulis that day; the drivers are aware of the problem, and will usually ask the name of your ship. If you took a train, you should allow a good half-hour for a possible search on foot.

The Akti Posidonos and Akti Miaoulis together, on the land side, offer you the meat market, the shipping branches of international banks and headquarters of Greek shipping and cruise companies, and hundreds of shops selling fast food, bread and cakes, video and tape-recorder cassettes, cheap luggage, clothing (including merchant navy uniforms) and shoes, the more portable aids to navigation and a full range of souvenirs. Towards the end of the last block before the Customs House and exhibition centre you will find the only shop in Piraeus stocking foreign newspapers and magazines.

Except for one at the underground station that could charitably be described as Balkan, the only other public convenience along the whole 2-km waterfront is at the exhibition centre, and even that is upstairs and unmarked.

There is no reason to venture into the maze of side-streets running up from the Akti Miaoulis unless you have business to transact. This used to be the red light district, once considered an essential service in any self-respecting port, until the Colonels cleaned it up.

By Zea, so much money!

If you have booked a yachting holiday, are the fortunate recipient of an invitation to spend a day under sail, or plan to reach the Saronic islands or the eastern Peloponnese by one of the Flying Dolphin fleet of Soviet-built hydrofoils operated by the Ceres Hellenic company of New York Greek shipowner George P. Livanos, you will need to go to the harbour of Zea-Freattys, formerly and still commonly known by its Turkish name of Passalimani.

A taxi from Athens will take you straight there, but if you have travelled to Piraeus by train or bus you will need to turn left at 2nd Merarchias Street (2nd Division Street), almost exactly half-way between the Cathedral and Customs House, and follow the road up the hill and down the other side until you reach the water.

You will be rewarded by a sight of real wealth: more than 2 km of quay, in an almost perfect circle, occupied by hundreds of yachts, cabin cruisers and catamarans flying the flags of practically every country with a shipping registry. The humble yellow-and-black hydrofoils have been allotted the right-hand corner as you face the water, not far from the naval museum.

As a port, Zea-Freattys is older than Piraeus; it was not until the fifth century BC that the expansion of Athens as a maritime power led Themistocles to propose construction of a new port at Piraeus along with the long walls linking it with Athens. This most snobbish of Greek marinas is a good place for a drink or a snack, at any of the dozens of waterfront cafés and bars, but for a meal you must press on a little further.

Mikro-limano – the place for fish

The next stop on the corniche road linking Zea-Freattys with the new coastal avenue to Athens – a road offering wonderful views of the distant capital and the Saronic Gulf from the hill of Kastella, it is served by trams and can be walked comfortably in an hour – is a gem of a harbour. The modern Greeks have renamed it Mikrolimano (Little Harbour) but most still refer to it as Turkolimano (Turkish Harbour); in ancient times it was Mounichia.

It accommodates smaller yachts than the Zea-Freattys marina and also, on a promontory at one corner, a building still known to its carefully vetted membership as the Royal Yacht Club despite the demise of the monarchy. The royal photographs have survived on the walls there and the royal toast is said to be occasionally offered; during the dictatorship the music of Mikis Theodorakis was played at low volume behind closed windows among consenting adults throughout Greece, in a similar display of reluctance to acknowledge defeat!

Little Harbour is Greece's biggest open-air fish-shop. Its twenty-two restaurants, which specialise totally in fish and seafood though they keep a few steaks in the refrigerator in case a customer has an allergy, line the quay from one end to the other. Their winter quarters are on the landward side, but in summer they lay out tables beneath awnings on the waterfront and are open for lunch as well as dinner.

Though the Greeks may have their particular favourites, by which they swear, there is really nothing to distinguish one restaurant from another either in range, quality or freshness of the fish, or price. It is definitely not a place to go for a cheap meal, or for a quick one: you might get away in one hour at Dr 2,000 a head but you would be safer to budget for three hours and Dr 3,000, or 4,000 if you start with lobster. A list in alphabetical order of those that appear to be best liked, or most adept at public relations, would include: Aglamair, El Greco, Kaplanis, Kranai, Kymata, Mavri Gida, Mouragio, Paragadia, Zephyros and Zorbas.

You will find a greater choice of table at lunch, when you will compete only with other tourists and a few Piraeus businessmen able to justify an expense-account meal. There is no real need to make a reservation for dinner either.

In the old days, fishermen would be waiting on the quay afterwards to row you across the bay to the New Phaleron station of the underground railway; with or without moonlight, it was an experience to be remembered. But that was when Greece was still a poor country. Equally, you will now be spared the procession of small boys offering to sell you matches or combs, or to polish your shoes while you eat.

Much the same fish can be eaten at half the price, though without any splendour in the surroundings, at the poor cousins of the Mikrolimano restaurants, further along the coast towards New Phaleron.

To reach Mikrolimano from Athens, you can take the train from Omonia Square to New Phaleron, last stop before Piraeus, or a green bus from Philhellinon Street to the New Phaleron train station. Your landmark then is the Peace and Friendship Stadium, Greece's largest and newest indoor sports/convention centre. After one disastrous attempt to hold a concert there, which will never be forgotten either by Leonard Bernstein or those who went in the expectation that they would hear as well as see, the Peace and Friendship is now most regularly filled when used for Socialist and Communist Party rallies. You cannot miss it.

The offshore islands

Though islands in general are outside the scope of this guide, mention should be made of those in the Saronic Gulf for two reasons: they are an integral part of a visit to Athens, and they are not places on which the average tourist is likely to stay.

There are five of them, known generically as the 'offshore islands': Salamis, Aegina, Poros, Hydra and Spetses. You can visit any of them in a single day and be back in your Athens hotel in plenty of time for dinner, though for Spetses – the more distant – this would allow only an hour or so ashore unless you went by hydrofoil. Alternatively, you can step ashore on three of them – Aegina, Poros and Hydra – as part of a one-day cruise.

If you did decide to stay you would find them well provided with hotels (with the exception of Salamis) but, from June to the end of August, crowded with middle-class Athenian families attracted by their proximity to home and the relatively cheap hotel accommodation.

Why should you go? To have the 'feel' of a Greek island if your itinerary includes none of those on which visitors would normally spend a week; as a break from sightseeing in Athens, and because it is most improbable that you would ever visit Greece just for them alone. It is much the same as going to Naples: once there you should take a look at Capri, but you would scarcely visit Italy just for the blue grotto and villa of Axel Munthe.

Salamis Salamis, with about 23,000 inhabitants, is easily the most populous of the Saronic five. But significantly, it has no hotel above third class, and none of any category with more than twenty-five rooms. At certain moments you may feel you are in a semi-industrialised suburb of Piraeus, though one with the traditional blue-and-white island colouring.

You might, however, be very attracted by the thought of seeing the narrow strait in which the great Greek–Persian naval battle of 480 BC was fought, and the hill from which Xerxes is said to have watched the destruction of his fleet and ambitions. Also, not even the worst sailor is likely to become seasick on the trip: it takes about twenty minutes by motor launch from Piraeus (Akti Posidonos) and is even quicker by car ferry from the suburb of Perama.

Salamis has a number of habitations too large to be villages but too small to be towns, linked by its own bus service, along with fish tavernas and some rather pebbly swimming. As a beauty spot it is definitely non-league, but even on the worst days it is outside the Athenian smog belt.

Where to   With three or four hours to kill in Piraeus, you could do worse
eat   than take the motorboat to Salamis to eat fish. You will spend considerably less than if you had dedicated the whole time to a meal at Mikrolimano! There is the Antzas taverna on Akti Karaiskaki; a little outside the town, you could try the Kanellos at Kaki Vigla or the Kapotsis on the road to Aindiou, where the local police like to eat. Some of the motorboats from Piraeus drop their passengers at

Ambelaki; there, at the opposite end of the Akti Themistokleos from the little white church, Votsalakis is probably the island's best fish taverna.

Aegina

Roughly in the middle of the Saronic Gulf (you will see it written also as Argosaronikos), Aegina is the island of which the northern shore and central mountains are clearly visible from the Acropolis. It offers something for the classical historian, the Byzantologist, the just-put-me-down-on-the-nearest-beach holiday-maker and even the numismatist.

History

With a population of around 6,000, Aegina was settled and fortified in neolithic times and was a shipping centre active in the pottery trade before the rise of Athens. Its coinage, most notably the Aegina turtle, was in circulation throughout the Mediterranean world, as was its system of weights and measures.

Aegina contributed thirty ships for the battle of Salamis but subsequently aligned itself on the wrong side in the struggle between Athens and Sparta. In what would today be considered an atrocity bordering on genocide, but which was then a humanitarian alternative to massacre, the great Pericles ordered the amputation of all the men's thumbs, followed by the expulsion of the island's inhabitants, and their replacement by colonists from Athens.

For the classicist, Aegina offers the Temple of Aphaia, crowning a wooded hill above the bay of Aghia Marina on the east coast. Built in the fifth century BC of local limestone, with twenty-two columns still standing, it is one of the best preserved Doric temples in Greece. To see its sculptures, however, you have to visit Munich, where they were taken after their purchase in 1812 by the father of King Othon.

What to do

At Aghia Marina you can take a swim from a good sandy beach, provided you have no objection to fighting for space and are impervious to flies. This is where you would probably stay if you thought Aegina was a holiday resort. You can reach it by bus or taxi from the port, a trip of about half an hour.

Well worth a call just for the beauty of the site, as well as for its Byzantine frescoes and wood-carving, is a small monastery with a long name, Chryssoleontissa, dating from the early seventeenth century. Collectors can pair it up with the island's other monastery, Aghios Nektarios.

In more modern times, Aegina served briefly, in 1828, as the seat of the first free Greek government before the capital was established in Nafplion. Also, until capital punishment was effectively suspended (though not abolished) some fifteen years ago, Aegina was one of Greece's principal execution sites; the gendarmerie firing squad would line up at dawn on a hillside near the prison, and for the next few days the island would mourn its reputation.

The visitor lands at the town of Aegina, by tender from a liner but otherwise via the gangplank, and can then do one or all of three things:

wander through the narrow streets of the town for a little shopping, sit at a quayside café or restaurant, or take a bus to Aghia Marina and the monasteries. Two islets, Angistri and Moni, can be reached by caique from Aegina for a midday meal and afternoon swim.

Best buys on Aegina are pistachio nuts and, although weighty, the traditional clay jars that really do keep water remarkably cool.

Where to stay

Two recommended Aegina hotels are the Danae and the Nafsika Bungalows, both second class, the former with a hundred beds and the latter with sixty-six.

Where to eat

You can eat well in town at the Vostitsanos restaurant behind the Aiakion pastry-shop, especially if you are prepared to pay for good fish, or at the Lalaounis restaurant on the waterfront for local specialities. You might also try the El Greco and Mourtzis in the harbour, Mihalatzikos one street back behind the Agapi café and, just outside the town but known to every taxi-driver, Baroutis and Vatzoulias.

Though the terminal for the Flying Dolphins as a fleet is at Zea-Freattys, the hydrofoils for Aegina leave from the Piraeus central port at Karaiskaki Square, on the Akti Posidonos, close to the moorings for the conventional ferries to the Saronic islands. While the hydrofoil shuttle service has opened Aegina to commuters, the conventional ferries are more like ships. The ferries take an hour and a half and the Dolphins about twenty minutes. Single fares in 1987 were Dr 500 first class and Dr 350 second class on the ferries, and Dr 550 on the single-class hydrofoil.

Poros

Next stop for the ferries and hydrofoils, thirty-six sea miles from Piraeus, is the island of Poros, which Henry Miller in *The Colossus of Maroussi* predictably likened to 'the neck of the womb'. Separated from the Peloponnese by the narrowest of straits, where the silence is palpable and the beauty overwhelming, Poros is inevitably an island that promises more than it could ever deliver. For after such an arrival, there can only be anticlimax.

You step out of the ship into the middle of the main street, lined with souvenir shops, restaurants and cafés. Across the water on the Peloponnese, the lemon groves of Galatas are lovely in all seasons, a cloud of blossom in spring, and only a ten-minute chug away in a fisherman's boat. If you have the time, you can take a taxi to the Temple of Poseidon where Demosthenes, when words ran out, committed suicide in 322 BC; equally, you can try the monastery of Panaghia, which can be reached also by motorboat.

Where to stay and where to eat

If you are on a one-day cruise, you will be allowed about an hour on Poros. It has a population of about 4,000 and thirteen hotels, of which eight are second class and the rest third class; only four of them can take more than a hundred guests and they rely mainly on Greek groups. Costas Alexopoulos, who runs a travel agency on Poros, sends his friends to stay at the Pavlou Hotel (second class, sixty-six beds) on the beach at Neorion, reached most easily by motorboat; or the Sirene (second class, 228 beds) at Monastiri, a few minutes outside the town by car or a half-hour's walk. His preferred tavernas are the Dolphin, on the steps near the Post Office, for fresh fish and Greek specialities, and the Panorama, a twenty-minute walk from where the ships tie up.

Other popular places for a meal include the Caravella and Lagoudera on the waterfront, the Epta Adelfia (Seven Brothers) in the main square, Dionysos near the Lahtsi Hotel, and Paradissos close to the Temple of Poseidon.

Hydra

While an hour may be enough for Poros, it is definitely not enough for Hydra. Just a quick lunch away from Poros on a slow boat, you need at least two hours, if only to walk about. You appear to be approaching a bare, treeless, uninhabited and totally inhospitable rock, then suddenly you turn into a tiny amphitheatrical harbour jammed with fishing boats and pleasure craft and backed by a hillside spread with white and grey red-roofed houses. Artists reach instinctively for pencils, and cameras acquire a momentum of their own.

Famed for its role in the 1821 Revolution, Hydra was given a second lease of life as a cosmopolitan tourist centre after the film *Boy on a Dolphin* was shot there in 1957; in that respect, however, it now plays a muted second fiddle to Myconos. Knitwear is a favourite purchase from the souvenir shops.

Where to stay

With a population of about 2,500, Hydra offers 401 beds in thirteen hotels, of which two are first class and six are second class. The largest have thirty-nine and thirty-six rooms, and the smallest have five and six. So if you do stay, at least you have nothing to fear from groups. Those who live on the island speak well of the air-conditioned Greco Hotel (second class, thirty-six beds) and the Leto (third class, seventy-four beds). The Orlof (second class, twenty-five beds), 250 m from the port, is too new to have been included in the most recent Hotel Chamber catalogue.

Where to eat

You can eat well, with a choice among international and Greek dishes, in restaurants in the town; equally well, and with more to watch, you can snack on the quayside. Among recommended restaurants are the Douskos in a large courtyard some 300 m from the port, the almost adjacent Tria Adelfia (Three Brothers), and the Kypos (Garden) next to the cinema. The Vlichos taverna on Vlichos beach can be well worth the half-hour's walk. If you feel in need of French cuisine, try the Grenouille.

Hydra is too small and barren, too lacking in greenery and sandy beaches, perhaps even too claustrophobic to be a place for a long holiday. But as one of three calls on a day's cruise, it is a real bargain.

In 1987, these day cruises were priced at just over Dr 3,000 a head, including pick-up and return by coach from the main Athens hotels, and lunch. They last about ten hours, and bookings may be made through hotels or any travel agent.

Spetses

Spetses, the most distant of the Saronic islands, fifty-two sea miles from Piraeus at the entrance to the Argolikos Gulf, is too far away to be included on a one-day cruise but is a delightful place to visit if you have a full day or preferably two at your disposal. The trip takes just over five hours by conventional ferry from Piraeus and up to half that time by hydrofoil, depending on the number of intermediate calls.

What to do

Easily the greenest of the five islands, Spetses could be mistaken at first sight for an Ionian transplant. It too has a Revolution history of note, and a picturesque harbour; it also offers good swimming, on the island itself or from Peloponnesian beaches half-an-hour away by caique, and comfortable hotels for an overnight stay. Offshore from Spetses, Stavros Niarchos occasionally holds summer court on his private islet of Spetsopoula, but for that you need an embossed invitation.

Spetses tends to be particularly crowded with Athenian holiday-makers in July and August, when there can be unseemly jostling for restaurant tables in the evening. But outside these peak months, it is a relaxing place in which to soak up sunshine and atmosphere, and take evening drives in horse-drawn cabs.

Where to stay

With a population of about 3,500, Spetses offers 1,081 beds in twenty-three hotels and not far short of that number in private houses; nevertheless, on a holiday weekend, it can sometimes be necessary to sleep on a beach. Most of the hotels, particularly the larger ones, are of tourist-era creation – clean, new and unremarkable. But there is one delightful survival from the last century, the first class Possidonian, with fifty-five rooms but only eighty-three beds, which will give you a taste of accommodation as it used to be in the days of the Lordi.

Where to eat

As for eating, in high season you might be better advised to grab the first table you can find; you can scarcely go wrong. The locals speak well of Lazaros Taverna close to the Tourist Police, the Psaropoulos near the Possidonian Hotel and, further along the same seaside road, the Patralis near the Anargyrion School. In the opposite direction from the port, the Trehandiri in the Old Harbour offers 'baked fish Spetsiotika' – cooked in slices with tomato, onion and garlic.

In 1987, the one-way fare to Spetses was Dr 1,000 first class on a ferry and Dr 1,600 on a hydrofoil.

The Messoghion and Sounion

It would be a pity, before leaving Athens, not to taste the Messoghion, the name given to the part of Attica lying between Mounts Pendeli and Hymettus and the coast from Sounion to Marathon. The degree of detail depends on how much time you have available and your means of transport, but it merits at least a day.

At one extreme, like dipping your toe in the water to say you have swum in the Mediterranean, you can take a half-day coach tour to Sounion that will allow you to see the Temple of Poseidon there, search out Lord Byron's initials scratched into one of the fifteen surviving Doric columns, and enjoy the views of the Saronic Gulf from the 65-km coastal road dating from the early days of post-war reconstruction.

You will see much the same at about a fifth of the price, though without the services of a guide, if you take a bus from the small square where Alexandras Avenue joins Patission Street, beside the Pedion tou Areos park. Departures are at hourly intervals: since some buses take the coastal road and others follow the inland route, the best plan is to go one way and return the other. Since the restaurant beside the entrance to the temple is unnecessarily pricy, your best bet is to take a packed lunch.

Drive or go by taxi if you can – it gives you greater flexibility. If you want a taxi, it is safer to make the arrangement through your hotel and obtain a price for the day than to leave it to the clock.

Glyfada   Choosing the coastal road, you pass Athens Airport and reach the suburb of Glyfada, where you might stop for an early morning coffee and croissant to contemplate the effects of tourism. Thirty years ago, Glyfada was a fishing village with a few villas, one of them belonging to Aristotle Onassis. Then the US Air Force set up a base at nearby Ellenikon, when Greece joined NATO, and bars of dubious repute followed. The narrow seaside road became a six-lane avenue, tourism seized the waterfront, and today Glyfada is all apartment blocks, hotels, restaurants, tavernas, nightclubs, 'pubs', and one of the two largest shopping centres outside central Athens (the other is at Kifisia, to the north). As of 1987 there were forty-seven hotels in Glyfada; by now the half-century should have been reached. The trouble with all of them is airport noise, which can take some getting used to, and their almost total dependence on package tours.

You can swim from a well-provided pay beach there, in water that is not so clear as it used to be before the fishing harbour became a yacht marina and the hotels were built. From July onward you should expect to collide with water melon peel. Four restaurants have survived all the development and competition with their reputations unscathed: Antonopoulos and Psaropoulos on the waterfront for fish, George's Steak House in the main square, and the Tzaki a few blocks further on.

There is nothing to distract you further until you reach Vouliagmeni; the intervening suburb of Voula is considered attractive only by the residents of the apartment blocks and Kavouri can be ignored unless you have a macabre interest in seeing the Pine Hill Hotel where

Dorothy Ann Chapman, the British journalist, was staying when she was murdered during the dictatorship – a crime that the Greeks seem curiously reluctant to solve even now.

Vouliagmeni

At Vouliagmeni you may briefly branch right along the Lemos peninsula to see how the wealthy, especially those with oil money, spend their holidays. After the best of the capital's pay beaches (not the one on the left, which is shallow and overcrowded, but the partly concealed one on the right), you come to the complex of Astir Palace Hotels owned by the National Bank of Greece. There, the magnificence of the surroundings and luxury of the appointments are matched only by the price; however, the view from the terrace is free if you first buy an ice-cream.

By now you are roughly half-way to Sounion, following a road that will take you through week-ender country: Varkiza, Aghia Marina, Lagonissi, Saronida and Palea Fokea are where middle-class Athenians by the thousands have built their country cottages (invariably referred to as 'villas') and where thousands of others spend comparatively cheap summer holidays in box-like hotels connected to their little patch of private beach by tunnels under the road.

At Palea Fokea close on a score of fish restaurants along the road set out tables under the trees or under awnings by the sea. Because they depend on the regular custom of Greeks, winter and summer alike, you eat better there and much less expensively than at Sounion or closer to Athens. You can get a meal from as early as 11 a.m., and at any time afterwards.

Sounion

At Sounion, a half-hour or so from Nea Fokea, you will see the temple on the headland, a landmark since antiquity for ships turning into the Saronic Gulf. If you can be there at sunset, the views are spectacular.

Back through the middle

Lavrion

Your next stop along the coastal road will be the squalid little port of Lavrion, where the now worked-out silver mines helped to finance the glory of the Golden Age and, through their devouring need for slaves, permit a suspicion that even in Ancient Greece war was an economic necessity. The long island opposite Lavrion, Makronissos, was used as a place of exile, euphemism for concentration camp, during the 1946–49 civil war.

Markopoulo

From Lavrion the road turns inland to Markopoulo, an undistinguished little town of just under 1,000 inhabitants but a communications hub for the whole Messoghion plain. Instead of continuing straight back to Athens, as the buses do, you should still have plenty of time to take the Porto Rafti road, where you recover the sea.

You can then drive all the way along the coast to Marathon, a journey that should not take more than three hours even if you stop for the Vravrona archaeological site and at one of the succession of small seaside resorts – Loutsa, Rafina, Aghios Andreas or Nea Makri.

Rafina

Rafina is the main fish port for Athens, with a cluster of fish restaurants. You can also catch ferries there for Syros, Myconos and Tinos, if you prefer a shorter voyage than that from Piraeus in less comfortable ships. This coast is where financially straitened Athenians take their summer holidays.

Nea Makri

At Nea Makri you have another opportunity to head back to Athens, by turning left and taking a twenty-year-old road along the slopes of Mount Pendeli through Dionyssos and Drossia to the ship-owner suburb of Ekali which the Finance Ministry assumes to be a den of tax evaders. But if the sun is still high, you could reach Drossia by a less direct route that takes in Marathon, where the battle was fought, and the lake/reservoir of Marathon with its marble-faced dam.

Marathon

At Marathon you will need to use a little imagination, since the battlefield is now covered with vineyards and orchards and there is nothing to see except the Mound, the collective tomb of the Athenian dead.

It was in the bay of Marathon, on which the mountains now look from a rather greater distance than in antiquity because of silting, that in the autumn of 490 BC the Athenians, assisted by a contingent of Plataians, demonstrated that the Persians were not invincible.

Although as in all ancient accounts numbers are unreliable, there seems little doubt that the Athenians under Miltiades were outnumbered at least six to one; on the other hand, they held the more advantageous ground. For this reason, the accounts say, the Persians after disembarking from their ships waited for the Athenians to attack them, while the Athenians waited for the expected arrival of help from Sparta. Finally, seeing the Persians re-embark their horsemen as a prelude to withdrawal, Miltiades decided to weaken his centre sufficiently to invite a Persian attack while strengthening his wings so as to envelop them if they accepted the bait. The tactics worked: the Persians were cut off from their ships in what would later have been described as a pincer movement, and were defeated.

While accounts are at variance on the Persian losses, they agree that 192 Athenians were killed and, as a mark of signal honour, cremated and buried in the collective tomb (Soros) that is now the starting point for Athens Marathon races and the annual Marathon peace march. The Marathon race, which made its début in international athletics at the first modern Olympiad in Athens in 1896, commemorates the fatal run by Pheidippides to announce to Athens the victory over the Persians. Since the exact route he took is still a matter of speculation and some dispute, the traditional 42-km distance is also an approximation. Modern runners follow the road.

Those who were Boy Scouts twenty-five years ago may have a sentimental motive for a quarter-hour detour to Shinias, the long and still unspoiled beach beside which Greece hosted its only World Jamboree so far. The tent city has long gone, but a taverna there, the Jamboree, keeps the memory alive.

Drossia and Kifisia

It should now be the evening of what has been a rather long day, but if you are not committed to a hotel dinner, Drossia offers numerous meat-over-charcoal tavernas with modest pricing. And Kifisia is a suburb of excellent restaurants – Greek, Italian, French, German and Chinese. Two that have been around for a long time are the Grand Chalet (a pricy restaurant with international cuisine and a pianist) at 38 Kokkinara Street, and the Gonia in Kefalari Square, a family-style Greek taverna. The Alt Berlin across the road is appreciated by Germanophiles, and those who like Chinese food swear by the nearby Red Dragon.

By turning back to the sea at Markopoulo you miss only the central villages of Koropi, Peania, Stavros, Spata, Pikermi and Pallini. This is concentrated taverna country, to which the Athenians drive on hot nights for grilled meat in cool surroundings. It is also the centre of retsina production, with the wine almost invariably sold *heema* (loose) from the barrel. With the minor exceptions of Peania and Spata, the villages have nothing to show until the tavernas open.

Peania

At Peania, those of speleological bent can visit the Koutouki Cave, on the eastern slopes of Mount Hymettus. Though not particularly cavernous even by Greek standards – there are far larger caves at Ioannina and in the southern Peloponnese – it is the best that Attica has to offer, and great pride is taken in the lighting of the stalactites and stalagmites.

Spata

Close to Spata, you pass a large expanse of dusty flatland that until a dozen years ago was rich vineyard. It was expropriated, razed and levelled before the money ran out and one day – but never ask when – it will become the new Athens International Airport.

Though distances on this trip will obviously depend on which of the roads you choose, you may expect to drive between 150 and 200 km, on roads that are good though not motorways. You will have seen the best that Attica has to show.

In summary

You might well devote four days to Athens: one for the city centre and the archaeological sites, one for the museums and shopping, one for exploration of Attica and one for a cruise of the offshore islands.

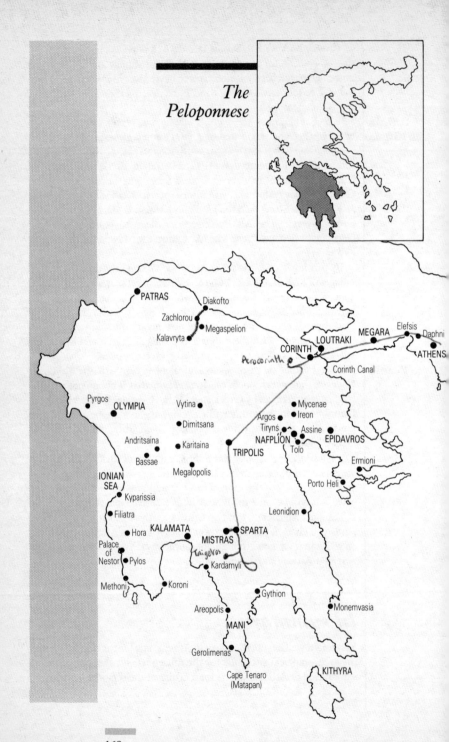

The Peloponnese

PATRAS
Diakofto
Zachlorou
Megaspelion
Kalavryta

CORINTH
Acrocorinth
Corinth Canal

LOUTRAKI
MEGARA
Elefsis
Daphni
ATHENS

Pyrgos
OLYMPIA
Vytina
Dimitsana
Andritsaina
Karitaina
Bassae
Megalopolis
TRIPOLIS

Mycenae
Argos
Ireon
Tiryns
Assine
NAFPLION
EPIDAVROS
Tolo
Ermioni
Porto Heli

IONIAN
SEA
Kyparissia
Filiatra
Hora
KALAMATA
Palace
of
Nestor
Pylos
Methoni
Koroni

MISTRAS
SPARTA
Taigetos
Kardamyli

Leonidion

Gythion
Monemvasia
Areopolis
MANI
Gerolimenas
Cape Tenaro
(Matapan)

KITHYRA

The Peloponnese

Introduction

With a population of just over a million, the Peloponnese would be Greece's largest island if canals dug with picks and shovels were regarded with the same awe as those created by natural forces. In fact, it is not an island, though it has the feel and name of one – Peloponnisos is literally the island of Pelops – and it is separated from the mainland by a canal through the Isthmus of Corinth that is no narrower than the one by which nature made an island of Lefkas.

Pelops was the son of Tantalus, on whom resistance to temptation was imposed; in legend they were the forebears of the House of Atreus, not a particularly nice family to know but the inspiration of Homer, the ancient playwrights and even Eugene O'Neill.

No other part of Greece offers the concentrated variety of this 21,383 sq km figleaf – or more properly mulberry leaf, the meaning of Morea (another name for the Peloponnese) – attached to mainland Greece by the stem of the Corinth Isthmus. Rocky coasts and sandy beaches, bare and tree-clad mountains, flourishing modern towns and dead cities from Ancient Greece and Byzantium, Frankish castles, historic monasteries where the monks are welcoming, not just Olympia and Mycenae but also the Mani and Monemvasia – it has everything the most exigent visitor could demand except perhaps a nightclub or symphony orchestra.

The Peloponnese has a generally Mediterranean climate, with winters a little more severe in the central mountains. It produces fruit and vegetables, olives, wine and currants, with little industry of any size. There is one university, at Patras.

The main cities are Corinth, Patras, Kalamata and Nafplion on the coast, and Sparta and Tripolis inland. It has good roads along most of the coast, and can be bisected north-to-south from Corinth through Tripolis to Kalamata and west-to-east from Olympia again via Tripolis to Nafplion.

The Peloponnese can be swept through comfortably in three days, the time allowed by many of the coach tours, but it really needs a week to be mulled over and absorbed more satisfactorily.

The route suggested here arbitrarily follows an anti-clockwise direction, and in general prefers coast to mountain. If you were not planning to return to Athens you could take it in reverse, by turning left at Corinth on the Nafplion road and, on finally reaching Patras, crossing by ferry for western Greece, Epiros and Delphi; you would then lose only the north coast of the Peloponnese.

Reliance on public transport would impose a longer time or a shorter route: you might then take the Olympia–Nafplion road, in either direction, and either forget about the southern Peloponnese or save it for a second visit.

As regards overnight stays, I have stayed in pleasant non-resort hotels in Diakofto, Patras, Olympia, the Mani, Sparta, Kalamata, Methoni, Tripolis and Nafplion. But Kalamata has had problems since a destructive earthquake in September 1986 which it may not yet have solved; and Methoni, the Mani and Diakofto offer limited accommodation for which it is certainly advisable to book in advance. In the other towns, rooms can usually be found at short notice or none at all.

If you are travelling without bookings, it might be wiser to start looking for a room about 5 p.m., before the arrival of the afternoon buses from Athens.

Athens to Corinth

Assuming no more than normal delays in reaching Elefsis and light traffic from the tollgate onwards, the 86 km of good though not particularly wide motorway from Athens to Corinth can be covered comfortably in an hour and a half; much faster and you risk a ticket, take it too slowly and you can be stopped for dawdling. The more romantic alternative to the motorway is the old road, which can be entered just before the tollgate. It always was and still is dangerous. Before, there was too much traffic on it; now it is not well maintained, and the drivers of the trucks and buses that serve the coastal settlements tend to drive on the assumption that they have the road to themselves. The same applies to the old road from Corinth to Patras: the motorway deprives you of the villages, but relieves you of the need to keep swallowing your heart.

Heading out from Athens towards the Scaramanga gap, you are driving parallel to, but will not see, the old Sacred Way to Elefsis. What you will see are successive small industries and, unless the construction sector has emerged from its slump, long ranks of unemployed equipment of the bulldozer family. You are, unavoidably, taking the ugliest of all the exits from Athens.

Daphni

Almost at the top of the incline, where the hills close in, you might consider a first stop at the monastery of Daphni, adjoining the site of the Daphni wine festival. Surrounded by battlemented walls, the monastery, founded in the sixth century, takes its name from the laurel, *daphni*, that was sacred to Apollo: there had formerly been a temple to Apollo on the site. The present church, the most important Byzantine monument within a short distance of Athens, dates from the end of the eleventh century: it was restored partially in 1893 and more completely after the Second World War. Its mosaics are unrivalled in the Athens area, and equalled only by those to be seen in Thessaloniki and at Ossios Loukas near Livadia; the Christ Pantocrator, surrounded by sixteen prophets between the windows, is regarded as a masterpiece of Byzantine ecclesiastical art.

The building across the road is Greece's largest mental hospital. A few hundred yards further and you descend into the pit. But take courage; Greece has nothing worse to show, and it lasts only a few kilometres. Shipyards on the left and oil refineries on the right, foundries emitting pungent reddish smoke which guarantees the survival of the Athens smog, and out in the bay – the island that encloses it is Salamis – dozens of laid-up oil tankers testifying to the world crisis in merchant shipping.

Elefsis

Somewhere in the murk are the few remains of ancient Elefsis, to which pilgrims once trekked twice a year for the Great and Lesser Mysteries. There is now almost nothing to see – a few pathways, a fallen pillar, ruined altars to lesser gods and some carved stone benches. The site is open daily from 9 a.m. to 3 p.m., except Tuesdays, and the Dr 200 entry fee includes admission to the museum.

Though the secret of the Mysteries was well kept, the general concept is clear enough: the winter mourning of nature and its resurrection in the spring, symbolised by the grief of the goddess Demeter for her abducted daughter and the rejoicing at her annual return on a six-month leave from Hades. For modern Elefsis, industry has ensured that there is no spring.

Megara

The pretty little town crowning the hill 800 m to your right just before the mountainous stretch of the road, 42 km from Athens and almost exactly half-way to Corinth, is Megara, population 17,000. A town with a long history and once a notable coloniser, it has two claims to modern fame: the chicken farms set back from the motorway which supply most of the eggs you will eat while in Greece, and which are mischievously reputed to have inspired the architects of some of Greece's newer public buildings, and a gentleman named Panaghis.

Panaghis

Panaghis of Megara was the archetypal professional bridegroom, pioneering a business that flourished in the decades immediately following the Second World War. His final coup was to promise marriage to three girls at the same time, pocket their dowries in advance, arrange simultaneous weddings in three different churches and, the night before, disappear from Megara for ever.

Jilted brides were a fleeting social problem at the time because of the shortage of men as a result of war, occupation, civil war and emigration. Shiploads of girls were sent to Australia on 'bride boats', after elementary training in Australianism in a school in an Athens suburb, to provide wives for newly arrived members of the Greek communities in Sydney and Melbourne. Men old enough to lay convincing claim to a business or career that inspired confidence (in Greece, it is said that you are what you assert yourself to be) were operating in a buyers' market. Times were hard, and a young girl's eligibility was measured by the value of her dowry.

Athens press reports of the period spoke of an estimated 5,000 cases of breach of promise brought before the Greek courts every year. There was no way of calculating how many other families preferred to swallow their losses rather than reveal their disgrace. Once fought with lawsuit or shotgun, breach of promise has become an infrequent subject of litigation since the formal abolition of the dowry, and only on Crete has it remained the occasional motive of an 'honour killing'. Nevertheless, Panaghis has an assured niche in modern folklore. His identification with Megara is particularly fitting, since Athenians have always laughed at Megarans.

The coasts of the Megara area were once famous for their olive groves, but these were all chopped down several years ago to clear the site for an oil refinery – it would have been Greece's fifth – which was never built. Naturally, they have not been replanted.

Once past the chickens, there is nothing of note before Corinth except Greece's most modern oil refinery, built during the dictatorship by the newly rich Vardinoyannis family from Crete who in addition own a fleet of oil tankers and the Meridien Hotel in Athens. They also own the Panathinaikos football club but, despite booster injections of oil money, the team defiantly refuses to repeat the glories it once knew when its trainer was Ferenc Puskas and it lost to Ajax in a European Cup final at Wembley.

Loutraki and Corinth: faded glories

Loutraki A branch road to the right immediately after the tollgate and before the Corinth Canal leads, after 6 km, to Loutraki, population 8,500, a faded summer resort set at the foot of tall cliffs in a position that suggests at once its original function as a spa. It is still the main source of

Greece's bottled mineral water, the brand marked as Ivi, which in Loutraki you can drink free from roadside taps. Loutraki is on the way down because the Greeks have learned to go further in order to drink their waters with greater discrimination, and also because there is no longer a casino there.

Where to stay

Though fashions in travel change, hotels survive. Should you decide on an overnight stay, there are thirty-six to choose from (eight first class, 12 second class, 14 third class and two fourth class) with a total of 3,235 beds; many of these sit side by side along the waterfront. The Club Poseidon (first class, 800 beds), 2 km outside the town, is the closest to a resort hotel, set among trees at the edge of the sea but without much of a beach. The more modest Pappas (second class, 153 beds) is a new hotel only 1 km outside Loutraki that describes itself as 'a complex full of pins and wild flowers' – but it is anything but a bed of nails! On the subject of pines, when the Mount Parnes hotel on the tree-covered slopes of the mountain of that name outside Athens opened some thirty years ago, its half-page advertising in English laid claim to a distinction that even now would be unusual: every room, it said, had a 'private bat'. It was not stipulated whether clients had to provide their own stake and garlic.

Where to eat

Two favourite Loutraki fish tavernas are the Delphini at 99 Poseidon Street and the Faros (Lighthouse) at 69 Eleftherios Venizelos Street; the latter also serves steaks. And one of the waterfront hotels is worth a visit even if you are not staying: whether because their residents tend to be elderly, seeking health through abstemiousness, or because of the water itself, they all serve the best cup of tea in Greece. The waiters appear to understand that tea tastes better when made in a pot with boiling water, and that the standard measure need not be one bag per person. They even offer a choice of milk or lemon. Across the water at the canal cafés, those who venture an order of tea will be squashing a bag against the side of a cup of tepid water and wondering whether adding the slice of lemon will remove the very slight stain of colour they have worked so hard to obtain; in other words, they will be drinking it Greek-style.

Ireon

Refreshed by tea and cake – Loutraki is not a great place to eat but it does specialise in a particularly sticky and nutty *baklava* – you can either turn back to Corinth or press on along a narrow road of second quality cut into the cliffs for a meal at Ireon. Situated on Lake Vouliagmeni – actually a lagoon, with the narrowest of openings into the sea – Ireon has been turned by its inexpensive fish restaurants into a favourite Athenian Sunday excursion. The question is whether that alone recompenses for the difficult access.

The Corinth Canal

And so to Corinth, the voluptuous city. But first you must cross the Corinth Canal. The canal would have been among the wonders of the Ancient World had Nero been able to finish what he began with a golden shovel in AD 67. Today, less than a century after its completion by French engineers, it is already becoming a museum piece. But it remains impressive, probably holding third place after Suez and Panama on anyone's list of canals, and is a kind of memorial to late nineteenth-century engineering.

Its purpose was to cut off 200 miles of sailing time, around the southern tip of the Peloponnese, for ships plying between the Aegean and Adriatic Seas. While a day saved is still a substantial economy, today's ships are simply too large for a waterway only 21 m wide at the water level and with a water depth of only 7 m. They are also too large for any conceivable widening and deepening of the canal to be economically justifiable.

The canal now serves mainly coasters and ferries and the occasional cruise liner, which scrape through with the help of tugs. Seen from the road and rail bridges 40 m above, the impression is of a narrow and absolutely straight ribbon much shorter than its actual 7.7 km length; seen from the deck of a ship, a sense of tension is amplified by the silence as the ship creeps through, sometimes with only inches to spare.

Unless you are planning to leave the motorway, the Corinth Canal provides the last opportunity for refreshment before reaching Patras 130 km further on, as well as the last petrol stations for 80 km. There is really nothing to choose between the rival cafés, all of which double as grocery and souvenir shops.

By this time you will probably have realised that in Greece the long-distance driver (the term, of course, is a relative one) is not as pampered as elsewhere, and must take the chance of a break where he finds one. The two motorways, though built considerably after the Second World War, pre-dated the growth of significant individual travel, Greek or tourist. For that reason it was not considered necessary to provide them with a succession of roadside restaurants; no one would have wanted to operate them because of the inevitable losses, and would not want to even today outside the tourist season. So on the 225 km from Athens to Patras you have only Corinth; on the 508 km from Athens to Thessaloniki your choice is between Kamena Vourla and the Vale of Tempe.

Corinth   Corinth, population 23,000, will almost certainly be a disappointment; it is best to think of it only as an easier alternative to Ireon for a fish lunch by the water. Repeatedly destroyed throughout history, sometimes for its ambitions and sometimes for its morals – those which so distressed St Paul – Corinth continues its tribulations: the new town has twice been shattered by earthquakes, in 1858 and 1928. For a while, when the canal was new, it seemed that it might reacquire a part of its old commercial importance, but in fact that never happened. Greeks hardly ever go there.

Corinth likes to sleep in the afternoon. Once, I disembarked there along with a dozen other passengers from an unexpected yacht and was told I would have to wait two hours to get my passport stamped. Murmuring 'You bet!', I continued to Athens. Subsequently, when asked by police how I happened to be in a country to which I had never returned, my explanation that I had come in through Corinth at four o'clock on an August afternoon was accepted without question.

The Corinth archaeological site, 9 km from the new city, is open from 8.45 a.m. to 3 p.m. daily except Tuesdays, with the Dr 300 admission including entry to the museum. The site contains ruins of the Roman agora of the first century AD, seven remaining columns of a temple of Apollo from the fifth century BC, and a theatre. The museum houses articles excavated locally.

Acro Corinth

Acro Corinth, the flat-topped rock with seemingly sheer faces which has been a landmark since you crossed the canal, is not quite as formidable as it seems. Though it is 575 m high, you can drive to a restaurant–bar just below the summit. From the top, you have a memorable view of the Saronic and Corinthian Gulfs and the mountains of the Peloponnese and mainland Greece. You can also wander among the ruins of a temple of Aphrodite where once a thousand priestesses gave the oldest profession the respectability of private worship, as well as later remains from the Byzantine, Venetian and Turkish periods.

On to Patras

The decision you have to make at this point, assuming Patras is your immediate destination, is whether to continue along the motorway or economise on tolls by using the old road through the coastal villages, which is still busy enough to be well maintained.

On the one hand, the villages are pretty, and you are close enough to the water for much of the way to end with salt on your car if the wind is from the north and the sea at all choppy. On the other, you lose nothing of the view, and have an easier and faster drive, if you prefer the motorway, which is never more than a kilometre from the sea.

Diakofto

Either way, however, one stop should be made, and could well be considered for an overnight stay. Diakofto (population 1,750) is not just a village in a sea of fruit trees, where the bees would be unworthy of their ancestors if they did not produce some of the finest honey in Greece, but also the terminal of a rack-and-pinion railway to Kalavryta. The village is built around a square at the end of the main railway line, with passable swimming from its beach and a choice of grill tavernas in the square and tree-shaded streets running from it. The best hotel is the twenty-six-room Chris-Paul (third class); the others, with a combined total of forty-six rooms, are all fourth class. So don't expect much comfort!

The rack-and-pinion railway

There is no more spectacular journey anywhere in Greece than the 23 km haul up the gorge of the Bouraikos, in and out of tunnels and over viaducts, along the route of a stream in summer and torrent after the autumn rains or when the snow is melting. Ideally perhaps, the 70-minute trip should be taken early in the morning in the heart of winter, when the river is full, the wind blows icy from the snow-covered mountains across the water and the best defence against the cold is a breakfast of brandy and *melomakarona* honey cakes bought at Diakofto, but on any day of the year it is a journey never to be forgotten. And no matter how hot it may be by the sea, a sweater is advisable if you are on the first train out or the last one back.

Megaspelion   Even this small journey needs to be broken half-way, at Zachlorou; from there it is an uphill walk or ride of between half and one hour, depending on lungs and legs, to the monastery of Megaspelion.

There is no monastery in Greece more incongruous. Built against a 122-m cliff that serves as its rear wall, the monastery displays relics dating from the tenth century but is itself barely fifty years old. Completely destroyed by fire in 1934 – lacking water, the monks could save only their treasures – it was rebuilt with indestructibility as the objective. Thus it is now an eight-storey religious hotel of concrete and glass, occupied by the few monks who are hardy or devout enough to accept the rigours of a mountain winter.

They will show you the great cave (*mega spelion*) from which the monastery takes its name: there, it is said, two monks named Symeon and Theodore, subsequently beatified, were led by a vision in the fourth century to the discovery of a miracle-working icon of the Virgin. Protected by a silver casing, the icon hangs in a niche of the original grotto church around which the monastery has been built. Certainly at Christmas, but also on other days if not too many visitors arrive at the same time, olives and a glass of wine will be offered in the refectory looking across to mountains where nothing ever changes.

Kalavryta   Returning to Zachlorou, you take the next train to the mountain town of Kalavryta, population 1,800, where the railway ends. Though offering fifty-seven hotel rooms, it not a place to stay except in an emergency. Kalavryta is Greece's Lidice: burned by the Germans in 1943, when more than a thousand of its inhabitants were massacred as a reprisal for attacks by resistance groups (an event commemorated by the Kalavryta Symphony of Mikis Theodorakis), it has been rebuilt in a particularly graceless style and could be ignored if it were not for the spectacular journey to it and the proximity of Greece's most famous monastery, that of Aghia Lavra.

Aghia   It was during a service at Aghia Lavra in March 1821 that Bishop
Lavra   Germanos of Patras raised the standard of revolt against the Turks which launched the Independence Revolution. Returning to Patras, he did the same there, while simultaneous uprisings were breaking out elsewhere in the Peloponnese. The Greeks as a result celebrate 25 March, the Feast of the Annunciation, as Independence Day. This monastery, alas, has also burned down, but has been rebuilt more tastefully in traditional style. It welcomes visitors.

It is possible to drive from Diakofto to Kalavryta, or to reach the town by a mountain road from Patras, but that is simply not the same thing as taking the train.

The Gulf of Corinth

You can take the 50 km from Diakofto to Patras at a run, unless your interests extend to the arms and cement industries of Aighion (population 21,000) or you are proposing to cross to mainland Greece by ferry from Rion to Andirion, at the narrows of the Gulf of Corinth. This is a twenty-minute crossing, suspended when the gales are westerly and due eventually to be replaced by a suspension bridge – exactly when is a matter of who will pay. The ruined castles on either side of the narrows are fifteenth-century Turkish, destroyed in the seventeenth century by the Knights of Malta and restored in the eighteenth by the Venetians.

Patras, the gateway port

Patras, with a population of 142,000, is Greece's third largest city after Athens/Piraeus and Thessaloniki (but fourth if Melbourne is included in the list!). It is the gateway port to Italy and by extension to the European Community: two or three passenger/car ferries (more in high season) leave every day for Brindisi, Bari or Ancona on the Italian Adriatic coast. As a result, transient tourism has become the city's main industry, taking over from the old trade in sultanas and currants.

Situated at the foot of Mount Panahaikon and subject to sudden thunderstorms as well as occasional earth tremors, Patras was razed by the Turks during the 1821 Revolution and rebuilt in the years immediately following Independence. It therefore has a homogeneity that is only now beginning to be disturbed by the inevitable apartment blocks. From the more distant past, it offers a Frankish castle and a Roman theatre, but its prettiest feature is its arcaded streets, which give shelter equally from rain and sun.

Getting there

Patras is well served by buses and trains from Athens. From Patras, there are trains down the east coast of the Peloponnese to Kalamata, and buses to Pyrgos, Tripolis and, in mainland Greece, Missolonghi, Agrinion and Thessaloniki. In addition to Italy, Patras is also the port for boats to the Ionian islands of Ithaka, Cephalonia, Paxos and Corfu, as well as to Igoumenitsa. However, most holidaymakers bound for Corfu prefer to drive to Igoumenitsa, where the ferries are more frequent and the crossing is shorter.

Main areas

Even though a large city by Greek measures, Patras is still essentially a waterfront; the train station is there, between the Customs House and the ferry docks, and so are the bus terminals, numerous hotels, and most of the restaurants and cafés. But it merits a little inward exploration for the attractive squares and cathedral of St Andrew, built on the reputed site of the crucifixion of St Andrew. Its greatest treasure is the saint's silver-mounted skull, returned to Patras in 1964 after five centuries in St Peter's, Rome.

The shopping is nothing special, even though Patras is the commercial capital of the Peloponnese.

Where to stay

The two most comfortable Patras hotels are the Astir (120 rooms) in Aghiou Andreou Street and Moreas (105 rooms) in Iroon Polytechniou and Kyprou (Heroes of the Polytechnic and Cyprus) Street. You can get a substantial breakfast at the Astir if you pay an extra Dr 500. Both rely on groups. The smaller second-class Galaxy (53 rooms) and Olympic (35 rooms) in Aghiou Nikolaou Street are rather more peaceful. If you prefer a hotel by the sea, try the Achaia Beach (second class, 165 beds) at Bozaïtika, 4 km back along the Athens motorway, or the Porto Rio, 10 km away at Rion: this is a 501-bed first-class hotel and bungalow complex on a beach and is particularly handy for ferries to the mainland (especially if you are delayed when they have been stopped by gales). There are also no fewer than fifteen camp sites in the immediate vicinity of Patras, all by the sea.

Nevertheless, you may well ask yourself whether you really need to stay in Patras, when you can be in Olympia in a couple of hours.

Where to eat

As may be imagined from the hundreds of thousands of tourists who pass through it on their way to or from Italy, or stop for lunch on Peloponnese coach tours, the city is full of restaurants, pizza parlours and sandwich bars.

If you are staying the night you may fare somewhat better by hunting out a restaurant deeper into the city, but you may congratulate yourself (or possibly question your own standards) should you regard your meal as in any way exceptional. It was different once, when the drive from Athens to Patras took the best part of a day and there were no ferries to Italy. As a place to eat, Patras has been ruined by the motorway and Brindisi.

Within the city, good eating is claimed for Trikoyias near the railway station in Othonos-Amalias Street, the Majestic Restaurant in Aghiou Nikolaou Street and, about 2 km from the centre, the Evangelatos and Kalypso a few blocks apart on Iroon Polytechniou Street; all four take credit cards. Patras inhabitants with cars prefer to drive out to their own favourites among the dozens of small fish restaurants along the coast on both sides of the city.

Useful addresses

The National Tourist Organisation of Greece (NTOG) has a regional office in Heroes of the Polytechnic and Cyprus Street (tel. 420.304) and the Greek Automobile and Touring Club (ELPA) has a branch office at 127 Korinthou Street (tel. 425.411).

Patras to Olympia

Pyrgos

From Patras there is, as yet, no more motorway, nor very much reason to stop along the 95 km to Pyrgos and the left turn for Olympia.

Pyrgos, population 22,000, has nothing to show the visitor but a main street and a few restaurants; with Olympia only 24 km away you need to be really hungry to stop for a meal.

Once you turn off the coastal road, you get a glimpse of the Peloponnese at its wealthiest. The coastal plain is well irrigated and intensively farmed to supply urban Greece with market garden produce and fruit. You follow broadly the course of the Alfios River (the 'Sacred Alph') to which the survival of even what is left at Olympia owes much. Silting of that river and its tributary, the Kladeos, covered the site with a protective blanket beneath which it snuggled through centuries of barbarism.

Olympia – old and new

Olympia never was and is not now a town: it was a sanctuary that came to life for a few days every four years. Now it is the remains of one, abutting a pleasant, unpretentious tourist village, population 1,100, which has no reason to exist other than to house and feed the passing stranger. The single main street is lined with restaurants and souvenir shops.

The ancient games

The Olympic Games were first held in 776 BC, acquired panhellenic significance a century later, and reached the peak of their glory in the sixth century BC. They were held in the full moon of July or August every fourth year in honour of Zeus, with contests that included foot, horse and chariot racing, jumping, discus and javelin throwing, wrestling and special events for boys and heralds. The prizes were wreaths of olive and the assurance of immortality. Before the games, messengers would be sent to all parts of Greece to proclaim a 'sacred truce' that halted all war for approximately three months.

Only once can it reasonably be suspected that the results were rigged: Nero won both events for which he entered, a chariot race in which he fell twice and a singing contest specially added to the programme because he was, after all, a musical emperor.

The 293rd Olympiad in 393 AD – 1,169 years after the first – was destined to be the last. The following year the games were banned by the Byzantine Emperor Theodosios I and thirty-three years later Theodosios II ordered the destruction of the temples as idolatrous. Today, only scattered stones remain from the once magnificent buildings. For centuries even the exact whereabouts of Olympia were forgotten, and it was not until 1723 that a French monk located the site. Desultory excavations were carried out by French archaeologists soon after Greece secured its independence, but the serious and systematic work that gave Olympia its present appearance has been done by German teams since 1875.

The ancient stadium, little more than a depressed running track, was fully unearthed between 1959 and 1961; it is a rare visitor who, looking down at it, cannot hear some distant echoes from the past. Unless your ambition is merely to say you have been, it is even more essential at Olympia than at the Athens Acropolis, Delphi or Mycenae to take the braces off your imagination before you enter the site. Olympia is not spectacular; it is evocative.

The archaeological site and museums

The Archaeological Site is open daily from 8 a.m. to 5.30 p.m., admission Dr 300.

The Olympia Museum, open daily from 8 a.m. to 5.30 p.m., Tuesdays from 12 to 5.30 p.m., admission Dr 300, houses a collection surpassed in Greece only by those of the Delphi and Athens Archaeological Museums. Pride of place is given to the marble statue of Hermes holding the baby Dionysos sculpted by Praxiteles in the fourth century BC, but one can also see more humble exhibits, such as the weights and dumb-bells used by athletes in their training. Unfortunately, the great ivory and gold statue of Zeus by Phidias was taken to Constantinople in the fourth century AD and destroyed in one of the city's many fires.

The Museum of the Olympic Games, open daily from 8.45 a.m. to 3 p.m., closed Tuesdays, admission Dr 100, displays material and literature covering the ancient games and their revival in 1896.

Where to stay

Olympia has twenty-four hotels with a total of 793 rooms. Of the three first-class, the veteran SPAP close to the museum is a little cheaper than the more modern Amalia and Antonios.

Where to eat

Recommended by Olympians are the Artis restaurant near the Xenias Hotel and the Praxitelis beside the Hellenic Telecommunications Organisation (OTE) building. From 1988 the Artis is to become a hotel also.

The centenary games

In Athens you will already have seen, though you will probably not have been able to enter, the marble stadium near the Zappeion Park built for the first modern Olympiad in 1896. That stadium is now far too small and narrow for athletic events; it is used, to the extent that it is used at all, for occasional pop concerts.

A modern Olympic stadium, completed only a few years ago halfway between central Athens and the hill suburb of Kifisia, gives a sense of the practical to Greece's determination to seek and secure the 1996 centenary Olympics, despite the drawback that the 1992 Games will also have been held in Europe.

The initial idea, however, was more ambitious: to apply not just for the centenary Games but for a monopoly of all future Olympiads. Floated at a time when successive Olympiads had been marred by terrorism or disrupted by international politics, the proposal made enough sense to be given serious consideration by the International Olympic Committee. The Greeks offered to create a new and permanent Olympic City, at a site close to but not actually visible from Ancient Olympia; it would have had something of the legal status of Vatican City, with its own authorities and a degree of autonomy from the Greek state comparable to that of the Mount Athos community of monks (see pp. 237–38).

The idea ran up against objections on two main counts. Archaeologists and conservationists, Greek and foreign, were unhappy over the proximity to Ancient Olympia. And there was concern over the cost of establishing and running a 'state' that would operate fully for only a fortnight every four years, but would still have to be provided from scratch not just with the normal requirements of an Olympiad but with hotel accommodation for spectators, a hospital, administrative buildings and communications.

From outside Greece, there was a natural resistance from countries that would be required to abandon their own hopes of staging future Olympiads. For better or worse, the idea of an Olympic State is now dormant and probably dead. In its trimmed-down form, the application will be simply for the 1996 Games, to be held in Athens.

Across the middle

If you are running short of time, or have decided to restrict yourself to the 'top half' of the Peloponnese, you can continue straight on from Olympia, along good roads, to Tripolis and Nafplion, enjoying picturesque mountain-and-valley countryside but meeting with nothing of exceptional interest along the way, except Bassae, near Andritsaina.

The more direct route from Olympia to Tripolis, an unhurried three-hour drive, will take you through only some small villages unless you make two short diversions, one to Dimitsana and the other to Vytina. The more southerly route from Olympia, taking possibly an hour longer, passes through Andritsaina, Karitaina and Megalopolis.

Dimitsana   Built amphitheatrically on two hills at an altitude of 960 m, Dimitsana was the birthplace of Bishop Germanos of Patras who raised the banner of revolution in 1821 (see p. 176) and whose family house can still be seen. Possibly for that reason, and also because it is small (population 600) and little visited, it has been declared a protected architectural area. Here you can see the traditional houses of the Morea, with wooden balconies projecting over narrow streets. For those who wish to stay, it has only one hotel – the third-class Dimitsana with twenty-seven rooms.

Vytina   At an altitude of 1,050 m and with a population of 860, this is a favourite place for weekending among snow-draped firs between December and March; its summer visitors are mainly hikers. Its most famous son was the late conductor Dimitri Mitropoulos. The visitor can choose from five hotels, second and third class, with 111 rooms between them: the largest is the Villa Valos, with fifty-one rooms, but only the Xenia Motel, with twenty rooms, has a full restaurant.

Andritsaina   With a population of 850, this is also a place, like Dimitsana, to see old stone houses with tiled roofs and to take a coffee beneath a huge plane tree that spreads over the central square. It has a library with rare sixteenth-century books and earlier manuscripts, churches of the eighteenth and nineteenth centuries, and three hotels of from second to fifth class with forty-seven rooms altogether; only one, the second-class Theoxenia with thirty-three rooms, serves meals.

Bassae
The main reason to stay at Andritsaina is to see the temple of Apollo Epikourios at Bassae (pronounced Vassae), 14 km away along a winding mountain road. Spectacularly placed on a plateau 1,500 m above sea level, the Doric-style temple was built by Ictinos, architect of the Parthenon, in about 420 BC as a thanks offering to Apollo 'who succours' (Epikourios) for his deliverance of the inhabitants from a plague. The well-preserved temple overlooks an ancient agora but the whole site, as so often in Greece, is most memorable for the splendour of the views.

Karitaina
Thirty-two km from Andritsaina on the road to Megalopolis is this picturesque medieval 'town' (population 300) situated above the bank of the Alfios River, where traditional stone-built houses of two and three storeys are still guarded by a thirteenth-century Frankish castle used by Kolokotronis during the Independence Revolution. The Byzantine church of St Nicholas is the showpiece among no fewer than forty old churches. There are fifteen beds on offer in private houses for the traveller wishing to stay.

Megalopolis
Founded in 371 BC as Megali Poli (Great City), this was the administrative centre of the Arcadian League. Fittingly, everything was large: there are the remains of an ancient theatre that could seat 20,000 and a place of assembly with room for 6,000 seated and 10,000 standing. Today it is dominated by a complex of thermo-electric power plants fuelled by lignite from open-cast mining in the area. The present population of 4,700 is double what it was in 1965 when the first of the power stations went into production. Nonetheless, it has only four hotels, all of fourth class, with a total of sixty rooms.

The west coast

Kyparissia
From Pyrgos, the coastal road south offers real rewards. Kyparissia, a quiet little town of 4,000 inhabitants crowned by a Byzantine castle, is worth a coffee break. But you can ignore the castle with a clear conscience, since better ones are ahead.

Just before Filiatra, if you think you catch glimpses among the trees of a great white horse climbing out of the sea, you are not hallucinating. Take the dirt road leading to it and you will find that in fact it is a house, with the door set into one flank; if it happens to be open that day you will see a small living room, bedroom, library and, in the tail, a bathroom. Alongside is a crenellated castle straight from the set of a Wagner opera!

Filiatra   Press on to Filiatra, an agricultural town of 4,900 inhabitants, and you will come to a replica of the Eiffel Tower the height of a three-storey building and, nearby, a 'unisphere' in need of a touch of paint. Now you know for certain that you have reached 'Fournierland'.

Dr Haralambos Fournarakis, born in Filiatra around the turn of the century and educated in France, became Dr Harry Fournier when he emigrated to the United States and set up an ulcer clinic in Chicago. In a rather eccentric manifestation of a long tradition among repatriate migrants, Dr Fournier returned to his birthplace after his retirement, rehellenised his name, and decided to devote some of his wealth to broadening the horizons of young Filiatrans – hence the Eiffel Tower, the unisphere and a sedately modern library – and to indulging his own love of Greek mythology. The equine house, his summer residence, was not, he was at pains to point out to curious visitors, the horse that led to the fall of Troy, but that of Poseidon rising from the sea.

On the subject of horses, Dr Fournier used to tell the story of how a Greek–American friend of his in his Chicago days, movie mogul Spyros Skouras, once unintentionally provided a novel twist to the culminating event of the Trojan War. Steaming into Hollywood for the first time, on a special train given to him by the studio he had just bought, he was confronted by a five-word banner: 'Beware of gifts bearing Greeks.'

Pylos   Pylos, population 2,500, deserves a visit of a few hours. This is the former Navarino, site of the 1827 naval engagement. You can lunch on the waterfront overlooking the bay where the battle took place, before or after a visit to the so-called New Castle above the town, built by the Turks in the sixteenth century.

The scene of the battle can be visited by small boat, and there are relics of the period in the small museum: open daily from 9 a.m. to 3 p.m. except Tuesdays, admission Dr 200. There are nine little hotels of second to fourth class, most of them near the water, for those who decide to spend the night safely away from groups. Try the Karalis Beach or Miramare for second class (twenty-eight and thirty beds respectively) or Galaxy in Three Admirals Square for third (sixty-two beds); the latter has a good view of the square and the harbour, but it can be noisy. Recommended restaurants are the Tria Adelfia (Three Brothers) on the waterfront and Patsouros in the main square.

The   One of the last of the age of sail, the battle was fought on 20
Battle of   October 1827, ending with the complete destruction of a Turkish–
Navarino   Egyptian fleet by a combined British–French–Russian squadron under the command of Admiral Lord Codrington. The third ship in the line on that day was HMS Albion; a photocopy of three pages of its log is on display in the Piraeus Marine Club. It makes piquant reading.

'2.45 o'clock: winds variable. Shortened sail and came to in the appointed station and commenced close action with a frigate on the larboard quarter. His bowsprit, in swinging, caught foul of the mizzen rigging.

'3 o'clock: boarded her and carried her. Found her to be on fire, cut her adrift and abandoned her. On her drifting clear, found ourselves opposed to two Turkish ships of the line on the larboard beam and one on the starboard. Commenced close action with them.

'4.40 o'clock: observed the main and mizzen masts of one of the ships engaged to fall and, in its fall, to take away the mast of the Turkish Admiral. We slipped the chain and springs to avoid the ships engaged, they being apparently on fire.

'6.20 o'clock: the action ceased throughout the line, the Turkish fleet being completely defeated, many having cut their cables and ships on shore on fire. Employed knotting and splicing the rigging and warping towards the Admiral. Received 46 Greeks on board, they having escaped from the Turkish ships during the action. Lost 10 killed and 52 wounded.'

Today, Pylos is such a peaceful little town!

Nestor's Palace   Though frequently dismissed as an anti-climax after Ancient Olympia, Nestor's Palace, which can be visited easily from Pylos, has the advantage that it was excavated comparatively recently (since 1952), is not particularly well known, and is rarely if ever included on the programme of a coach tour.

About 10 km from Pylos and 4 km from the medieval town of Hora, the palace was the home of the 'wise old man' of the Trojan War. However, he was not sufficiently wise, or wealthy, to avoid building with wood in a hot country, and the palace was destroyed by fire around 1200 BC.

The remains give a clear ground plan of what was once a two-storey construction in three main blocks, including a throne and hearth room, kitchens, bathroom and guard towers. The Hora museum, built in 1966, displays a watercolour impression of the palace in its original form, tomb furnishings, weapons and cups, beautiful frescoes, pottery and some tablets found during pre-war exploration that helped in the deciphering of Linear B script. The most important of the finds, however, are in the Athens Archaeological Museum.

Hora   The site is open standard hours, and closed Tuesdays. The museum, with the same opening hours, is in Hora, population 3,100. There are two small hotels there of second and fifth class with a total of thirty beds.

Methoni–Kalamata–Sparta

Methoni   Once a strategic military port but now little more than a village 13 km down a side road south of Pylos, Methoni tends to be ignored by guidebooks or generously allowed just a sentence, for the soundest of reasons: it involves a diversion, it is not very well supplied with hotels, and it is certainly not a place to swim for those who prefer their beaches long and sandy, and their sea bottom uncluttered with weeds.

The Venetian castle

But there is an excellent reason not only to visit, but to stay there overnight: it has the most magnificently sited and best preserved of all the Venetian castles in Greece, not this time on a hill but on a promontory at the end of the beach. Just to walk around the castle requires the better part of half a day, if you are to allow time to appreciate why it was built exactly where it is, what made it so strong, and what it must have been like to take refuge there – or to defend it – in the dangerous Middle Ages.

Where to stay

Methoni had a population in 1981 of 1,251, including the three inhabitants of the offshore islet of Sapientza. The eight hotels, from second to fifth class, together offer eighty-eight rooms; while this is an advance on the one hotel of twenty years ago it still secures protection against groups except, just possibly, at the twenty-room Alex. Probably the pleasantest is the second-class Methoni Beach, with twelve rooms, beside the water; it and the third-class Alex 50 m back from the sea are the only ones providing even breakfast, but there is no shortage of fish tavernas and of families ready to start your day with a frying of *marides*.

You can reach Kalamata from Methoni either by back-tracking to Pylos or continuing across the tip of the peninsula to Koroni and from there taking the coastal road.

Koroni

Koroni, population 1,380, is the site of the 'companion' fortress to that of Methoni; the two together were once known as 'the eyes of the [Venetian] republic'. While the Koroni castle is the less impressive, it does offer a view across the gulf to Taygettos and the mountains of the Mani. The town has four hotels of second to fifth class, with a total of ninety-one beds; easily the best is the forty-bed Auberge de la Plage just 70 m from the beach.

Kalamata

Kalamata, some 50 km along the direct road from Pylos, lies at the head of the Gulf of Messinia. Until a Saturday night in September 1986 it would have been the obvious place to spend the night. The end of the line for the Peloponnese railway, it was a busy port city of some 42,000 inhabitants, with good hotels, excellent beaches along water deep enough to stay refreshingly cool even in the heart of summer, restaurants of note and an interesting Frankish–Venetian fortress dating from the thirteenth century. But then it was wrecked by the worst earthquake to strike a Greek city since those soon after the Second World War that levelled Cephalonia in the Ionian islands and Volos on the east coast of Greece.

Kalamata has a long and arduous period of reconstruction ahead of it before it regains its old position as a popular holiday resort. It is not a matter only of actual damage; the Greeks are excessively timid about tremors, for all that they have to live with them, and there is no collective belief that the safest place of all is one that has just had its disaster. So they still flock to Iraklion in Crete despite the converging opinions of statisticians and predictions of astrologers that it would perhaps be safer not to.

Sparta

Provided there is still sufficient daylight it might be better to press on to Sparta, a short (60-km) though dramatic drive along the flanks of Mount Taygettus, at 2,407 m the tallest in the Peloponnese, on a road that is among the first to be closed by winter snows. Taciturn and singleminded, the Spartans of Ancient Greece must have been dull companions to spend an evening with. The same applies to their modern successors. But the city does have plenty of hotels, because of its importance as a road junction and capital of the province of Lakonia (from which the adjective laconic derives), and because it is only a few kilometres from Mistras.

Getting there

Sparta is well served by buses from Athens, 255 km on the direct, but less interesting, route through the central Peloponnese, and has local bus connections with Tripolis, Kalamata, Monemvasia and Gythion, the gateway to the Mani.

What to see and where to stay

Sparta has a population of 12,000, a statue of Leonidas, a museum (open from 9 a.m. to 3 p.m., closed Tuesdays, admission Dr 200) with exhibits from the Mycenaean and Roman eras, but practically nothing to show in situ from its ancient past – this is scarcely surprising, since the Spartans were better at destroying than building. Mainly to serve the Greek excursion trade (weekenders from Athens spend Friday and Saturday nights in Sparta and devote Saturday to exploring the Mani and Monemvasia), it has twelve hotels of second to fifth class with a total of 417 rooms. If you select from those that have restaurants – the Lida, Menelaion, Apollo, Dioscouri and Sparta Inn – you will be spared the search for a table elsewhere.

Mistras

Mistras is unique. How long you devote to it will depend on the extent of your interest in Constantinople. And also, perhaps, on the temperature, the condition of your legs and lungs, and the comfort of your shoes. For Mistras, uphill all the way, is no place for the faint of heart.

On one of the foothills of Mount Taygettus, 4.5 km from Sparta, Mistras is an uninhabited city from the Byzantine era, with fortress, palaces, churches, monasteries and the houses of the wealthy and the poor. It is comparable only with Mount Athos in its concentrated essence of Byzantium.

How did it happen?

After the Crusaders had captured Constantinople in 1204 the Franks extended their sway over much of the Peloponnese, and in the middle of the thirteenth century one of them, Guillaume de Villardhouin, built a castle on the hill then known as Myzithra. Less than a decade after its completion, de Villardhouin was captured in battle against the Byzantines and forced to cede the castle, along with

Monemvasia and the province of Mani, as ransom. Under the Byzantines it became a fortified town and a place of refuge in times of danger for the inhabitants of Sparta.

During the two centuries of Byzantine rule, Mistras was the capital of the Morea and seat of the Governors (Despots), a post normally held by a son or brother of the ruling emperor. The last Byzantine Emperor, Constantine Paleologos, was crowned in the cathedral of Mistras. Captured by the Turks a decade after the fall of Constantinople, Mistras continued to flourish for another 300 years, with a population that at its peak exceeded 40,000. Following an unsuccessful revolt it was sacked in 1770 by the Turkish sultan's Albanian forces; after a second and final burning during the Independence Revolution it was never repopulated.

What to see

The churches have particularly fine Byzantine frescoes; the cathedral of St Dimitrios is where Constantine Paleologos had his coronation and there is a museum in its grounds. The palace of the Despots stands among the ruins of some 2,000 houses both grand and ordinary. And, at the top of the 621-m hill, the castle of de Villardhouin remains along with the soldiers' quarters and the reservoir.

How long does it take?

To see it all fully, you should allow at least four hours. Two will be enough if you give the castle a miss. If you are on an organised coach trip you may unfortunately be given only an hour, just long enough to acquire an idea of the lower town and buy some postcards. The archaeological site is open daily from 9 a.m. to 3 p.m. The entrance fee of Dr 300 includes admission to the museum, which is closed on Tuesdays. There is only one hotel at Mistras, the second-class Vyzantion with twenty-two rooms.

An unusual souvenir, to pin on a wall rather than to fly from a pole in your garden, would be a yellow Byzantine flag bearing the two-headed eagle that looks both east and west. The Greeks used to dream that one day it would fly again over Istanbul, which helps to explain why Mistras is sometimes approached in a spirit of pilgrimage.

Monemvasia and the Mani

From Sparta it is a drive of only 96 km along an adequate road to Monemvasia, so it would be a lost opportunity not to take a look at it, but you will have to take the same road back again. Also largely Byzantine, Monemvasia is a kind of Gibraltar in miniature. Its name – 'single passage' – derives from its position at the end of a headland; the cut made by the Byzantines in the narrow isthmus, to reinforce its defences, is now spanned by a stone bridge. The 'town', population 630, huddles on the lower slopes of a 300-m rock crowned by Venetian fortifications dating from the sixteenth century.

Is it really worth a total of some 200 km just to see yet another castle and a cluster of Byzantine churches? The answer depends on your enjoyment of a wonderful view, a swim from one of the finest beaches in the southern Peloponnese, and fresh fish – sometimes lobster – in tiny wooden-floored restaurants hanging over the sea.

Known in the Middle Ages as Malvoisie to the Franks and Malmsey to the English, Monemvasia gave its name to a sweet dessert wine that was produced there but also on Tinos and other Aegean islands, and probably had been since the time of Ancient Greece. However, the cask of Malmsey reputedly used as the means of execution of the Duke of Clarence is said to have come from Madeira. While Monemvasia ceased to be an exporter of wine after the Turkish occupation in the early eighteenth century, some authorities hold that the muscats of Samos, Cyprus and even Spain are produced from descendants of vines transplanted from Monemvasia. In Greece today the better wine merchants stock red and white *moshato*, from Samos or other Aegean islands, but report little demand for that or any sweet wine. You would receive only a blank stare if you asked for Malmsey, Malvoisie or Malvasia.

Ten hotels, the largest with eighteen rooms, offer a total of only 107 beds, so Monemvasia is no place for groups to stay. Groups do pass through, however, so the equally tiny restaurants can easily be overwhelmed.

Monemvasia is a 360-km drive from Athens; to reach it by bus requires a break in the journey at Sparta. There are also ferry and hydrofoil services from Piraeus.

The Mani   The Mani is the region extending from the entrance port-town of Gythion to Cape Tenaro, perhaps better known as Matapan, at the southern tip of the central prong of the Peloponnese. Wild, inaccessible, never really conquered by the Turks and once a nest of pirates and last stronghold of the vendetta, the Mani is very much an acquired taste. Its natural beauty is undeniable but it is hard to get to; it is not worth starting out unless you are prepared to allow it a day. It is traditionally divided into Exo (Outer) Mani from Kalamata to Areopolis and Mesa (Deep) Mani south of Areopolis to Cape Tenaro, one of the mythical entrances to Hades.

Gythion   Gythion, the Mani capital, is a 46-km drive from Sparta. A small fishing town with a graceful waterfront and tile-roofed houses, it has a certain old-fashioned charm. It was the ancient port of Sparta and to some extent is the modern one also: Paris and Helen are said to have slept there, whether 'together' is not specified, on their way to Troy after their elopement. The remains of the ancient harbour can still be seen beneath the clear waters of the bay. The ancient theatre of Gythion comes to life for three days every August during the Gythion Festival. The town, population 4,350, has ten hotels with 767 beds – two first-class, two second-class and the rest third- and fourth-class.

Areopolis

Areopolis, 'the town of Aris' (Mars), is 26 km further. At once a small village (population 611) and transport centre for the Mani, it has bus services to Kalamata, Gythion, the Dyrou caves and Gerolimenas. The 'town' is dominated by the cathedral in the central and only square, the best taverna is said to be the one where the buses park, and there is a third-class hotel, the thirty-bed Mani, as an alternative to the NTOG 'tower' (see below).

The caves

The main point of many people's visit to the Mani are the caves of Dyrou and Alepotripa, 7 km from Areopolis. The Dyrou cave is a subterranean river more than a kilometre of which can be explored in small boats and another half-kilometre on foot. The nearby Alepotripa cave, consisting of vaults and corridors joining two lakes, is still being studied by scientists, so it is not always fully open. Both are remarkable, but certainly not easy to reach.

Gerolimenas

Gerolimenas, literally 'old harbour', population seventy-five, was in fact built in the 1870s by a Maniot merchant for his own trade. It has the air of being at the end of the world, until you reach Vathia.

Vathia

A collection of Maniot towers standing on a low hill overlooking the sea, Vathia has a population of forty and absolutely no facilities for tourists, but it does offer memorable sunsets. Gerolimenas, in contrast, has two fifth-class hotels with a total of twenty-two beds.

Kardamyli

Back in Exo Mani, on the road to Kalamata, Kardamyli is a beautiful village, population 280, with a cluster of tower houses, the ruins of an acropolis, a sixth-century church, St Spyridon, and a twelfth-century castle. There are two family-run hotels of third and fifth class with thirty beds, rooms to let in private houses, and fine tavernas along a pebble beach fronting groves of olives.

A hard land of stone and thirst, the Mani began to lose population as soon as the rest of Greece became as safe a place to live in freedom, and today there are more Maniots in Athens than in the peninsula itself. As a result, the old fortified houses, in which families lived as clans and preserved 'the law of the west' longer than anywhere else, have been crumbling into ruin. Eventually, the more suitable are to be turned into small guest houses, as part of a National Tourist Organisation of Greece programme of 'traditional settlements'. But so far, NTOG has listed only one such settlement in the Mani: the seventeen-bed, six-room Kapetanakos Tower at Areopolis, at prices ranging from Dr 3,000 a day for a double room to Dr 6,000 for the one with five beds.

The north-east corner

Tripolis

Whether directly from Sparta or after side-trips to Monemvasia and the Mani, it is now time to head north for Nafplion. The direct route is from Sparta to Tripolis, 65 km along a scenic road. Tripolis, the capital of Arcadia with a population of 21,000, stands 660 m above sea level but nevertheless is surrounded by mountains. Its twelve hotels and assorted restaurants and tavernas are adequate if you arrive too late to press on to Nafplion, 70 km away through the high pass of Achladokambos, but otherwise it is not necessarily a place to stay.

Nafplion can also be reached along the coast from Sparta, via Leonidion, but it is questionable whether the effort and extra distance are really repaid by the views.

Nafplion

If Greece wanted a resort for the bathchair years of retired diplomats and generals, Nafplion would be the obvious choice, only 146 km from Athens at the end of a road that, since it involves no sea crossing or mountain passes, presents no risk of winter isolation. In fact, Greeks in retirement either lie beneath the tree from which they fell – which usually means Athens, if they reached the upper branches – or head for an island. But should fashions change, Nafplion, written also as Nauplion or Nauplia but pronounced with an 'f', is available.

Peaceful as well as picturesque, this city of only 10,600 inhabitants is situated at the head of the Bay of Nafplion, sheltered from the northerly gales of winter but cooled in summer by the sea breezes. It was founded a long time ago – reputedly by Palamides, son of Poseidon and inventor of dice – but does not have much of an ancient past to accommodate; just the ruins of an acropolis where the main attraction today is the sunset.

What to see

Out in the bay there is the Venetian island fortress of Bourtzi, and at the top of a 216-m hill at the east end of the city the restored Franco–Venetian–Turkish castle of Palamidi. Palamidi has been made more accessible by the completion of a road, but if you take the old steps (guidebooks speak of 1,000 or 999, but both figures could be a form of poetic licence), you will have no need to jog for the rest of the day.

The city itself, set on a promontory between Acronafplia and the Akti Miaoulis and Bouboulina (two quays named after Revolutionary heroes), can be explored easily in an hour. Largely dating from the first decades of Independence, it is a harmonious combination of neo-Classical and modern, with cafés in shaded squares, several very comfortable hotels, and hardly ever a suggestion of bustle.

From 1829 until 1834, Nafplion was the first capital of the new Greek state: Capodistrias put order into the administration from there, and King Othon held court in the Palamidi fortress until he moved to Athens. You should visit the Church of St George, where Capodistrias and Othon both took their oaths (the former of office and the latter of allegiance), and the Church of St Spyridon, where Capodistrias was assassinated in 1831.

Capodistrias

John Anthony Capo d'Istria, as he was before his name was hellenised, was an early example of the Greek emigrant who made good and came home. A doctor of medicine from Corfu with a bent for diplomacy, he moved to St Petersburg, entered the Russian diplomatic service, and was ambassador to Switzerland when the Greeks invited him back and gave him supreme power. Energetic but too autocratic for some of the old Revolutionary fighters, he made enemies and was shot.

Nafplion is an excellent place to spend the night, not only to enjoy the city itself but to be able to start out early for a full day visiting Mycenae and Epidavros.

Getting there

Nafplion can be reached from Athens by an almost hourly bus service, and from Piraeus by hydrofoil. It has its own bus services to Corinth, Tripolis, Sparta and Kalamata, as well as to the Saronic spa of Methona.

Where to stay

Nafplion is one place where a touch of extravagance might be considered, with a stay in one of the three links in NTOG's 'Xenias' chain: the deluxe Xenia's Palace and Xenia's Palace Bungalows, and the first-class Xenia, all at Acronafplia, at double-room prices of between Dr 4,000 and 6,000 a night. You can be comfortable elsewhere at half the price, but the difference is perceptible.

Xenia apart, you will do well at the first-class Amphytrion (eighty beds) or, at a considerably lower price, at the second-class Agamemnon (seventy-four beds), both on the Akti Miaouli. If you are really economising, try the fourth-class King Othon in Farmakopoulou Street (twenty-three beds), a converted old house with a spiral staircase where you will be served breakfast in the garden.

Where to eat

Nafpliotes like to eat out at the Savouras, a fish taverna on the waterfront in Bouboulina Street, or the nearby Kolios which serves both fish and meat. A popular general restaurant is the Hellas in Constitution (Syntagma) Square.

Museums

The Nafplion Museum (exhibits from Ancient Greece and the Revolutionary period) is open from 9 a.m. to 3 p.m., closed Tuesdays, admission Dr 200. The Palamidi fortress is open daily from 10 a.m. to 4.30 p.m., at Dr 200. There is also a Popular Art Museum, open from 9 a.m. to 1 p.m. and from 5 p.m. to 7 p.m., closed Tuesdays, admission free.

What to do

Apart from Mycenae and Epidavros, Nafplion is a jumping-off place for a trip to Tolo, 12 km away, for swimming from a superb sandy beach lined with hotels and fish restaurants, or for Porto Heli and from there along the coast to Ermioni.

Swimming can also be enjoyed from an inferior but less crowded beach at Assine, 2 km from Tolo, with the bonus there of the remains of an acropolis, fortifications and tombs of the Mycenaean and later periods, excavated in the 1920s by Swedish archaeologists, and a fifteenth-century Byzantine church. Assine has the Domesday distinction of a mention by Homer. The present village, population 950, is listed as offering ninety-four beds in furnished rooms.

Porto Heli and Ermioni

The coast between the two attractive fishing townships of Porto Heli (population 750) and Ermioni (population 2,100) is one of the most intensively developed resort areas of mainland Greece, with more than 5,000 beds in fourteen major hotel and bungalow complexes. It is also an example of broken promises: the hotels were constructed between fifteen and twenty years ago on the basis of an assurance that Nafplion would be provided with an airport, which has never been built. As a result, a tourist arriving at Athens Airport can fly on to an island more quickly and easily than he can reach this 'local' resort area by coach or hydrofoil; Porto Heli hoteliers have been reduced in consequence to fishing mainly in Greek waters, where the catch is less remunerative. You need not stay there, but Porto Heli and Ermioni are worth a visit if you have half a day to spare.

Mycenae

To the modern imagination Mycenae is the creation of Homer and Heinrich Schliemann; the former told of the misdeeds of the House of Atreus and the curse that lay on it, and the latter found the place, some 6 km off the Argos–Corinth road and an easy 20-km drive from Nafplion.

You enter the acropolis of Mycenae through the famous Lion Gate, a cyclopean lintel supporting a triangular slab on which two lionesses are depicted standing on their hind legs, their forepaws resting on a column. Within the walls are the six shaft graves excavated by Schliemann, from which he took the gold treasures now displayed in the Athens Archaeological Museum. Of the beehive tombs outside the reconstructed walls, the largest is commonly described as the Treasury of Atreus or Tomb of Agamemnon, though archaeologists insist that it was neither. The so-called Tomb of Clytaemnestra is closer to the citadel.

Try to visit Mycenae early, while both the morning and the imagination are fresh and the day-trippers from Athens are still on the far side of the Corinth Canal. Half the magic is lost, along with the silence and distant tinkle of sheep-bells, when the groups queue for their turn and you must either slip in among them or look from a distance. Leave Tiryns and Argos for the way back.

The archaeological site is open daily from 8 a.m. to 5 p.m., admission Dr 300.

Argos

Archaeologists say that Argos, once a powerful town, began to decline in the seventh century BC: the casual visitor may well believe the process has not yet ceased. However, for those impervious to dust and noise – it is now a hive of commerce with 20,000 inhabitants – it offers the ruins of a fourth-century BC theatre, an agora and Roman baths, has a nicely arranged museum, and exchanges a magnificent view from the citadel for the effort of a 274-m climb. Its 194 beds in five hotels of third and fourth class suggest that as a place to stay it is favoured mainly by businessmen without expense accounts and backpackers.

Tiryns: the Cyclopean walls

A rather more rewarding diversion, past Argos and 4 km from Nafplion, takes you to Tiryns, where easily the most impressive of the ruins are the Cyclopean walls, so called because the Ancient Greeks believed that only a race of giants, the Cyclops, could have moved the stones that built them.

Eight metres high and ranging in thickness from eight metres to almost twenty where they enclose corridors or casements, the walls include stones estimated to weigh up to fourteen tons, hauled into position during the Mycenaean period by means that are still mysterious. Some of the underground galleries have curiously polished patches, where centuries of sheep using them for refuge in bad weather have brushed against wall or roof.

One version of the legend has Tiryns as the birthplace of Hercules, but the present remains, including the fortress palace, date mostly from the thirteenth century BC, when Tiryns was among the most important Mycenaean cities.

The modern village of 500 inhabitants is close to an agricultural prison (under a system where one day's work on the land counts as two days of sentence); it was originally Greece's first agricultural school, founded by Capodistrias. A first-class hotel, the Amalia, about 1 km from the historic site, offers 319 beds, a restaurant and swimming pool, and is open all year round.

Epidavros

Unlike at Mycenae, numbers do not really matter at Epidavros; the theatre there, the best preserved in Greece, can hold 16,000 spectators in fifty-five tiers of seating, so there is plenty of room even on the busiest day. For that reason, if you are staying in Nafplion go first to Mycenae, early, and then double back for the 30 km drive to Epidavros.

Epidavros, written as it is pronounced but sometimes seen in English as Epidaurus, was a sanctuary of Asklipios, to the Romans Aesculapius, the ancient god of medicine; it lies in a cool, wooded valley where a failure to recover would be almost an insult to the doctor. Treatment in this most ancient of sanatoria, though tinged with magic, was based essentially on what today would be described as a health diet, reinforced by fresh air, herbal medicines and occasional surgery. Only the foundations of the various buildings can be seen today, but the museum displays models of Epidavros as it was at the peak of its renown, between 2,000 and 2,500 years ago.

The theatre is now used on summer weekends for Epidavros Festival performances of ancient Greek drama and comedy; it is famous for its pin-drop acoustics.

The archaeological site and museum are open daily from 8 a.m. to 5 p.m., with the Dr 300 admission covering entry to both.

From Epidavros you can return to Corinth along a beautiful new coastal road, a drive of only 45 km which takes less than an hour.

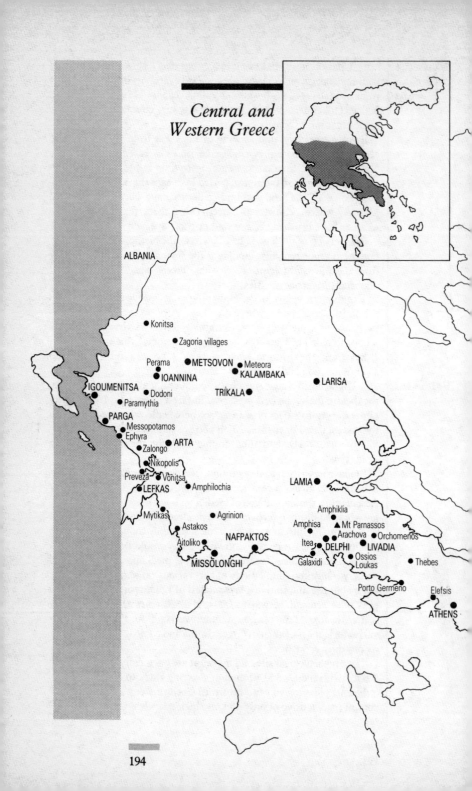

Central and Western Greece

ALBANIA

● Konitsa

● Zagoria villages

Perama ● ● **METSOVON** ● Meteora

● **IOANNINA** **KALAMBAKA**

IGOUMENITSA ● Dodoni **TRIKALA** ● **LARISA**

● Paramythia

PARGA

● Messopotamos

Ephyra

● Zalongo ● **ARTA**

● Nikopolis

Preveza ● Vonitsa

LEFKAS ● Amphilochia **LAMIA** ●

Amphiklia

Mytikas ● ● Agrinion

● Astakos Amphisa ● ▲ Mt Parnassos

NAFPAKTOS Arachova ● Orchomenos

Aitoliko Itea ● **DELPHI** **LIVADIA**

● Ossios ● Thebes

MISSOLONGHI Galaxidi Loukas

Porto Germeno Elefsis ●

ATHENS

Central and Western Greece

Introduction

The mountainous heart of central Greece is neither accessible by roads worthy of the name, nor does it offer rewards sufficient to justify the risk of accident or breakdown. But road construction over the past twenty years has made possible a circular tour along the edges that requires of the driver only a degree of stamina.

The proposed route covers a total distance of between 1,400 and 1,600 km, depending on final choices between alternatives on certain stretches and whether or not you make detours. It includes Delphi, Missolonghi, Ioannina and the monasteries of Meteora.

The adoption of a clockwise direction is not entirely arbitrary, but is intended to facilitate those who may have abandoned Athens as a base. Thus the route could be joined from Patras by crossing on the Rion-Andirion ferry; Delphi could then be a one-day diversion, approached along the coast before returning inland through Amphisa. Also, anyone not returning to Athens could branch left at Trikala for Larisa, Volos and the drive along the coast of eastern Greece to Thessaloniki.

The suggested overnight stays, at Delphi, Ioannina and Kalambaka, would involve two days of short driving (less than 200 km each) and two strenuous days behind the wheel, but would allow full afternoons for explorations of Delphi and Meteora. Abbreviating the visit to Delphi (not much of a sacrifice, since the archaeological site closes at 5 p.m.) would permit the first night to be spent instead at Nafpaktos, one of the most beautiful little ports in mainland Greece, and would shorten the drive on the second day. The second day could equally be made less tiring by stopping at Parga instead of Ioannina.

Side-trips could also be made to the Ionian islands of Lefkas and Corfu, the first without leaving your car and the second by a short sea-crossing.

Central and western Greece, once Delphi is behind you, is not an area of heavy group traffic where hotels are likely to be full. Reservations might be advisable at Parga, where there are only two hotels of more than forty rooms, but elsewhere along the route accommodation can generally be found without notice.

As in the Peloponnese, two-thirds of the journey would be along or in sight of the coast, on roads that are adequate but are not motorways. But after turning away from the sea at Igoumenitsa, you would be passing through spectacularly mountainous countryside.

This route should not be attempted by car in less than four days; if you use buses, it would be better to allow a week. The railway takes you only to Livadia for Delphi, and to Kalambaka for Meteora.

You should not expect to see much sign of industry, except at Thebes, nor of intensive farming. The centre and west is where the mountains come right down to the sea, and Greece's rich agricultural land is elsewhere.

Athens to Delphi

Thebes

You set off as if for the Peloponnese but at Elefsis, well before the toll gate, branch right for Thebes (Thiva). Just over 80 km from Athens, Thebes is a place to pass quickly through with thoughts of Oedipus. A town of 18,700 inhabitants, it is today a centre of small industry with 120 factories; to the passing stranger, it offers *souvlaki*, some little regarded archaeological sites, and a museum that is open until 3 p.m. and closed on Tuesdays. Most travellers prefer to press on to Livadia, 45 km further, though if your interest lies in observing how the poorer Greeks spend their summer holidays, fork left 20 km before Thebes to look at the resort of Porto Germeno.

Livadia

Livadia, population 17,000, is a great place for coffee and cake before entering Parnassos country. Greece has seven mountains taller than Parnassos, which is 2,457 m, but, with the exception of Olympos itself, none has a more extended dominance over its approaches. The NTOG ski centre on Parnassos, reached from Arachova or Amphiklia, doubles as a summer resort for those whose main concern is to avoid the heat, but that is scarcely a common ambition among tourists.

For a time during the Turkish occupation, Livadia was the second town of Greece. At an altitude of 200 m, it stands along the banks of the small but fast-flowing River Erkinas at a point where it emerges from a deep gorge. Cool in summer, it is bitterly cold on a winter's morning when Parnassos, confusing itself with Mont Blanc, is an even quicker restorative than a cold shower after a long night in a taverna.

Take note of the Turkish bridge, clamber up to the fourteenth century castle if you like, but spare half an hour for refreshment at the foot of the rock where the river spills out of the gorge.

Arachova

Arachova, 168 km from Athens and only 10 from Delphi, at an altitude of 960 m on the slopes of Parnassos, is a wonderful mountain village of 2,700 inhabitants that poses as one long souvenir shop. The houses climbing the steep slopes are to be admired: the embroideries, hand-woven blankets, flokati rugs and sheepskins in various adaptations – floor, chair and bed covers and shepherds' coats – are very much for sale; with a little time, prices can become perceptibly lower than in the Athens Flea Market. The brusque red wine of Arachova is much praised.

You should be in Delphi in plenty of time for an early lunch, and will then have until 5 p.m. to explore the ruins after the morning wave of day-trippers has set off back for Athens.

If you chance to be ahead of the clock, or prefer to save the Delphi exploration for the cool of the following morning, two side-trips could be inserted between Livadia and Arachova.

Orchomenos

A 13-km drive from Livadia along the Lamia road will bring you to Ancient Orchomenos and the 'Treasury of the Minyans', a Mycenaean domed tomb excavated by Schliemann in the 1880s, as well as a fourth-century BC theatre and a ninth-century Church of the Dormition restored just under a century ago. Inhabited uninterruptedly from neolithic to Macedonian times, Orchomenos was one of the largest cities of the Mycenaean era and its 'treasury' is closely related to that of Atreus at Mycenae. You can climb to the small acropolis with its well-preserved remains of ancient Greek fortifications and also take a look at the nearby acropolis of **Gla**, the most striking of a string of fortresses built by the Minyans.

Modern Orchomenos, population 5,400, has a single fourth-class hotel, the fifteen-bed Elli.

Ossios Loukas

The other diversion, involving a left turn about 20 km along the road to Arachova and from there a 12-km drive each way, will take you to the monastic complex of Ossios Loukas and some particularly fine Byzantine mosaics. The monastery bears the name of a local hermit, Blessed Luke who, after his death in about 950, was beatified in recognition of his healing and prophetic powers. The present buildings date from the eleventh century. The best of the mosaics are considered to be those depicting the crucifixion, resurrection, Thomas inserting his finger into the wound of Christ, and Christ washing the feet of the Apostles.

The complex includes a restaurant and a small tourist guest-house with six rooms, and is a favourite picnic spot for Greeks on a day's excursion from Athens.

Delphi

From an admittedly prejudiced point of view, the Athens Acropolis, Olympia and Mycenae are to be visited once, but only Delphi can be considered a place of pilgrimage. Somehow, it enforces awe. You come across Delphi suddenly, as is proper: rounding the cliff of one of the two Phaedriades rocks, you find it spread out in front of you like an amphitheatre. To the left, a sea of olive trees, the 'Sacred Valley', stretches down to the Gulf of Itea in the distance; to the right loom the peaks of Parnassos, where even now you may dream of seeing an eagle.

Getting there

Delphi can be reached by bus from Athens (a three-hour trip) and from Amphisa.

History

The Ancient Greeks held Delphi to be the centre or the navel of the world, as determined by Zeus in his great-geographer mood; he freed two eagles at the ends of the earth to fly in opposite directions, and they met at Delphi. The exact age of Delphi is not known. But it is mentioned by Homer, and the Mycenaeans were still the dominant power when the sun god Apollo displaced the older deities and became sole guardian of its oracle. By the sixth century BC it had developed into a diplomatic and cultural centre and an athletic forum, and was very rich indeed.

Fame, power and wealth derived from prophesy, delivered by Apollo through the medium of the Pythia, a priestess required to be at least fifty years old and chaste. During the peak period of Greek colonisation, cities which had resolved to found a colony would first consult the oracle: one of her responses, to the Megarans, resulted in the establishment of Byzantium by an expedition led by Byzas, today the name of the Megara football team.

Before the sixth century BC, divination took place only once a year, on the day held as Apollo's birthday. Later, it became a monthly ceremony, and the Pythia was provided with two apprentices. The ceremony itself is broadly known, though some details are still mysterious. The priestess would cleanse herself in the Kastalian spring and immerse herself in the smoke of laurel leaves while seated on the sacred tripod of Apollo, the sun god's throne which, equipped with wings, had once carried him on his daily journey across the sky. She would then, in a trance, deliver an inarticulate prophecy which would be interpreted in verse by the priests and presented in writing to the pilgrim.

Even then, the replies remained subject to misinterpretation: Croesus, told he would destroy a great power if he made war on the Persians, went home filled with confidence, and destroyed his own.

What to see

Before it fell into ruin, under the twin assaults by philosophers on superstition and by Roman and barbarian raids on its treasures, Delphi was a magnificent cluster of buildings. The central and largest structure, the Temple of Apollo, of which six columns have been restored, was similar in design to the Parthenon. Around it, temple-like treasuries were constructed as store-rooms for the gifts to Apollo; one of them, erected by the Athenians after the Battle of Marathon, has been rebuilt with funding from the Athens municipality.

Above the Temple of Apollo is the fourth-century open-air theatre, seating 5,000 and still used for occasional performances of ancient drama. Even further up the hill, the stadium recalls the ancient

Pythian Games, once second in importance only to the Olympics. Some 70 m long with twelve tiers of seats, the stadium could accommodate 7,000 spectators.

Having drunk from the ice-cold Kastalian spring and climbed by the Sacred Way to the Temple of Apollo and, beyond, to the theatre and stadium, you will find the museum deliciously cooling. It is definitely not to be missed, even if only for the magnificent fifth-century BC bronze of the Charioteer.

Both the archaeological site and the museum are open from 8 a.m. to 5 p.m., except that the museum is closed on Tuesdays. Admission to each is Dr 300.

Modern Delphi

The modern village, population 2,500, has a single main street lined with hotels, cafés and souvenir shops. It is all that remains of a larger village which had sprawled across almost the whole site when excavations were begun by French archaeologists in 1892.

Where to stay

You have a choice of twenty-eight hotels of all categories, except deluxe. A favourite is the first-class fifty-eight-room Vouzas; the Amalia, with 185 rooms, is a safer bet if you arrive without a booking. By dropping to any of the smaller second- and third-class hotels you should be able to avoid groups.

Where to eat

People who live in Delphi, at least during the tourist season, insist that, so far as food is concerned, there is little to choose between the plethora of restaurants and tavernas. But the Vacchos in Apollonos Street is mentioned for its view to Itea and the Gulf of Corinth, and the Asteras in Pavlou Street is not without its supporters.

To Nafpaktos and Missolonghi

Amphisa

If you were to visit Greece with maps borrowed from an older generation, you would conclude at this point that the only way to Nafpaktos was by the inland road through Amphisa, an attractively situated market town of 7,100 inhabitants just 22 km from Delphi. This is indeed beautiful foothill country, with a succession of mountains of above 2,000 m in the middle and far distance on your right and, on your left, dense concentrations of olive groves. The olives and oil of Amphisa are rated second only to those of the Kalamata region, in the southern Peloponnese, among connoisseurs – which all Greeks consider themselves to be. However, you do now have an alternative, by a new road along the coast completed only eight or ten years ago.

The distance by either road is about the same: just over 70 km through Amphisa and about 80 km along the coast. But the route by the sea is recommended for three reasons: the views are stupendous; though you lose Amphisa you gain Galaxidi; and, since you are not competing with trucks and farm vehicles, the driving is more relaxed.

Itea

You take the 15-km downhill road from Delphi, winding among olive groves and vineyards, to the tiny port of Itea, population 4,400. Once the main means of access to Delphi, with a ferry service from Corinth, Itea is now used only by the occasional cruise liner on an Ionian instead of Aegean itinerary, and by Soviet freighters loading bauxite ore from mines in the Delphi area.

Since bauxite is the basic raw material of alumina, which is the intermediate stage between ore and aluminium, the Greeks have for a long time been eager to replace their low-value bauxite exports to the Soviet Union at least with alumina. This led to a Greek–Soviet agreement to set up a joint venture alumina plant in the area of the mines, and therefore close to Itea. The result was anguish among Greek and European archaeologists and conservationists over the possibility of pollution damage to the Delphi monuments. Though the government denied that there would be any damage, or that the industry would even be visible from Delphi, it finally yielded to pressure in the summer of 1987 and agreed that the industry should be sited at a safer distance from Delphi, despite slightly higher transport costs for ore and alumina.

From Itea (at most a coffee stop on the quay) you could reach Nafpaktos in about an hour with fast driving, but should allow yourself a couple so as to enjoy the view: tall mountains on the right, and on the left the shimmering blue of the Gulf of Corinth and, beyond, the north coast and mountains of the Peloponnese.

Galaxidi

You pass through successive fishing villages in bays and sheltered coves. One of them, Galaxidi, is so startlingly suggestive of a stage setting that you will be tempted to linger. Galaxidi, 17 km from Itea and with a population of 1,200, is all nineteenth-century waterfront without a single unharmonious note. Abandoned *archontika*, the homes of once wealthy families, and a tiny museum, recall the time when Galaxidi was a notable provider of caiques, the once traditional but now largely superseded Greek fishing craft. Since tourism has not yet stepped in to fill the gap, probably because the beauty does not extend to sandy beaches, it is still unspoiled.

Though Galaxidi can be reached directly by bus from Athens (210 km, five hours), it has only three hotels with a total of eighteen rooms. Stay there only if you are happy to do nothing at night but eat fish, drink wine and watch the lights across the water.

Nafpaktos (Lepanto)

Nafpaktos is developing rather faster than Galaxidi, and would be my personal recommendation for an overnight stay. A port-town of 9,000 inhabitants, there was a time not so long ago when it attracted nobody. Now it has been opened up by the new road from Delphi and, more importantly, by the Athens–Corinth–Patras motorway. Situated only 8 km from the Andirion terminal of the Rion–Andirion ferry, it has been brought to within four hours of Athens along the motorway route. Weekenders can now leave the capital when offices close on a Friday afternoon and can spend the night there with the whole of Saturday to explore the west coast.

Nafpaktos is served by two buses a day from Athens (a four-hour trip including the ferry) and is on the route of a Thessaloniki service through central Greece to Missolonghi and Agrinion in the west. At Nafpaktos you are less than 50 km from Missolonghi, on a new road that could almost qualify as a motorway.

Lepanto to the Venetians who twice occupied it in the fifteenth and eighteenth centuries, Nafpaktos was the port from which the Turkish fleet sailed to its destruction at the 1571 naval battle – an encounter in which the Spanish wounded included Cervantes, author of *Don Quixote*.

Before the Second World War, when more freight travelled by sea than road, Nafpaktos was a transshipment port for Peloponnesian products destined for western Greece. Today, the small, quaint harbour protected by a medieval breakwater is little used except by yachtsmen. With good beaches in the immediate vicinity and new hotels, it is slowly becoming a tourist spot, but not yet painfully so.

It offers 265 rooms in eleven hotels, of which the three largest – the Lepanto, Xenia and Akti – account for 153. All the hotels are of second to fourth class. There is good but simple eating, mainly at fish tavernas. Easily the best year-round taverna is Stavros, near the Xenia Hotel. In the summer only, Molos on the waterfront is preferred for fish and the nearby Cavo d'Oro for general dishes.

Missolonghi, sometimes written to accord with its Greek pronunciation of Messolonghi, has to be visited: not for what it is – a depressing modern town with nothing to offer but views of a lagoon that might qualify as sleepy but is more attractive to the eye than the nose – so much as for what it briefly was. Byron died of fever outside its walls, in 1824, and every April Greece's head of state, whether king or president, goes there to lead celebrations of the Exodus.

The Exodus is a reference not to the Biblical event but to the second siege by the Turks in 1825, during the Independence Revolution. In April 1826, facing starvation, the defenders of Missolonghi decided to attempt a break-out, in the hope of joining up with forces encamped on nearby Mount Zygos. Accounts vary as to what exactly went wrong – whether they made too much noise or, in the version according more closely with national sentiment, were betrayed. In any event they were massacred, and Missolonghi was razed to the ground.

The commemoration is held in the gloomy Park of the Heroes, close to the few remnants of the old wall; since you are in the 'Sacred City' you should take a look at the park, and the statues of the heroes of the Revolution. You could also stroll along the causeway to the lagoon, to see the curious fishermen's huts built on piles at the edge of the water.

The lagoon used to produce *avgoteraho* (mullet roe) and mosquitoes; the former has become too expensive for any but the most affluent among the Greeks and the latter have been eradicated along with the malaria which, some believe, may have been the 'fever' that killed Byron. *Avgoteraho*, dried and coated with beeswax as a preservative, is on sale in half-kilo packs in Athens delicatessens; it is sometimes eaten in small quantities as an accompaniment to *ouzo*. The smooth, pink *taramousalata*, on the other hand, is manufactured from the roe of more common fish imported by the barrel from Scandinavia and the Soviet Union. It has nothing to do with Missolonghi.

Getting there

Missolonghi is served by nine buses a day from Athens (a four-hour trip), and has its own bus service to Ioannina and intermediate west coast towns.

Where to stay

The city, population 11,300, is hot and humid and not a popular place to stay; if it were, it would need more than its 195 rooms in seven hotels of second to fifth class.

Aitoliko

On your way out, spare a glance for Aitoliko, 10 km away at the narrowest point of the lagoon. A heavily populated islet, its 4,300 inhabitants like to think it bears a resemblance to Venice, and it is certainly unusual. It is joined to the mainland by three bridges, one of them 300 m long dating from 1848. The restaurants offer fish from the lagoon, including eel.

Through Aitoloakarnania

From Missolonghi you have a choice of routes through this Greek department (*nome*), with the tongue-twisting name: you can take either the commercial or the touristic.

Agrinion

It is only 87 km to Amphilochia by the main road, which you have to take if you feel you must see Agrinion and have no objection to fighting it out with trucks, buses and coaches. A town of 35,000 inhabitants and a centre of the tobacco industry without a single first-class hotel, Agrinion is not a town that you should worry about missing.

The new coastal road, half as long again and still under construction at a few points but perfectly safe and little used, passes through one beauty spot after another. It emerges on to the Amvrakikos Gulf

Vonitsa

at Vonitsa, where you turn right for the 40 km drive along the southern shore of the gulf to Amphilochia. Turn left at Vonitsa and you are only about 20 km from Lefkas, if you want a quick glance at the closest of the Ionian islands (you cross from the mainland by bridge). Vonitsa itself, a town of 3,800 inhabitants, need not detain you.

Astakos

On the way there you will see Astakos, a delightful fishing village, population 2,700, with forty-seven rooms in three hotels, where you could stop for a meal or take a ferry to Ithaka.

Mytikas

Then there is Mytikas, an even smaller village of 756 inhabitants but with forty-nine rooms in four hotels from where, before or after a meal, you could take a fishing boat across to the Lefkas offshore islet of Kastos which has a population of just sixty-eight.

Somewhere between these two charming villages, two questions will begin to form in your mind. How did it happen that such a breathtakingly beautiful stretch of coast, with long beaches, tiny coves and bays, and offshore islets all the way, should have no sign of a tourist movement? And why has such an obviously expensive road now been built effectively to nowhere?

The answer lies in the bridge that is one day to be constructed across the narrow mouth of the Amvrakikos between Aktion (Actium), where Antony and Cleopatra came to grief, and Preveza. Once the bridge is in place, the new road will become the direct route from Missolonghi to Epiros and Igoumenitsa, and there will be no need to suffer either Amphilochia or Arta. But until that day, the right turn at Vonitsa is the only solution.

Amphilo-chia

Amphilochia, at the head of the Amvrakikos Gulf, is a long one-street town which lives on its lunch trade; you have a choice from at least a dozen restaurants and no reason to prefer one over another. Ignore them all at your peril: you will then be condemned to eat at Arta or fast until dinner.

To do it justice, Amphilochia does have a certain picturesqueness. Founded at the end of the eighteenth century by the notorious Ali Pasha of Ioannina (see p. 208), it was known until 1907 by its Turkish name of Karvasaras. At night the waters there have a curious phosphorescence not seen elsewhere in Greece. It has a population of 4,300 and 147 rooms in five hotels of third and fourth class.

Arta–Parga–Igoumenitsa

Arta
Getting there

Arta, 360 km from Athens and 420 km from Thessaloniki, is served by buses from both cities, and has its own buses to Ioannina and Preveza, 90 minutes and 75 minutes away respectively. It takes six hours by bus to Athens and eight hours to Thessaloniki.

The important difference between Agrinion and Arta is that you can avoid the former. Arta there is no way round. So having got there, you may as well pause to photograph the bridge and look at one or two of the churches. Situated on the Arachthos River, with a population of 18,000, Arta is entered across an ugly new concrete bridge built parallel to a graceful stone-arched medieval bridge which is at once the town's showpiece and the source of one of Greece's most durable legends.

History

The story and supporting folk-song tell of forty-five masons and sixty apprentices who returned to the bridge every morning to discover that what they had built the day before had collapsed during the night. A bird then whispered the secret to the master builder. Sadly but obediently, he sent for his wife and told her that his wedding ring had fallen into the foundations. She volunteered to retrieve it, clambered down, and was at once immured. Fortified by the sacrifice, the bridge stood firm, as the bird had said it would and as it still does.

Just a tale, of course. But one day, when archaeologists of the distant future excavate the ruins of modern Athens, they may be puzzled to find chicken bones at the bottom of some of the support pillars of what they will conclude must have been apartment blocks. Most civil engineers will deny that they do it, on the day the first cement is poured; the few prepared to admit it will do so shamefacedly, insisting that the chicken died at the demand of purchasers of the apartments. Though suggestive more of Ancient Greece than the bridge of Arta, it is still a kind of poetic justice on the bird family as a whole for the widowing of the master builder.

Arta knew its greatest prosperity in the thirteenth and fourteenth centuries, when it was the capital of a Byzantine principality. The Church of the Panaghia Parigoritissa above the market-place dates from that period and is in an excellent state of preservation. Though they are more easily overlooked, the same is true of the churches of Aghia Theodora and Aghios Vasilios, and the nearby monasteries of Vlachernai and Kato Panaghia.

Vlachernai, it may be recalled, was also the name of a palace in Byzantine Constantinople. One theory of the origin of the name is that, through the same process by which the Greek for 'in the city', *eis teen polis*, was corrupted into Istanbul, so the invocation to the Virgin, *val ta heria*, 'extend (the protection of) your hand', became Vlachernai. Perhaps, perhaps not.

Where to stay

If you do stay, you will have plenty of time to visit the medieval fortress and remains of an ancient theatre and to see the Byzantine mosaics in the museum. There are 171 rooms in five hotels of second to fifth class; best of the hotels is the second-class Xenia (forty beds) at the castle, which also boasts the town's top restaurant; largest are the 110-bed Amvrakia in N. Priovolou Street and the 102-bed Chronos in Kilkis Square, both third class.

Where to eat

Artans say that, in the hot weather at least, they generally eat at one of the four or five tavernas in the central Ethnikis Antistasios (National Resistance) square which have tables outside.

At Arta you are only 80 km from Ioannina by the old, direct route, first through a plain of citrus orchards and then up the gorge of the River Louros. But the new road along the coast to Igoumenitsa and from there to Ioannina through a different set of mountains, though a drive of almost 250 km, is in every way preferable.

Taking the Ioannina road out of Arta but turning left for Igoumenitsa at a well-marked fork, you cross some rather uninteresting plateau land and then drop down to the sea near Zalongo. The road should by now be finished; at worst, there will be a few stretches not yet asphalted and one or two short diversions.

Preveza

You may, on reaching the coast, consider your own short diversion to Preveza, a town of 12,500 inhabitants at the entrance to the Amvrakikos Gulf with some fine old houses and churches and a Venetian castle offering splendid views of the Ionian Sea.

Nikopolis

You will certainly not want to miss Nikopolis, 'Town of Victory', founded and so named by Augustus in 30 BC to commemorate his victory at Aktion (Actium). It was given an instant population, apparently through the same kind of enforced resettlement later practised by Stalin.

Remains at Nikopolis include 3 km of Byzantine walls, a theatre, Roman temples subsequently converted into Byzantine chapels, an agora, gymnasium, baths, and a restored Roman odeon used for occasional performances of Ancient Greek drama.

St Paul wrote his Epistle to Titus while staying at Nikopolis. Plundered by the Goths, the city was rebuilt by the Byzantines on a more modest scale; four early Christian churches with attractive mosaics date from this period. The site and museum, the latter displaying mainly Roman finds, are open from 9 a.m. to 3 p.m. except Tuesdays.

You may prefer to leave Preveza for a future visit since, assuming the bridge has been built, you will then pass through it anyway. Sometime, not many years in the future, the whole coast from Preveza to Parga will inevitably have become Greece's western riviera; at the moment, it is astonishing for its lack of development. You pass sandy coves without even a footpath into them, and long beaches of fine sand so pale that it is almost white, and you ask yourself where are the people, where the hotels.

You also begin to understand why this road and the new one from Missolonghi to Vonitsa were built, and how essential they have made the realisation of the Aktion–Preveza bridge project. There is a whole new resort area waiting to be created, barely a twelve-hour ferry crossing from Italy. So enjoy the peace and primitiveness while you can.

Parga

Parga, 70 km from Preveza and 48 km from Igoumenitsa, is for the moment the only township along the whole coast relatively well supplied with hotels, for all that it has a population of only 1,700. The fact that the hotels were built despite the former difficulty in getting to them testifies to the region's attractiveness. Lying at the head of a bay at the foot of wooded hills, constructed amphitheatrically and dominated by a thirteenth-century castle, Parga was once a Venetian outpost. Occupied by the Turks in 1817, after a brief period under British rule, it became part of Greece only in 1913.

Just offshore is the islet of Panagia; beyond lie the Ionian islands of Paxi and Antipaxi and, to the north, Corfu. Some one-day cruises from Corfu already include a brief call at Parga, and are due to be augmented by regular crossings from the south Corfu resort of Kavo as soon as a new jetty has been constructed at Greece's closest approximation to a British colony.

A short drive from Parga will take you to the Necromantion of Ephyra near Messopotamos, a place where in Ancient Greece the dead were believed to reveal the future to the living. Excavated less than thirty years ago, the Sanctuary of Persephone and Oracle of the Dead require a contribution from the imagination – a process helped by the grim corridors and windowless rooms both above and below ground. In mythology, this was where Charon rowed the dead across the dark waters into Hades.

What to do   If you stay at Parga you can, apart from swimming from sandy beaches, visit the castle and the twelfth-century monastery of the Virgin, make a caique crossing to Paxi 12 nautical miles away, and take a motorboat trip along the coast. The main danger in spending a night there is a probable reluctance to leave in the morning.

Where to stay and where to eat   Should you arrive without a booking, your best bet would be first to try the second-class Parga Beach and Lychnos Beach hotels, which together account for 160 of the 470 rooms on offer in twenty hotels. They are also the only ones at which you can get a meal; elsewhere you will rely on the nearest fish taverna.

Igoumenitsa   By contrast, Igoumenitsa presents no accommodation problem, despite the fact that it has only 294 rooms in fourteen hotels. The explanation is simple: the most common reason for an overnight stay there is miscalculation.

Hemmed in by mountains and without a sign of a beach that would tempt even a child to paddle, Igoumenitsa, population 5,800, runs no risk of becoming a tourist resort. It is a cluster of modern houses built after the old town was destroyed in 1944, with a waterfront dedicated to shipping agencies and cafés. But ten years from now it may conceivably be challenging Patras as Greece's main western port.

It is a matter equally of trade and tourism. Lying at the head of a long, sheltered inlet so deep as to be suggestive of a fjord, Igoumenitsa began to develop when post-war road construction made it easier to reach Corfu by ferry from there, a crossing of 18 nautical miles, after an eleven-hour bus journey from Athens. Formerly, the only way to get to Corfu was a twenty-four-hour sea trip from Piraeus. Now, the Igoumenitsa ferries are the sole alternative to flying from Athens for most travellers, with seventeen sailings a day in summer and nine in winter; the occasional boats from Patras to Corfu via Igoumenitsa are slow but too uncomfortable to qualify as romantic.

Already, many of the Greek–Italian ferries from Brindisi, Bari and Ancona make a call at Igoumenitsa for tourists whose objective is northern Greece. When the west coast fulfils its promise as Greece's newest resort, Igoumenitsa will be its port of access.

In addition, there are plans for a new motorway through and sometimes under the mountain ranges of central Greece to Volos on the east coast, to provide a shorter route for European and, in particular, Italian trade with the Middle East. At present, the Volos ferries to Syria serve mainly freight routed by road through Yugoslavia. In the meantime, because of congestion on Yugoslav roads, freight ferries have been put on a route from Igoumenitsa to Trieste in the north of Italy. This is still a somewhat tentative service, but one that is likely to grow and also eventually to acquire a tourist aspect.

So, although Igoumenitsa might seem of greater interest to the speculator than the holidaymaker, it would be purposeless to calculate whether you should buy up half or only a quarter of the town. Its proximity to Albania puts it in a 'frontier region' and it is therefore closed to land-purchase by foreigners.

Getting there

Igoumenitsa is easy to reach by bus from Athens or Thessaloniki, and has its own services to Ioannina, Arta and Preveza.

Where to stay

If you need to, you can stay pleasantly at the second-class Xenia Motel (seventy-two beds) with its garden and beach or, in third class, at the new Jolly (fifty-one beds) in King Paul Street or the Oscar (sixty-two beds) in Aghion Apostolon Street near the port.

Where to eat

Recommended for meals are the Strada Marina on the waterfront close to the terminal of the Corfu ferries and, for fish, the Droponos Beach restaurant 3 km outside the town.

Mountain villages

Should you have stayed in Parga and be planning your next night in Ioannina, you would have plenty of time for a side trip either to Paramythia (35 km) or Souli (73 km) to gain an idea of how harsh life used to be, and to some extent still is, in the high mountains of Greece. The roads are adequate and require only strong nerves.

Ioannina to Kalambaka

If you have declined the direct route from Arta to Ioannina, the road from Igoumenitsa is now your only way to the historic capital of Epiros and, beyond, to the towns of central Greece. You should allow rather more than two hours for the 104-km drive, because of the mountain terrain and the hairpin bends rather than any temptation to stop along the way.

Ioannina

Ioannina, which you will see spelt also as Yannina, Jannina, and in any of the three versions with a single 'n', is the capital and largest town of Epiros. With a population of 45,000, it stands on the banks of a lake at an altitude of 520 m and is 445 km from Athens and 370 km from Thessaloniki on the most direct routes.

Getting there

There are eight buses a day from Athens and three from Thessaloniki (seven and a half and seven hours respectively), and local services to Arta, Agrinion, Preveza, Igoumenitsa, Patras,

Trikala, Larisa, Kozani and Kastoria. Olympic Airways flies at least once a day from Athens, and twice a week from Ioannina to Thessaloniki.

History

Believed to have been founded by the Byzantine Emperor Justinian in the sixth century AD, it became an important centre of Byzantine art in the thirteenth century and was captured by the Turks in the fifteenth, twenty years before the fall of Constantinople. It was finally reunited with Greece after the 1912 Balkan War.

Ali Pasha

Curiously, Ioannina acquired its greatest splendour as the most important province of the Ottoman Empire, and centre of an early Hellenic cultural revival, under the rule of an Albanian adventurer whose cruelty has gone down in Greek folklore. Ali Pasha of Tepeleni governed the Pashalik of Epiros, an area considerably more extensive than the present province, from his appointment by the Sultan in 1788 until he launched a revolt in 1820 that served as a kind of signal for the Greek Independence Revolution. Killed by the Sultan after his revolt was crushed, Ali was buried partly in Ioannina (his body) and partly in Constantinople (his head). Though much of Ioannina was destroyed during the siege, much also survives from the days of Ali and earlier.

What to see

The citadel, dating from the eleventh century, is worth a visit, and so too are the seventeenth century Aslan Pasha Mosque, now a museum of Epirote arts and crafts, and the Fethie Mosque with the tomb of Ali Pasha outside. Numerous houses of the Turkish period survive, as does the old Jewish quarter (the Jews themselves were transported to the Nazi death camps in the Second World War and few returned). Above all, go to the island in the lake, population 460, for the old churches and monasteries there; it takes five minutes by motorboat. The island contains six Byzantine and post-Byzantine monasteries, in one of which, Aghios Pandeleimonos, Ali was killed; you can visit the bedroom where he went down fighting and see the bullet holes in the walls. You can also eat well at any of several island restaurants specialising in trout from the lake; they are kept in tanks, and the one you choose is executed at your command, then fried or grilled.

What to do

Ioannina is excellent for shopping: in the bazaar area you can find gold and silver jewellery, articles of copper and brass, and traditional Epirote embroideries. Also, there are good local wine and Turkish-style cakes.

Where to stay

Although there are 923 rooms in twenty-two hotels, Ioannina has only two of second class – the 135-room Palladion and sixty-room Xenia. None of the twenty-two would take your breath away.

Where to eat

You can eat well at the Litharitsa restaurant at the southern end of the central park near the castle, and in the garden restaurant of the Xenia Hotel. On the island, Ioanninans insist they choose on the basis of 'the fish that day' and play no favourites among the restaurants.

Perama

You should certainly find time to visit Perama, just 4 km outside the town. Opinions differ on whether Perama is a 'better' cave than those of the Mani, but it is certainly more accessible. Discovered only in 1942 by villagers seeking a refuge from bombing, it runs more than a kilometre into the mountainside through a succession of galleries where the stalactite and stalagmite formations have been cunningly illuminated and inevitably accorded their identifications: Marble Forest, Candlesticks, Organ Pipes, Artichokes and, for less obvious reasons, Persephone and Pluto. It is a forty-five-minute walk through the cave, during which you will be escorted by guides.

Dodoni

Dodoni, 22 km from Ioannina, is a must. The site of the oldest oracle in the Hellenic world, considerably predating that of Delphi, it was a religious centre from about 1900 BC, with worship first centring on the Earth Mother. But from approximately 800 BC the site was dedicated to Zeus, whose voice would be interpreted by the priests from the rustling of leaves in a grove of sacred oaks.

Razed in the sixth century by Alaric and his Goths, even the site was lost until the end of the nineteenth century. Most Greeks now associate Dodoni with its ancient theatre, even larger than that of Epidavros, and go there for summer performances of ancient drama; during the Roman period the same theatre was used for gladiatorial contests. But Dodoni is also one of the most important archaeological sites in Epiros, with remains of the sanctuary, a citadel and an early Christian basilica.

The site is said to be open from 7.30 a.m. to 7.30 p.m. in the summer (later if there is a performance at the theatre) and from 9 a.m. to 6 p.m. on Sundays; in the off-season, from 9 a.m. to 5 p.m. weekdays and from 9 a.m. to 3 p.m. on Sundays. But at some point it has to be observed that for the so-called 'lesser' sites (not, of course, for the Athens Acropolis, Delphi and Olympia) opening hours reported by NTOG do not always accord with those actually applied by the Culture Ministry, which has to provide the guards and pay their salaries. This unsatisfactory situation is unlikely to be resolved until a Ministry that is in other directions spendthrift abandons its penny-pinching attitude towards the provision of tourist services.

Metsovon and Zagoria

The 120-km drive from Ioannina to Kalambaka, via Metsovon, takes you through the heart of the Pindos mountains and across the Katara pass, the highest in Greece and the first to be closed by winter snows. With successive peaks of up to 2,600 m, the view is Alpine and so is the temperature; a sweater should be kept close at hand.

Metsovon

At the halfway point of the road, Metsovon (sometimes written Metsovo) is well worth a pause. Perched at a height of 915 m with a population of 2,700, it is something between a village and a town. It was the birthplace in the late eighteenth century of Michael Tositsas and in the early nineteenth century of George Averof. Both moved to Egypt, where they prospered, and both used their wealth to finance the construction of public buildings in Athens after it had become the Greek capital. The Averof family also financed the old battleship of that name now moored between Athens and Piraeus.

Metsovon is interesting for its traditional houses. One of the larger ones, belonging to the Tositsas family, is now a folk museum, with a guest-house for scholars and an excellent library (non-scholars have a choice of ten hotels). While Metsovon is really a winter resort, with snow regularly from December to April, the ski lift to Karakoli at a height of 1,500 m also operates during the summer. It is one of the last parts of mainland Greece where national costume is still worn as a matter of course; and it produces the hard and salty Metsovon cheese to be found in the better supermarkets.

The Zagoria villages

While in the area, though this is entirely a matter of taste and time, you could devote a day to an exploration of the forty-six Zagoria villages sited along the slopes of Mount Timfi in the triangle bounded by Ioannina, Metsovon and Konitsa in the north. When the Turks conquered Epiros in the fifteenth century, the inhabitants of these villages secured an agreement by which they retained a large degree of autonomy in return for payment of an annual tribute. As a result, they were able to offer asylum to what today would be called political refugees from the Ottoman Empire, who brought their traditional crafts with them, and also developed an extensive trade network into the Balkans.

Largely depopulated during the migration to the cities after the Second World War, the villages are now acquiring new life as more holiday-makers discover them, and a few hostels have been constructed to supplement rooms on offer in the houses. The villages are best appreciated on foot, but can be sampled by car or on one of the buses that leave Ioannina in the morning and return in the early evening.

Kalambaka and Meteora

Kalambaka

Though Kalambaka (population 5,700) is undeniably picturesque, built at the foot of the Pindos range, it is really only a place to bed down for the night and enjoy a simple meal accompanied by the excellent local wine. But while you are there you might as well take a look at its cathedral, a three-aisled basilica dating from the early fourteenth century with some noteworthy frescoes of the same period and a much admired marble pulpit.

Kalambaka can be reached by train from Athens or Thessaloniki (change at Paleo Pharsala) or by bus via Trikala. It offers 311 rooms in twelve hotels of all categories, with 187 of the rooms in the two first-class units, the Divani and Xenia Motels. The best places to eat are the Nikos taverna and Pindos restaurant, both on the central Riga Ferraiou Square.

The Meteora monas-teries

The main reason for Kalambaka is Meteora, 2 km out of town. Its monasteries, of which there were once twenty-four but are now only five, occupy the summits of pinnacles of grey rock at a point where the Pinios River emerges from the Pindos mountains, at the edge of the plain of Thessaly. Their history goes back to the fourteenth century, but even earlier than that, monks of ascetic tendency had sought refuge in cliffside caves there, and a Byzantine imperial edict of 1143 contains a reference to the area as having been a religious retreat since the previous century.

In the fourteenth century, however, when warfare between Byzantium and Serbia washed over eastern Greece and brigands, as always, flourished in its wake, the monks were required to contemplate their security in the present world as well as their salvation in the next. They could have fled, but instead they climbed higher. As their numbers grew, the original wooden shelters were transformed into the monasteries of stone and wood that can be visited today.

Considerations of safety demanded that the monasteries, indefensible with the weapons available to religious communities, should be impregnable. The solution was to build no roads or paths, but to provide access only by jointed, removable ladders. Later, windlasses were added by means of which monks could be winched home in boxes or nets. Some of these survive, but are now used only for hauling up provisions; for the visitor, they have been replaced by stairways or steep ramps. There was a legendary monkish reply to those who timorously wondered how often the ropes were replaced: 'When the Lord lets them break!'

Though uniquely situated, the monasteries themselves are of typical design. They have a central courtyard formed by the monks' cells, the chapels and refectory. The main church, the *katholikon*, occupies the centre of the courtyard. 'Catholic' in Greek has retained its meaning of universal, and the *katholikon* is the all-purpose church open to visitors and used for general services, as distinct from chapels that may be reserved for the monks.

In the late Byzantine period and after the Turkish conquest, the Meteora monasteries became the sanctuary of the persecuted as well as the devout, and also one of the more important centres of Byzantine art. Decline set in from the seventeenth century, and today only four of the monasteries are inhabited: the Great Meteoron, Aghia Trias (Holy Trinity), Aghios Stefanos and Aghios Varlaam. The 1981 census recorded sixty-four monks in residence.

The **Great Meteoron**, founded in the mid-fourteenth century, originally applied the cenobitic rules of Mount Athos, with women rigorously excluded, but is now open to visitors of both sexes. The foundation stone of its Church of the Transfiguration (Metamorphosis) bears two dates: the year of the world 6393 and the year of Our Lord 1388. The **Varlaam** monastery, founded in 1517 by two brothers from Ioannina, displays frescoes painted in 1565 and restored in 1870. **Aghios Stefanos**, an hour's walk from Varlaam, is connected to the main cliff by a bridge over a deep crevice. Below it is the nunnery of Aghia Roxanne. **Aghia Trias**, established in 1476, sited on a particularly beautiful pinnacle, is reached by a circular flight of steps cut into the rock. Originally a hermitage, it was turned into a monastery in the fourteenth century by the Byzantine Emperor Andronicos.

Not so long ago the monasteries demanded of a visitor strong legs and a head for heights; if you happened to be caught half-way up one of the pinnacles in a sudden storm you felt like a fly on a wall and wished you had made your will. Now they can be visited in succession along a paved road, with only some easy steps to climb, on a round trip from Kalamata of barely 20 km. They offer breathtaking views of mountains, river, plain and woods.

Decorous clothing, is, of course, a condition of admission, but the required garments are available on loan. As a general rule, though not one followed by all the monasteries every day, the monasteries are open daily to visitors in the morning, close for a siesta around 12.30 or 1 p.m., and reopen for a couple of hours at or soon after 3.30 p.m.

Back to Athens

Trikala

If it is still early or you do not wish to eat a second time in Kalambaka, you could drive 20 km to Trikala for lunch. The ancient Greek Trikki, reputed birthplace of Asclipios, Trikala (population 45,000) is a modern city with ruins of a sanctuary to the physician-god, a Byzantine castle nearby and, in the town itself, Byzantine churches and a nineteenth-century Turkish mosque. The Varousi quarter, built 200 years ago under Turkish rule, contains homes once regarded as rich and stately and now protected by law from demolition – an unusual example of the Greek state closing the stable door with the horse still inside.

From Trikala you have a choice of routes back to Athens. The easiest and most direct is to take the road due east to Larisa, 61 km away, and there join the north–south motorway.

Larisa and Lamia

Larisa, 361 km from Athens, is a big city (population 102,000) of vital significance to Greece's agricultural economy. It is stiflingly hot in the summer and no Greek would dream of going there for a holiday.

Karditsa

The same applies to Lamia, population 41,000 and 146 km closer to Athens. The motorway skirts both cities, and you may do the same.

An alternative route is to reach Lamia via Karditsa, a drive of 118 km of equally little interest. Either way you should allow about seven hours for the drive from Kalambaka to Athens, even though the buses do it in six.

Eastern
Greece

● THESSALONIKI

KATERINI ●   Thermaikos
                Gulf
Mt Olympos ● Dion
Litohori ●● Plaka
Aghios ●   Leptokaria
Dionyssios ● Platamonas
Elassona ●   ● Vale of Tempe
         R.Pinios ● Ambelakia
Tyrnavos ●   ▲ Mt Ossa

LARISA ●

          Mt Pilion Portaria
Makrynitsa ● ▲ ● Zagora
VOLOS ●   ● Tsangarada

Pagasitikos Gulf

LAMIA ●
Thermopylae ●   ●
   Kamena Vourla

                ● HALKIS
                 ● Avlis
Skimatari ●

            ● ATHENS

Eastern Greece

Introduction

It is quite possible to leave Athens after a leisurely breakfast, stop for an early lunch at Kamena Vourla or a late one at the Vale of Tempe, and be in Thessaloniki 508 km away in plenty of time for a shower before dinner. Most Athenians, whether driving north on business or to start a holiday, do exactly that.

For about four-fifths of the distance, the motorway passes by or in sight of the sea. When it turns inland you have a view, illuminating rather than enthralling, of some of the rich agricultural land that makes up the plain of Thessaly; it will be covered by the smoke of burning stubble after the crops are in. Unless you branch off, you will miss the large commercial centres of Lamia and Larisa, but these are cities which Greeks visit only for business or family reasons.

However, there are two temptations along the way. Yield to both and you will need three or four days to reach Thessaloniki, with one or two nights spent at Volos and another on or near Mount Olympos. You will then have been introduced to Greece's two finest mountains, Olympos and Pilion.

Other temptations are provided by opportunities to visit the off-shore island of Euboia (pronounced Evia) without leaving your car, and Skopelos and Skiathos in the North Sporades group by ferry from Volos. If you take in all of these, you will turn the trip into a week's holiday.

A word on the motorway The Athens–Thessaloniki motorway is styled National Road No. 1 (*Ethnikos Dromos Ar 1*). It is referred to as a motorway because this is the literal translation of the Greek *aftokinitodromo*, and one should be polite when politeness costs nothing. But the Greeks themselves agree that it does not really qualify. One day it might, as a result either of European Community financing or its incorporation into the great Trans-European Motorway (TEM) that is one day to run from the north of Poland to Italy, Greece and Turkey. For the moment, however, it requires vigilance, and is best avoided at night.

Pending reconstruction, it has no central island for most of the way, and can only be loosely described as accommodating two lanes of traffic in each direction. It is provided sparsely with lay-bys and generously with entries for lorries and farm vehicles; it is sometimes poorly cambered, and sequined with blind corners. Nonetheless, it is considerably safer than the old road it was built thirty years ago to replace, and is incomparably superior to the Yugoslav *autoput* with which it connects at the border north of Thessaloniki.

Police patrols and radar traps have not yet wholly persuaded the drivers of inter-urban buses, tourist coaches and long-distance TIR lorries that speed should be determined by road conditions and traffic signs rather than engine-power, but driving standards are slowly improving. Even so, on most holiday weekends there are more deaths on this particular motorway than from the greater number of accidents at slower speeds in the rest of the country.

So while for once you may take a motorway for the pleasure of the route, you still need to drive defensively.

Athens to Volos

Regardless of the time at your disposal, and of whether you have decided to cover eastern Greece in a day or tour it in depth, you will face no choices between leaving Athens, through Kifisia, and reaching the tollgates about an hour later.

The unusual distance of the tollgates from Athens – you may have begun to think you were getting it all for nothing – should not be attributed to state generosity. Enticed by tax and other concessions, which in turn were inspired by the worsening Athens air pollution, dozens of industries have set up or relocated along both sides of the first 50 or 60 km of the motorway. The need to lay on buses for their workforce was acceptable, but the cost and delay of tolls would probably not have been.

At Skimatari, 70 km out of Athens, you can turn right for Avlis and Halkis, a distance of 18 km.

Avlis   Avlis or Avlida, only a village now, was where the Greek army and fleet assembled for the Trojan expedition and where Agamemnon was persuaded to sacrifice Iphigenia in return for a favourable wind. The remains of a temple to Artemis may be viewed in passing.

Halkis   Halkis, which you will also see written as Khalkis and as Halkida or Khalkida, is the capital of Euboia, Greece's second largest island after Crete, with an area of 3,653 sq km. It is scarcely rated by the Greeks as an island, however, because of its proximity to the coast and capital.

A city of 45,000 inhabitants, Halkis spreads along both sides of the Evripos straits at a point where the island is only 40 m from the mainland, to which it is linked by a swing-bridge. Attractively sited, with the old town on the island and new town on the mainland, and with good swimming in the immediate vicinity, it is favoured by elderly

Athenians for unambitious summer holidays or weekend breaks. While the eye is caught by an unusual Byzantine church with Gothic overlays, the island's real beauty spots lie further afield.

Back on the motorway, you have only the sea to enjoy until reaching Kamena Vourla, 170 km from Athens. The lake on your right just before you come in sight of the sea is Yliki, which feeds into Marathon and helps ensure against Athenian water shortages.

On your right a few kilometres before Kamena Vourla you can hardly fail to notice Levendis, Greece's biggest roadside café. The first refreshment and toilet stop for almost every bus out of Athens, Levendis serves the normal range of snacks: and soft drinks. If you prefer a full meal you should continue to Kamena Vourla, where you can have one seated.

Kamena Vourla

Kamena Vourla, the only built-up area through which the motorway actually passes, has managed to come to terms with the traffic. On the right, the beaches; on the left, the hotels, shops, restaurants and cafés; behind them, the mountains that look on Thermopylae. It ought to be a town, with 128 hotels providing 2,257 rooms and a nightlife that includes discos, 'pubs' and bouzouki centres. In fact, it is a squashed little village, with a resident population of only 2,000. The explanation is that it is one of the few Greek spas that combine mineral water of repute with good sandy beaches. It is therefore a popular year-round resort which rapidly becomes overcrowded in the summer, but it has no hinterland to allow room for expansion.

Stay there only if you enjoy crowded beaches, the steady growl of traffic, and a catch-me-if-you-can adventure every time you cross the road from where you swim to where you eat. However, the number of those taking the waters ensures that the food is good, plentiful, varied and cheap. It is your last chance for lunch until you reach Volos or the Vale of Tempe.

The best hostelry is the 231-bed first-class Galini, where you can take the waters on the premises. Recommended among the cluster of second class are the Sissy (190 beds) and the rather newer Possidon (176 beds). The Radion (second class, ninety-four beds) has built up a loyal clientele over the decades but is beginning to look its age. For a meal, try the Delphini or Asteria restaurants on the beach, Argyris on the National Road, or Mouries, 50 m back from the beach in the middle of the 'town'.

Thermopylae

A few minutes after leaving Kamena Vourla you will reach what was once the pass of Thermopylae, where Leonidas and his 300 Spartans fought to the death against the Persians in 480 BC. As recently as 1941, some military planners, apparently more familiar with Ancient Greek texts than modern maps, actually dreamed of halting the German invaders there. The sea has now receded so far that it is just a ribbon on the horizon; the white observatory-like building in the far distance is Greece's satellite ground station for international telephone calls and communication with the far-flung merchant navy.

The modern bronze statue closer to the road is of Leonidas, who went down fighting. Further along, this time on the left, is a memorial to another Greek hero, Athanasios Diakos, an 1821 Revolutionary who was caught by the Turks and, in the custom of the times, impaled on a spit and roasted over a charcoal fire.

Thermopylae today is a village of 401 inhabitants, with ninety-one rooms in two hotels. The site of the ancient battle and the tomb of those who fell have been located, but there is really very little to see.

The part of the road from Lamia to Larisa, a stretch of about 150 km, passes through farmland that was added to Greece only in 1881 when the protecting powers were persuaded that, without it, the Greeks could not feed themselves. About half-way between the two cities, a well-marked turn leads to Volos, 25 km off the motorway.

Volos and Mount Pilion

Volos, population 71,400, is Greece's main east coast port and sixth largest city, after Athens/Piraeus, Thessaloniki, Patras, Larisa and Iraklion in Crete. Situated close to ancient Iolkos, from where Jason set out in the Argo to seek the Golden Fleece, Volos was devastated by an earthquake in 1955 and is now a modern city with an extensive industrial zone on its outskirts and little to commend it except its good hotels and attractive quayside restaurants.

The restaurants are there because the hotels are, and the hotels, all twenty-two of them with 733 rooms, are there because Volos, though scarcely a place for a holiday, is the natural base for exploration of Mount Pilion and the terminal for passenger ferries to the northern Sporades islands, mainly Skiathos and Skopelos but also Alonysos; Skyros can be reached from Volos, but is far closer to Kimi on the east coast of Euboia.

Getting there Volos can be reached from Athens by bus (five hours) or train (seven hours, allowing for a change at Larisa). It has its own bus services to Larisa, Lamia, Karditsa and Patras, and a train that runs to Kalambaka and the Meteora monasteries. It is 319 km from Athens, a comfortable five hours' driving, and 215 km from Thessaloniki.

Where to stay and where to eat Well regarded among hotels are two of second class, the 225-bed Park and 134-bed Alexandros. Favourites of the Volos people for a meal out are the Metaftsis and Dzafolias restaurants on Argonafton Street, the latter open only for dinner. Argonafton is the waterfront; the restaurants, cafés, snack-bars and such are at the part closer to the ferry terminal for the Sporades islands.

Excursions – Mount Pilion and its villages

Once you have walked along the quayside, looked at the Pagasitikos Gulf and tried not to notice the terminal of the freight ferries to Syria, and enjoyed some large or little fish at one of the waterfront restaurants, there is really nothing else to do except what should have brought you to Volos in the first place. Head for Mount Pilion.

The twenty-four Pilion villages begin only 5 km from Volos and can be toured comfortably in a day, using your own car, an hourly bus service or taxi. If there is need for compression, preference might be given to four of them: Portaria, Makrynitsa, Zagora and Tsangarada.

Unlike most Greek mountains, Pilion (1,601 m) is well watered and green, with woods, groves and orchards of beech and chestnut, walnut, peach, apple, cherry and olive. Of the villages, some are at altitudes of from 300 to 900 m and others skirt lovely beaches and deep coves. They retain their original architectural forms, and under postwar Greek legislation will continue to do so.

Pilion was essentially free under the Turks, who were always lazy conquerors, and the houses were therefore free to spread without need for considerations of defence. Traditionally of three storeys, with the upper floor the reception area, many still survive and some have been turned by NTOG into small hostels.

The villages flourished particularly in the eighteenth and nineteenth centuries, when the region was a cultural centre for Thessaly and an exporter of silk and wool to the large cities of Europe. Visit them and you will appreciate that mainland Greece can be lush, and that there is far more to it than the Golden Age.

Portaria and Makrynitsa

Portaria (population 769), 14 km from Volos, and Makrynitsa (population 546), 3 km further along the same road, are built on steep slopes with spectacular views of Volos and the Pagasitikos Gulf. Makrynitsa was originally built as a fortress to protect the other villages, and has a Church of the Virgin dating from 1222. Cars have to stop just outside the village, since they could scarcely be driven through the steeply cobbled streets.

Zagora

Zagora, 47 km from Volos at an altitude of 500 m, is the largest of the Pilion villages with a population of 2,680. Situated on the Aegean side of the mountain, it is almost lost among chestnut and plane trees. The monastery of the Saviour, dating from the twelfth century, might be visited in passing.

Tsangarada and Milopotamos

Tsangarada, 15 km from Zagora on the same road, is 450 m up the mountain and has a population of 646. Numerous turnings off the Tsangarada–Zagora road lead down to the seaside villages, such as Aghios Ioannis (population 143) and Milopotamos, where the swimming is unsurpassed and the fish, if your timing is right, make the arrow-flight journey from sea to frying pan almost before they have ceased to twitch.

For sound environmental reasons, there are no large concrete-and-glass hotel and bungalow complexes on Pilion. Makrynitsa, for example, has eight hotels with a total of sixty-five rooms, Tsangarada seven with 149, and Portaria nine with 215. This means that only small and unobtrusive groups can be booked there; it also means that if you arrive in summer without a reservation you had better resign yourself to staying in Volos.

You can taste the area in half a day, but a full day is better – and essential if you are using the Volos buses.

Dimini and Sesklo

West of Volos, two left turns off the Larisa road lead 3 km and 4 km respectively to Dimini and Sesklo, a couple of archaeological sites that really require a degree of specialised interest but are so easily reached that it would be a pity not to consider them. At Dimini you can see remains dating from the neolithic to the Mycenaean periods. Sesklo, once one of the most important neolithic settlements in south-eastern Europe, offers ruins of an acropolis, palace and neolithic housing.

Dimitrias and Pagasai

Even closer to the Lamia road, but therefore a little out of your way if your objective is northern Greece, are the ancient sites of Dimitrias and Pagasai. Dimitrias has remains of ancient fortifications partly restored by the Romans, an aqueduct, a temple and a theatre, while Pagasai, which gave its name to the Pagasitikos Gulf on which Volos stands, either was itself, or was very close to, Jason's Iolkos. Both are near to good beaches with fish restaurants.

Olympos country

The Vale of Tempe

From Volos you can quickly rejoin the motorway for the 80-km drive to the Vale of Tempe. Only 12 km long and not particularly deep, Tempe is exquisitely to scale: wooded slopes on either side, the once mighty Pinios river now a fast-flowing stream at the bottom, and the single-track rail line from Athens to Thessaloniki on the opposite bank. Tempe passes all too quickly, though there are lay-bys to permit a more leisurely contemplation or picnic. Half-way through Tempe you may just discern the ruins of the Frankish castle of Orias, one of four which once guarded the pass. It is equally easy to overlook the hamlet of Tempe, concealed among trees and home to just seventy-five people.

The tollgate (the exit gate for those driving north) is situated just before the valley, alongside the second large restaurant serving motorway traffic. Unlike Levendis, this one seats its clients, but for that reason you need to allow yourself more time.

Ambelakia

If you have a couple of hours to spare and an interest in the oddities of social history, you can turn off the motorway beside the tollgate for the winding drive to Ambelakia, a village of 490 inhabitants perched 450 m up the slopes of Mount Ossa. Its claim to fame derives from the establishment there, in the seventeenth century, of the first cooperative movement ever to be formed in Greece. Set up for the production and marketing of cotton and silk, it eventually attained a membership of 6,000 and sufficient wealth from exports to Europe to be able to pioneer what today would be regarded as a miniature welfare state, providing a health service for its members and free distribution of basic foodstuffs to the poor.

The cooperative was ruined in the early nineteenth century by Ali Pasha of Ioannina (see p. 208) who raised the taxes; the collapse of a Viennese bank which held its capital; and the disruption of its market by the Napoleonic Wars. Two houses, those of the Schwartz brothers, merchants and bankers, remain from the period of Ambelakia's prosperity; one of them has been turned into a museum for the display of folk art, embroidery and manuscripts, and opens when it has a visitor.

Once past the ruined thirteenth-century Crusader castle of Platamonos that guards the northern approaches to the Vale of Tempe, you are fully in Olympos country.

A not-quite holiday resort

As a tourist region, the Olympos coast of the Thermaikos Gulf has never quite lived up either to its promise or the expectations at one time placed in it by Greece's tourism authorities and hoteliers. It has the beaches, hotels and campsites, and Olympos with its cloud-wreathed summits as backdrop; what it does not have is much of a holiday movement.

It would be easy to say, now, that those who put their money into the Olympos coast during the great tourist boom of fifteen to twenty years ago, when hotels were springing up in every corner of the country, should have known better. But at the time it seemed that no one could lose, and far worse blunders were committed elsewhere.

The Olympos hoteliers were hurt first and most of all by the faster and more luxurious development of the Halkidiki peninsula on the other side of the gulf. For the tourist, and for the Athenian venturing a holiday in the north, the saving of three or four hours of travel time was a minor consideration in the context of a week's holiday.

Halkidiki was promoted abroad, legitimately, as the only real resort area of mainland Greece. Deprived of significant package tours from Europe, and largely ignored by Greek travel agents in their own programmes, the Olympos coast languished. It nevertheless offers two advantages for the independent traveller with his or her own means of transport. It is far more peaceful for an overnight stay than Thessaloniki, not much more than an hour's drive away. And the next morning can be devoted to Olympos itself and a visit to Greece's newest ancient site, that of Dion.

Where to stay

You can find hotels in almost all of the coastal villages along the 30-km drive from Platamonas to Katerini and, if Olympos is not an attraction, between Katerini and Thessaloniki. If the smaller ones happen to be full of local holiday-makers in July and August, you should have no trouble at the Olympian Bay at Leptokaria (228 rooms), the Platamon Beach or Maxim at Platamonas (174 and 73 rooms respectively), or the Lito or Olympios Zeus at Plaka, the former with 93 rooms and the latter with 100 bungalows.

No place for beginners

Anyone planning to climb Olympos must make arrangements in advance, through a travel agent or, better, through a mountaineering club; Olympos is definitely not a hill for the inexperienced.

The tallest mountain in Greece, at 2,917 m, it was the obvious place for the ancient gods to set up home; awe kept out the believers, and inaccessibility the sceptics. The latter deterrent also guarded it from successive armies of invasion or occupation, including those of the Turks during 'the 400 years', and allowed Olympos to become a stronghold of the *klefts*, literally robbers but rather the equivalent of guerrillas. If redemption were needed, they obtained it with the 1821 Revolution.

There are two main peaks, Mytikas ('The Needle'), of which the first recorded ascent was made in 1913, and the slightly lower Skolion. About the closest you can approach to either by car, and the safest way to circle the mountain, is to drive from Larisa through Tyrnavos and Elassona to Katerini, where you rejoin the motorway. You can get a little higher, if you wish, by taking any of the side roads upwards to where they or your fortitude come to an end.

Elassona, 61 km from Larisa, is the main Olympos town, with a population of 6,500, and access point for the winter sports facilities on Kato (Lower) Olympos. A monastery of the Virgin there, dating from the twelfth century, displays a notable collection of ecclesiastical treasures and manuscripts. Curiously, Elassona has only two twenty-room hotels, both of fourth class.

A shorter but steeper route, involving a left turn off the motorway half-way between Platamonos and Katerini, leads to Litohori, population 6,100, where there are three hotels with seventy-six rooms. You would take this route if you intended an attempt on the summit or a visit to the Byzantine monastery of Aghios Dionyssios. It makes a good excursion, but you have to return the same way.

The Old Man of the Mountain

If you are a collector of modern primitive art, you may have heard of Vassilios Ithakissios, two of whose works are said to be hanging in the White House in Washington. You may not be aware that for twenty years his postal address was the Cave of the Muses on the Table of the Gods, Mount Olympos. Ithakissios, who died in his nineties in an Athens old people's home, lived for two decades at the 1,700 m level, in a cave that was both home and studio.

Son of a boat-builder on the island of Mytilene, he was apprenticed to a hagiographer for icon painting, won a scholarship to the Athens Fine Arts School, studied portraiture in Belgium, and migrated to Smyrna, now Izmir. Caught up in the Asia Minor disaster of 1922, when the city fell to the Turks and was burned along with all his paintings, he arrived in Athens a penniless refugee.

Aristotle Onassis, who was almost as penniless then, made the same journey at the same time, though on a different boat. He went to Buenos Aires and grew rich; Ithakissios went to Olympos and acquired a different and more local kind of fame. He lived there from 1926 to 1946, wintering in Litohori. During the Second World War, he said in an interview shortly before his death, the German occupation forces stole most of his paintings but let him stay on the mountain. The communist guerrillas who held Olympos during the civil war stole or destroyed the rest, and drove him out. At the age of seventy he was back in Athens in almost the same condition as when he first arrived a quarter of a century earlier.

Ithakissios paintings are apparently scattered throughout the world – he said he identified the two in the White House from illustrations in a magazine article – and Greek dealers are on the watch for those that occasionally surface. Between 1926 and the invasion of Greece in 1940, he said, more than 700 climbers spent a night in his cave, enjoying the hospitality of a simple meal and glass of wine. Since he left, Upper Olympos has been uninhabited again.

Dion of the Macedonians

As an archaeological site, Dion, near Litohori (you take a left fork off the motorway 3 or 4 km past that for Litohori) is not yet in the big league, and will never challenge Delphi, Olympia or Mycenae. It is of interest mainly because the discoveries there are relatively recent, and because Dion was once the sacred city of the Macedonians.

Philip II celebrated his victories at Dion, and it was there that Alexander the Great sought the favour of Zeus before setting out for the east. Greek and Roman theatres have so far been excavated, along with sanctuaries of the gods, including one of the Egyptian goddess Isis, and hundreds of inscriptions which shed fresh light on the Macedonian period. Excavations have also brought to light the ground plan of a city going back as far as 550 BC, with streets, houses, workshops, public buildings, baths and an unexpectedly advanced water supply and drainage system. There is a small museum at Dion, open from 9 a.m. to 3 p.m., closed on Tuesdays, admission Dr 200. It is a good way to spend a couple of hours.

Katerini

You could also take a look at the capital of Pieria province, Katerini. It has a population of 38,000 but really nothing to offer except hotel rooms (124 in five of third to fifth class) for those in desperate need.

Better to press on to Thessaloniki (see p. 227), through the heaviest traffic you will have encountered since leaving Athens and with only eyesores to observe. Since 1954 Thessaloniki has successfully turned into Greece's second industrial city; the cost has been paid by its approaches.

Northern Greece

YUGOSLAVIA

BULGARIA

Orestias

Didimotichon

● Promahonas

● Sidirokastron

Soufli ●

● Evzoni

DRAMA ●

XANTHI ●

● KOMOTINI

● SERRES

● Philipi

Kipi Bridge ●

● Kilkis

Avdira ●

R. Evros

● KAVALA

ALEXANDROUPOLIS

TURKE

● THESSALONIKI

THASSOS

HALKIDIKI

SAMOTHRACE

Polygyros ●

● Ouranoupolis

● Gerakini

● Nea Moudania

Sithonia

▲ Mount Athos

● Kassandria

● Porto Carras

Cassandra

● Torone

224

Northern Greece

Introduction

Macedonia is divided into three parts for administrative purposes – west, central and east Macedonia which, together with Thrace, geographically comprise an entity that is at the same time the north of Greece and the Aegean outlet of the Balkan peninsula.

By the time you reach Thessaloniki you begin to appreciate that Greece is what its government declares it to be: Balkan as well as Mediterranean and European. The rolling, tree-covered hill country of much of Macedonia and most of Thrace resembles southern Bulgaria and Yugoslavia more than central Greece, let alone the Peloponnese. The climate is more extreme, colder in winter, at least as hot in summer and with a greater likelihood of sudden storms. The rivers you cross are for Greece both wide and swift-flowing, since they rise in the watersheds of the northern neighbours, where some of them have different names during their longer courses: Yugoslavia's Vardar, which links with the Danube, becomes the Axios for its final 76 km; and the Nestor and Strymon, with flows in Greece of 130 and 118 km, were the Mesta and Struma respectively before crossing the border from Bulgaria.

In Balkan fashion, the rivers divide more than they unite: the 204-km Evros is the actual border between Greece and Turkey; there is an unresolved dispute between Greece and Bulgaria over distribution of the water resources of the Nestor/Mesta, while realisation of the old dream of a navigable waterway through the heart of Europe from Thessaloniki to Rotterdam depends on action with regard to the Vardar that Yugoslavia appears neither able nor willing to take.

Go anywhere north or east of Thessaloniki and it is hard to escape the sense that you are in border country. The signposts on main roads speak of Evzoni, Promahonas and Kipi, villages known to every Greek as the border crossings for Yugoslavia, Bulgaria and Turkey respectively. At Thessaloniki railway station, Greece's biggest, the trains are announced as departing for Munich, Vienna, Paris, London or Istanbul.

Greece's army, relatively large for a country of fewer than ten million people, is in evidence, with major headquarters in Thessaloniki and Komotini. Regardless of whether it is currently fashionable to speak of a threat only from the east (Turkey) and no longer from the north (Bulgaria), it remains true that this is a comparatively recent development. Greece was last invaded by and through Bulgaria in 1941, and without the support provided by Yugoslavia to the communist guerrillas after the Second World War the 1946–49 civil war would have been shorter and less destructive. For whatever reason it may now stay in the alliance, Greece did not originally join NATO to protect itself from Turkey.

To the holiday-maker, northern Greece is the Halkidiki peninsula, in particular the western and central of its three prongs which jut out into the North Aegean: there is a resort hotel at almost every turn of the road. The island of Thassos, an emerging alternative, still carries the handicap of distance and insufficient infrastructure.

Unless their objective is a beach umbrella on Halkidiki and their wanderlust is assuaged by a one-day coach excursion from there to the borders of Mount Athos, most travellers through central and eastern Macedonia and Thrace are heading for somewhere else: Istanbul, through Sofia to Bucharest and Budapest, or through Skopje and Belgrade to Austria or Italy.

Yet there is much to see, in a region that was united with Greece only during the first two decades of the present century. There is the green and well-watered hinterland of the long North Aegean coast and, to the west of Thessaloniki, Greece's most rugged mountain country, as well as its finest woodlands on the approaches to Halkidiki. There are ancient sites such as Vergina, Pella and Philipi, and busy modern cities which are always interesting and sometimes picturesque. From Kavala you can visit Thassos, and from Halkidiki you should at least cruise off the shores of Mount Athos and catch glimpses of the magnificent monasteries. You can shop for silk at Soufli and fur at Kastoria, and for almost anything you can imagine in Thessaloniki.

It is 344 km from Thessaloniki to Alexandroupolis, the last town before the Turkish frontier, and 229 km from Thessaloniki to Kastoria, the last before the Albanian frontier. To cover the north in reasonable depth on two excursions, returning each time to Thessaloniki, would involve distances of something between 1,400 and 1,600 km and require at least a week to allow time for leisurely exploration. But it is quite possible to dip selectively.

My personal choice, if time were particularly restricted, would be to arrange a timetable that provided one night in Halkidiki, one in Kavala and one in Kastoria. Much would inevitably be missed, but everything essential would be seen.

In any case, allow the best part of a day for Thessaloniki.

Thessaloniki

In 1985 Thessaloniki celebrated the 2,300th anniversary of its foundation. It is the capital of northern Greece and offical co-capital of the country as a whole, seat of the Ministry for Northern Greece and focal point of celebrations for Greece's second national holiday, that of 28 October, which marks the Italian invasion that brought Greece into the Second World War.

It is Greece's second largest urban conglomeration: the city has a population of 406,000 and Greater Thessaloniki, an area that includes the adjacent municipalities, 871,000. It is also Greece's second port after Piraeus, handling export–import trade for the north and some transit trade for the Balkans, and the second largest industrial region after Athens. As Greece's 'fairs city', it possesses the country's largest exhibition grounds and stages the Thessaloniki International Exhibition every September and other fairs during the rest of the year.

As a shopping centre many consider it superior to Athens, and for this reason it attracts many tourists from nearby Yugoslavia. Other visitors are drawn by the Ancient Greek, Roman and Byzantine remains, the city's pole position on road and rail communications with the Balkans, Europe and Turkey, and simple business requirements. One way or another, Thessaloniki hoteliers are not complaining; they may not have a resort reputation, but they have more of a year-round movement than anywhere else in Greece.

Thessaloniki has nothing to envy Athens in terms of cultural life: it has a symphony orchestra and a state theatre, a better concert hall than any yet completed in Athens, the 'Dimitriada' (equivalent of the Athens Festival), annual film and song festivals and, to give culture its full dimensions, a host of good restaurants.

It has Greece's second oldest and second largest university, possibly its best hospitals and, in the form of the Ministry for Northern Greece, certainly its most elegant public building. Its tree-shaded streets are pleasant and cool to stroll in, its squares are sufficiently peaceful to allow for low-voiced conversation at restaurant and café tables, and there is nothing else in mainland Greece to compare with the seaside promenade between the docks and the White Tower.

It is not a city its inhabitants are eager to leave. Otherwise ambitious civil servants have been known to turn down promotion rather than move to Athens.

A word on the name   By all means call it Salonika (Salonica) if you find that easier. The Greeks are easygoing about place names, do not expect you even to be aware that Corfu is properly Kerkyra, and would regard you as pedantic if you spoke of Rodos, Kriti, Athenai or Piraefs. But since they are making an effort to establish the international usage of Thessaloniki, your contribution would be an appreciated politeness.

Getting there   Thessaloniki can be reached from Athens by air, rail or bus. Olympic Airways puts on at least six flights a day, and more in summer; the duration of the flight is 50 minutes. There are seven trains a day from Athens (a nine-hour trip) and nineteen buses, fourteen of them run by the state railways (just under eight hours).

It is also possible to reach Thessaloniki by boat from Piraeus, though the schedules are irregular and involve calls at a number of east Aegean islands.

From Thessaloniki there are Olympic Airways flights (less than daily) to Ioannina and the islands of Crete, Limnos, Mytilene, Rhodes and Skiathos. Trains can be taken to the main cities of eastern Greece, Macedonia and Thrace. There are bus services to all the main cities of the north, and almost hourly to Halkidiki.

There are also boat connections (less than daily) to Chios and Mytilene.

Getting out   You take Monasteriou Street (past the railway station) for the roads to Yugoslavia and to Veria/Edessa; Langada Street if you are headed for Seres and Kavala; and, in the opposite easterly direction, Vassilisis Olga for the airport and the coastal route to Halkidiki.

Main Areas   The great advantage for the visitor is that almost everything that needs to be seen lies between King Constantine Quay (Vassileos Konstandinou), which is now officially named Nikis Quay, and the seventh parallel street back from the water; the quadrilateral is bounded by the exhibition grounds on the east and the grimly utilitarian segment between the docks and the bus terminal and railway station in Monasteriou Street on the west. The station is within walking distance of the centre but it is also within the minimum taxi fare, so this is one economy that need not be ventured.

The waterfront   Walk along the promenade and you have magnificent views of the Thermaic Gulf; on a clear day, you can just discern Mount Olympos in the far distance. In the opposite direction, the city climbs the lower, wooded slopes of Mount Hortiatis, with here and there the remains of old Byzantine fortifications. By the water, the fishing boats bob at anchor, and nets are spread to dry in the morning. Across the road are some of the best restaurants, among office blocks and consulates. Where the promenade ends, at the White Tower, you can cross a stretch of garden to the archaeological museum, beside the main entrance to the fair grounds.

The city's two main squares, Aristotelous (where Greece's political parties traditionally hold their opening general election campaign rallies) and Eleftherias (Freedom) abut the waterfront. There you can sit in comfort for light refreshments or a full meal.

The closer parallels to the waterfront – Mitropoleos, Tsimiski, Ermou and Ignatia – are the main shopping streets, and between Ignatia and Aghiou Dimitriou Street are the most important of the Roman remains.

Railway Station

Monasteriou

Aghiou Dimitriou

Ignatia

Eleftherias

Aristotelous

Vassileos Konstandinou (King Constantine Quay)

Mitropoleos

Tsimiski

Ermou

Aghia Sofias

Gounari

Places of Interest:
1 Tourist Office
2 White Tower
3 Arch of Galerius
4 Rotunda (Church of St George)
5 Roman Market
6 Birthplace of Kemal Ataturk

Churches
7 St Dimitrios
8 St Sophia
9 Virgin Akheropiitos
10 Panaghia Halkeon
11 Holy Apostles

Museums
12 Archaeological
13 Folklore

Megalou Alexandrou (Alexander the Great Quay)

Vassilissis Olga

THESSALONIKI
STREET MAP

229

Your hotel is likely to be in this same general area, or on or just behind Alexander the Great Quay (Megalou Alexandrou), the continuation of King Constantine Quay on the other side of the White Tower. You will have little need to go further afield either for good restaurants, simple tavernas or fast-food eating. Thessaloniki is not a city where you need to acquire familiarity with the public transport system. It has much to offer, but compactly.

History

Alexander the Great's father, King Philip of Macedonia, whose casket in the Thessaloniki Archaeological Museum should not be missed, returned home from conquering Thessaly to find that his wife had given birth to a daughter, Alexander's half-sister. He named her Victory-in-Thessaly, *Thessalo-niki*. She grew up to marry the Cassander who succeeded Alexander as King of Macedonia and who, on founding his new capital in 315 BC by uniting existing settlements at the head of the Thermaic Gulf, gave it his wife's name.

Thessaloniki flourished under the Romans as the main staging post and administrative centre on the Via Ignatia, the road linking Italy with Byzantium across what is today Albania. Christianity took root after the visits of St Paul and spread from there into the Balkans and southern Russia. The second city of the Byzantine Empire, it survived 500 years of Turkish domination, and was finally reunited with Greece in 1912.

In 1913 King George I was assassinated there after a half-century's reign. In 1915 it was the headquarters of the Allied Expeditionary Force sent to establish the Macedonian Front, and for a time was the seat of the provisional government of Greece during the breach between Eleftherios Venizelos and King Constantine. In 1917 most of the central areas were gutted in 'the fire of the century'; as a result, the main port of the city dates largely from the 1920s.

What to see
The White Tower

At the end of the quay close to the entrance to the exhibition grounds, the White Tower is both the landmark and symbol of Thessaloniki. Built by the Venetians in the fifteenth century, it is all that remains of the original sea wall. Once used as a prison for recalcitrant janissaries, it will almost certainly feature on whatever souvenir you may buy of Thessaloniki - plate, ashtray, scarf or tee-shirt.

Roman remains

Seek out the Arch of Galerius, built in AD 303 to commemorate the triumphs of Galerius over the Persians six years earlier, and the nearby domed rotunda, now the church of St George but believed to have been intended by Galerius as his mausoleum. The original Galerius complex also included a palace and hippodrome, but all that remain today are the western half of the arch, with its relief sculptures, and the converted rotunda.

The rotunda was consecrated as a church by Galerius' successor, turned into a mosque by the Turks (the minaret outside is the only one surviving in central Thessaloniki), and restored as a church after the 1912 liberation of the city. You reach the arch, and the rotunda just behind it, by turning sharp right along Gounari Street one block before the White Tower. A left turn either along Ignatia Street at the arch or Philipou Street at the rotunda will bring you to the Roman market, which is of rather less interest than the Byzantine churches that surround it.

Byzantine
churches

Half a dozen easily accessible churches are well worth a visit, and a dozen more if your interest is less than casual (see following page).

Turkish
reminders

The Turks have left little behind them, surprisingly for a people who held the city for close on 500 years, but less so in view of their undistinguished history as builders and the 1917 fire. One house that could be visited, however, adjoining the Turkish Consulate in Aghiou Dimitriou Street, is the birthplace of Mustafa Kemal Ataturk, the founder of modern Turkey.

St
Dimitrios:
church
and person

Rome and Byzantium come inextricably together in the Cathedral of St Dimitrios, dedicated to the city's patron saint and naturally standing in Aghiou Dimitriou Street. Born to an aristocratic Thessaloniki family in the third century, Dimitrios joined the Roman army and, at some point in a distinguished career, was converted to Christianity. For him, the end of the road was inevitable martyrdom.

Believers retrieved his body and buried it in the precincts of the prison where he had been held. Almost at once there was talk of miraculous cures, and in the fifth century the first of several churches was built on the site. The cathedral, Thessaloniki's largest church, was completed only in 1948; it looks and is new, but it is a painstakingly exact reconstruction of the one destroyed in the 1917 fire. In the crypt below, discovered during the rebuilding, you can see a metal drain in one wall through which perfumed oil 'from the body of the saint' is said once to have flowed, with healing properties; for this reason, Dimitrios is sometimes addressed as *myrovlitis* – the 'sweet-smelling'.

It took several centuries of miracle-working to turn St Dimitrios from a healer into the protector of Thessaloniki. According to the legends, during a siege in the sixth century he was seen on the wall in full armour, hurling down the first barbarians to reach the top. A later siege ended abruptly when the attackers fled before an apparition of myriads of soldiers led by a man on a white horse enveloped in flame. Still later, the image of the saint walking along the walls was sufficient to discourage another besieging army. In 1912 – probably a matter of the campaigning season and careful timing – the Greek army made its triumphant entry into Thessaloniki on 26 October, the Feast of St Dimitrios.

All the churches of St Dimitrios in every corner of Greece are dedicated to this martyred convert. So too is every Dimitrios and Dimitra, Dimitrakis, Dimitroula and Dimis who, in the Greek name-day tradition, offer cakes to relatives and friends on 26 October. Though occasionally you will meet a Pericles or Xenophon, a Sophocles or a Miltiades, the general practice is for a Greek baby to be given the name of a Christian saint, and one name only. In the Russian style, both boys and girls bear a personal Christian name and that of their father in the genitive – for example, Dimitrios (or Dimitra) Georgiou (of George) Papadopoulos. A married woman commonly, though not necessarily, replaces her father's name with her husband's, also in the genitive. Greeks celebrate not their birthday but the patronal festival of the saint whose name they bear. Intended to emphasise the eternal over the ephemeral, it is a great boon to those with no memory for dates and guards against one source of marital discomfiture.

Byzantine
churches

The numerous Byzantine churches in Thessaloniki apart from the cathedral are of interest for particular rather than general reasons. There are four in the central part of the city, all within easy walking distance of the White Tower.

● The eighth-century Church of St Sophia in St Sophia Square (Aghia Sofias) is considerably older than its more famous namesake in Istanbul. It is the earliest example of a traditional basilica with a cupola added.

● The fifth-century Church of the Virgin Akheropiitos in St Sophia Street is one of the oldest early Christian churches. Built after the third Ecumenical Council in 431, it is in the form of a basilica with central nave and aisles on either side. It has Roman mosaics as well as eleventh-century frescoes.

● The Panaghia Halkeon in Ignatia Street dates from the eleventh century, and is the oldest of the strictly Byzantine churches, with an unusually tall dome and ornate frescoes.

● The Church of the Holy Apostles at the end of Olympou Street is considered by many to be the most beautiful of the Thessaloniki churches. Dating from the fourteenth century, it has a dome decorated externally with mosaics and, on the inside, with frescoes from the period of the Paleologos family of Byzantine emperors.

The Jewish
community

The Thessaloniki Jewish community, which was easily Greece's largest, dated from the second half of the fifteenth century when the Turks, seeking to reduce their dependence on the Greek element for administration and trade, encouraged the Sephardic Jews of Spain and Portugal to seek refuge from Catholic persecution in the city.

In 1940, the 56,000 Thessaloniki Jews supported thirty-six synogogues, a few of which can still be seen (in Greece as a whole there were 77,000 Jews in twenty-five communities). At the end of the war there were 10,000 left in Greece and only 1,900 in Thessaloniki, from where 46,000 had been deported to the Nazi death camps in twenty-nine shipments. This is one reason why Austrian President Kurt Waldheim will not be paying an official visit to Greece.

Some of the Jews who survived owed their lives to Greeks who gave them shelter, and others to false papers supplied to them by the then Athens police chief, Angelos Evert, whose son Miltiades Evert is now Mayor of Athens and may soon be Prime Minister.

The deportations led to one famous incident. Archbishop Damaskinos, the Primate of the Orthodox Church in Greece, insistently protested about the deportations, and at length was warned by the Nazi commandant of Athens that a firing squad could be assembled for him too. His reported answer has gone down in modern Greek annals: 'Hierarchs of the Greek Church, General, are not shot but hanged. I would beg you to respect this tradition.'

Museums

While in Thessaloniki, you can make half-day excursions to two nearby archaeological sites from the Macedonian era, Vergina and Pella (for more on these, see p. 245 and p. 248). But if you are pressed for time, you can 'cover' them quite adequately by going instead to the Archaeological Museum. Among Greece's plethora of museums, this is one of only four – the others are those of Athens, Delphi and Olympia – that should under no circumstances be missed.

The Archaeo-logical Museum

It has been converted into an inconceivable omission by Professor Manolis Andronikos, Greece's most renowned living archaeologist and the only peer in the present century of the late Professor Spyridon Marinatos, whose Minoan discoveries on Santorini (Thera) are in the Athens Archaeological Museum.

The Vergina treasures

Vergina is a village outside the city of Veria, about an hour's drive from Thessaloniki, where in 1977 Professor Andronikos looted a tomb. The treasures he found, comparable among grave furnishings only to those discovered by Schliemann at Mycenae, are now in the Thessaloniki museum. They include:

● an 11-kg gold casket, standing on lion's feet and embossed with the star symbol of the kings of Macedonia, containing bones identified with reasonable certainty as those of Philip II, father of Alexander the Great;

● a smaller gold casket, weighing 8.5 kg, containing bones believed to be those of Philip's second wife, Cleopatra;

● silver utensils, weapons, articles of body armour such as a breastplate, ceremonial shield and a pair of greaves, carved ivory heads and the most exquisite examples of Macedonian jewellery ever discovered.

In interviews at the time of the discovery and subsequently in his book, *Vergina*, Professor Andronikos told of the day on which he struck gold at a site where he had been excavating, on and off, since 1937. It was almost at the end of the 1977 digging season, he said, when an apparently unlooted tomb was discovered. Because the weather was about to break and 'we had to know what we had found', rather than slowly clear the approaches to the door, he removed a stone and went in through the roof. For safety, the treasures were moved at once to Thessaloniki in the boot of the Professor's car before word of the discovery could spread.

Other exhibits

Other galleries of the museum display prehistoric pottery from all parts of Macedonia and Thrace; archaic and Classical sculptures along with Roman copies; finds from excavations at Ancient Olynthos (a city destroyed by Philip in 348 BC); Roman sculptures of between the first and fifth centuries AD; Roman sarcophagi and mosaics found during excavations in Thessaloniki; and bronze and silver vases, weapons, gold, glass and alabaster ornaments from tombs at Derveni of the fourth century BC.

The museum is open daily from 8 a.m. to 6 p.m., but is closed Tuesdays; the Dr 300 admission covers both the museum as a whole and the Vergina room.

The Folklore Museum   An interesting museum to which admission is free (it too is closed on Tuesdays but on other days is open from 9 a.m. to 2 p.m.) is the Folklore Museum in Vassilissis Olga Street. It displays traditional local costumes from Macedonia, Thessaly and Thrace, hand-woven fabrics, wood carvings and metal objects.

Where to stay   There are hotels in Thessaloniki to suit every pocket, from the deluxe Makedonia Palace where a room can cost you Dr 20,000 a day in peak season, through the first-class Elektra Palace (Dr 7,500 a day peak season), to any number of comfortable second- and third-class units in the Dr 6,000 to 3,000 range. Among second-class hotels, you may stay modestly at the 224-bed Metropolitan at 65 Vassilissis Olga Street or the 208-bed Olympia at 65 Olympou Street. For third-class, the 124-bed Amalia at 33 Ermou Street and 217-bed Delta at 13 Ignatia Street should prove adequate. Even if you drop down to fifth class you can expect to pay at least Dr 2,000 a day, so the savings to be made in return for loss of comfort are not all that significant.

Try to avoid the area of the railway station, which is highly commercial and extremely noisy. The Capsis, for example, Thessaloniki's biggest hotel, can accommodate 823 guests in 428 rooms, but it is too often a travel agent's favourite for his own convenience. It has a lounge which, when all the groups are back, is deficient only of a platform to become part of the railway station the hotel was built to serve, and it will still charge you Dr 7,000 a day in peak season.

Similarly, there is no real point in choosing a hotel in one of the hill suburbs, for example Panorama, unless you are planning an unusually lengthy stay in Thessaloniki – at least the duration of one of the trade fairs. Stay central and close to the water and you cannot go far wrong at least for a night or two; this, as you may have gathered, is advice that applies almost everywhere in Greece, except to Athens.

Where to eat   It is difficult to eat badly in Thessaloniki, if you watch where the Greeks go. For those who wish to stay close to the waterfront, best bets are probably the Olympos/Naoussa and the Stratis at 5 and 19 King Constantine Quay respectively (the quay's new name, Nikis, 'Victory', has yet to catch on), and Elvetiko at 40 St Sophia Street. Proxeno Koromila Street, one back from the waterfront, has the restaurants Clochard (No 4) and Votsala (No 17) as well as two good tavernas, Ta Nissia (No 13) and Kapilio (No 26). Just behind Alexander the Great Quay, Vassilissis Olga Street houses the Steki tou

Nioniou (No 31) and two of the best grill-rooms, Kameni Gonia at No 72 and Takis at No 15.

A little further out, at Nea Krini, you can find four of the most highly regarded fish tavernas – Archipelagos, Miami, Hamodrakas and Paradissos. Up in the hills, the Panorama suburb offers the Dionyssos and Asteria restaurants and the Kioskia taverna.

Excursions

Half-day excursions listed by Thessaloniki travel agents include a city tour, separate trips to Dion and Pella for the archaeological sites and museums, and a cruise off the coast of Mount Athos. One-day excursions include Kavala and Philipi, an 'Alexander the Great' tour (Pella, Edessa, Veria and Vergina), Litohoro and Kalambaka for Mount Olympos and the Meteora monasteries, and the Halkidiki peninsula with the Petralona cave.

Useful addresses

The National Tourist Organisation of Greece (NTOG) has an office at 34 Mitropoleos Street (Tel. 271.888) and an information booth at the airport (Tel. 412.261).

The Hellenic Automobile and Touring Club (ELPA) has a branch office at 228 Vassilissis Olga Street (Tel. 631.920).

Outward bound from Thessaloniki

Without being dismissive of north-eastern Greece, there are only three common reasons for going east from Thessaloniki: a holiday in Halkidiki or on the island of Thassos, to reach Bulgaria or to get to Istanbul.

To Promahonas

If your immediate objective is Sofia and a little Balkan slumming, there is nothing much you can or need to do to improve the journey. Within a couple of hours you will be at the Promahonas border crossing and, a couple of hours after that if your luck holds, you will have overcome a set of controls on both sides of the border that will give you pause for thought.

At most you may fortify yourself with coffee at Serres, an important agricultural city of 46,000 people, 95 km from Thessaloniki and about 50 km short of the border, with little to offer the visitor except a Byzantine castle. You could allow a half-hour for a stroll through the old Turkish quarter, but the ruined castle hardly merits the climb. Sidirokastron, the last town before Promahonas, with a population of 6,100, has even less to offer.

The border can be reached less directly through Kilkis, population 11,000, a town that lists as its attractions one church and a cave.

The Halkidiki Peninsula

Halkidiki, an hour-and-a-half from Thessaloniki on one of the buses that leave at almost hourly intervals in the summer, is the holiday camp of northern Greece. The Germans in particular have adopted it and it is the most accessible resort for anyone driving to Greece through Yugoslavia.

To reach it by car from Thessaloniki you have a choice of two roads, the fairly new one along the coast (you fork on to it opposite the airport) and the old one through Polygyros. For once, it might be preferable to travel inland, so as to pass through some of the few really beautiful wooded hills of Greece. It is a jewel of a region of which the Greeks themselves are only just becoming aware.

What to see   Most of all, you will enjoy the countryside: wooded hills, blue water for those who venture away from the hotel swimming pools, sandy beaches along more than 500 km of coastline, opportunities for walking in the cool of the morning or early evening, one-day tours of the three peninsulas laid on as a routine hotel service and, if you have your own means of transport, always a seaside taverna or fish restaurant within 10 or 15 km of where you are staying.

Where to stay   Since Halkidiki is still Greece's only real resort area on the mainland other than that between Athens Airport and Sounion, you will probably have taken your decision on whether to stay there before coming to Greece. The Halkidiki hoteliers deal mainly with tour operators, but somewhere there is always room for the individual.

Only twenty years ago, guides to Greece were cautioning their readers: 'The present condition of the roads does not facilitate travel in the Chalcidice peninsula.' This is certainly no longer true; the roads have been built, and at the latest count there were sixty-five hotels with 10,669 beds: one deluxe, seven first-class, eighteen second-class, seventeen third-class, fifteen fourth-class and seven fifth-class.

The deluxe hotel is the Meliton Beach at Porto Carras on the Sithonia peninsula, part of a three-hotel complex (the others are first and second class) with a total 2,096 beds.

Other hotels with more than 500 beds are on the Cassandra peninsula: the first-class Athos Palace and Pallini Beach at Kallithea (1,130 and 938 beds respectively); the second-class Gerakina Beach at Gerakina (955 beds); and the second-class Sani Beach at Sani (886 beds).

No matter how many reservations you may hold about 'resort' hotels and their implied dependence on package tours, an exception may be made for Halkidiki for the simple reason that there are no large towns to offer nightlife; most of the hotels are close to nothing but the sea or to a village with two or three hundred inhabitants which may or may not have a taverna. It follows that more hotels than usual have restaurants, and that it might be preferable to use them. The alternative is to drive to the nearest village (it may be a long walk) and hope, if you are out of the main season, to find a taverna that is open.

Polygyros   Polygyros, 67 km from Thessaloniki with a population of 5,200, is the capital of the *nome* of Halkidiki, one with a total population of only 61,000. Built amphitheatrically at the foot of Mount Holomon, it is a delightful place to linger over coffee while reflecting on the injustice to which history has subjected it: Polygyros was the first town in northern Greece to join the 1821 Revolution but among the last to achieve its freedom, nearly a century later. Driving south from Polygyros for 13 km, you join the coastal road at Gerakini; there you either turn left for the Sithonia and Athos peninsulas or right for Cassandra.

Cassandra

The most developed of the three peninsulas is the western one, Cassandra, entered through Nea Moudania, the second town of Halkidiki with a population of 4,100.

Sithonia and Porto Carras

Sithonia, the central prong, is still a little more primitive for all that it is the site of Porto Carras, a 1,001-room resort complex consisting of three hotels of deluxe, first and second categories with a golf course, yacht marina and open-air theatre that on occasion has been used for symphony concerts. Porto Carras also produces its own wine – red, rosé and white – marketed under that label throughout Greece.

The Petralona cave

On your way to Nea Moudania you could branch off for a quick look at the Petralona cave. You will see some not particularly remarkable stalactites and stalagmites; but what should excite you is the thought that recent discoveries in the cave point to its occupation possibly half a million years ago by some early independent travellers to Greece.

Torone

On the Sithonia peninsula you could also be among the trailblazer visitors to Greece's newest minor ancient site, at Torone, where the excavations at a city dating from the eighth century BC were carried out by a team from Sydney University as agents of the Athens Archaeological Society.

You cannot go into Mount Athos, the easternmost peninsula, unless you have made arrangements in advance, and you cannot go at all if you are a woman. To enter this, the 'Holy Community' of monks, you need a permit either from the Foreign Ministry in Athens (Directorate of Churches, 3 Akademias Street) or the Ministry for Northern Greece in Thessaloniki (Directorate of Civil Affairs, Platia Dioikitiriou).

Mount Athos

Getting in

Theoretically, you require a justifiable academic reason to visit Mount Athos but, in fact, permits are normally issued on the basis of a letter of recommendation from an embassy or consulate. However, since there is a ten-a-day limit on the entry of aliens there tends to be a waiting list. If you happen to be a clergyman, you will require an additional authorisation from the Ecumenical Patriarchate of Constantinople. Obviously it is advisable to plan a visit months in advance; then you can deal with the procedures by letter and ensure yourself a safe place on the list. NTOG offices around the world can offer additional information and assistance.

The permits are for a four-day stay in the community, but extensions of a day or two can usually be arranged once you are in Karyes, the Mount Athos administrative capital and port of entry from Ouranoupolis.

History and status

The monastic 'republic', established by a Byzantine imperial edict of 1060, is frequently but erroneously described as 'autonomous'. In fact, it is a self-administered part of the Greek state, subject to the laws of Greece, with Greek state control exercised by a civil administrator under the terms of a charter of 1926 which determines the system of local administration.

Once part of the Byzantine empire, Mount Athos was recovered from the Ottoman empire in 1912 and definitively recognised as subject to Greek sovereignty by the Treaty of Lausanne of 1923. Its status was not affected by Greece's European Community accession: a special declaration signed as part of the agreement guarantees that the 1926 charter will remain in force and will take precedence over any Community law that would conflict with its spiritual and religious contents. In simpler terms, Community progress towards sex equality stops at the border of Mount Athos, and so do women.

In the eleventh century there were 180 monasteries on Mount Athos. By the middle of the fourteenth century their number had fallen to twenty-four, with some 5,000 monks. Today, the monasteries are down to twenty and the monks to about 1,400. Spiritually, the monasteries are under the jurisdiction of the Ecumenical Patriarchate of Constantinople; administration is exercised by a council of twenty representatives, one for each monastery.

Weather permitting, it is possible to see some of the monasteries from a distance without actually setting foot on the peninsula, by caique from Ouranoupolis. Since the caiques stay outside the Community's 'territorial waters', women have the same right as men to the long view.

Ouranoupolis

Ouranoupolis, population 647, is the last 'town' before the border of Mount Athos and is an easy drive from either Cassandra or Sithonia. Even on days when southerly winds make the caique trip impossible, you can still enjoy a swim from a sheltered beach, a meal at one of the fish restaurants and high tea at the Eagles' Palace Hotel, the closest approach of worldly luxury to the Republic of God.

On the road to Istanbul

While you can make Kavala just a lunch break, it is better to spend an afternoon and a night there to allow time the next day to see Komotini and Alexandroupolis and, if that is your destination, still be in Istanbul for a late tea.

Kavala

Kavala, population 56,000, is arguably Greece's prettiest mainland port. You drop steeply into it, passing beneath a disused aqueduct of the sixteenth century, and find yourself in a most elegant harbour with a view across to Thassos. Until the middle of the 1970s,

Kavala's commercial importance was a matter of tobacco production and marketing, and cigarette manufacturing. Now oil and natural gas have been added, pumped from the Prinos offshore field between the port and Thassos. Both the shore installations for the oil, and the fertiliser industry to utilise the natural gas, have been sited some way out of the town, to create jobs but not disfigurements.

Getting there

There are two Olympic Airways flights a day to Kavala in the summer, flying time one hour. The airport, however, is 35 km outside the town. There are two buses a day from Athens (an eleven-hour trip) and seventeen a day from Thessaloniki (two and a half hours). Kavala can also be reached by occasional boats from Piraeus, which take from 16 to 25 hours for the voyage depending on the number of islands visited en route.

Kavala has bus services to the cities of eastern Macedonia and Thrace, and ferries (less than daily) to Samothrace, Alexandroupolis, Limnos, Mytilene, the Dodecanese islands and Crete. It has daily ferries to the island of Thassos.

History

Originally named Neapolis, the city was founded in the seventh century BC as a colony of Thassos and became the port for nearby Philipi. After St Paul landed there on his way to Philipi, it became the first European town to accept Christianity and, in honour of the event, was renamed Christoupolis by the Byzantines in the ninth century. Occupied by the Turks in 1387, it acquired its present name in the fifteenth century, possibly from the Italian for the horses that were changed there. It was liberated in 1913, and after 1922 its population was almost doubled by an inflow of refugees from Asia Minor.

What to see

Kavala's greatest charm is undeniably its situation, with the long curving quay. You can also explore the fourteenth-century castle, take a look at the aqueduct, and visit the house where Mehmet Ali, subsequent founder of an Egyptian royal dynasty, was born in 1769; its harem is particularly well preserved.

Where to stay

Kavala has sixteen hotels with a total of 1,030 rooms. Probably the pleasantest in the centre of town, by the water, is the second-class Galaxy; some twenty years ago it was one of the first in Greece to place a refrigerator in every room. A little further out are the first-class Tosca Beach with a hundred bungalows and the second-class Lucy with 217 rooms.

Where to eat

There are excellent quayside fish restaurants among the clump of trees at your far left as you face the sea. Greeks returning from coach excursions to Istanbul head straight for them, to enjoy a meal in which they can have confidence. Since the restaurants depend on local custom and the local fishermen depend on the restaurants for the disposal of their catch, they have to be good; provincials in Greece are not so easily fooled as Athenians. Zafira is a firm favourite. For a good meal with a beautiful view of the harbour, try the Stathis restaurant next to the Galaxy Hotel.

Philipi

Philipi, 37 km from Kavala along a good road, is one of Greece's more evocative ancient sites: the scene of the battle between Octavius and the army of Brutus and Cassius in 42 BC, and of St Paul's first sermon on European soil in AD 49.

The site

In the centre of the site lie the ruins of the city's Graeco–Roman agora, once lined on three sides by arcades and temples. There are also the ruins of two early Christian basilicas and of the city's public latrine with a number of marble seats still in place. A crypt dating from the Roman period is thought to have served as a prison for St Paul.

The museum

The museum contains finds from the Hellenistic, Roman and early Christian periods, and also some from a nearby neolithic settlement. Performances of ancient drama are occasionally given in the restored ancient theatre, which dates from the fourth century BC, was remodelled by the Romans, and at one time was used as an arena. So far as is known, despite the setting of its last act, Julius Caesar has not yet been presented there.

The theatre

The archaeological site is open daily from 9 a.m. to 5 p.m., admission Dr 200. The museum is open from 9 a.m. to 3 p.m., but is closed on Tuesdays.

The 175-km drive from Kavala to Alexandroupolis will take you through Xanthi and Komotini. You will be crossing the length of Thrace, a geographical area combining a coastal strip with an unusually striking mountain hinterland. Everywhere you will see evidence of the continuing importance of tobacco to the local economy: fields of tobacco plants in the early summer, and later the leaves threaded on strings to dry out in the sun before baling and sale at tobacco auctions. Fortunately for Thrace, while the rest of the world may be weaning itself from the habit, cigarette consumption in Greece still sets new records every year.

You can also reach Xanthi by way of Drama, a drive of 132 km instead of the 60 km by the direct route, if you wish to see a city whose name conveys excitement, and to pass through the mountains rather than the coastal plain.

By either route, you will see more indications of Anatolia than anywhere else in Greece with the possible exception of Rhodes. Greece's Muslim minority, concentrated in Thrace despite the exchange of populations after the 1922 Asia Minor disaster, has fared considerably better than its counterpart, the Greek community in Istanbul. Equality of rights is enshrined in the 1975 constitution, and extends to religion, language and a degree of autonomy in regard to education, as well as representation in the Greek parliament.

Drama

A city of 36,000 inhabitants well off the tourist track and scarcely worth a diversion, Drama offers a view of Byzantine walls in the centre of the town and a couple of Byzantine churches, the Church of the Archangels and Aghia Sophia. Occasionally, river trout from the area is on restaurant menus, along with such Anatolian specialities as *soutsoukakia* and *pastourmas* if you want to sample Turkish food before crossing the border.

It is well connected by rail and bus with Athens, and shares an airport with Kavala. Those who stay overnight, usually for business reasons, can find accommodation in seven hotels of second to fourth class, with a total of 248 rooms. Three which are new or newly restored are the second-class Xenia (eighty-eight beds) in Ethnikis Amynas Street; the Apollo (seventy-five beds) in Lambrianidou Street and the Marianna (eighty-five beds) in George Vorazani Street, both third class.

Good restaurants in the city include the Nissaki in Aghia Varvara (St Barbara) Street and Metaxas near the Apollo Hotel. The Korivolos on top of Korivolou hill offers spectacular views of the city from a height above sea level of close on 1,000 m.

Xanthi   With a population of 31,000, Xanthi is an old town which is beginning to take on a modern appearance, but still has some well-preserved old houses, as well as a Turkish-style market similar to that on Rhodes.

Avdira   Its main attraction for the traveller is the opportunity to visit the site of Ancient Avdira, 26 km away. Situated 3 km from the modern village of the same name and with 2,000 inhabitants, Ancient Avdira's main claim to fame is as the birthplace of Dimocritos, the 'smiling' philosopher who postulated the theory that there is nothing smaller in nature than the atom, a word derived from the Greek for something that cannot be cut or split. Greece's nuclear research centre in Athens is naturally named 'the Dimocritos'. Avdira itself has only some Greek and Roman remains, but the site is pleasant.

Xanthi can be reached by bus or train from Athens (journeys of twelve and fourteen hours respectively) as well as from Thessaloniki (four hours), and has local bus connections with Kavala, Drama and Komotini. It has ten hotels, of second class downwards, with 351 rooms. The two larger are probably the most comfortable – the 127-bed Motel Natassa and 142-bed Nestos in Kavala Avenue, both second class. The town's two best restaurants are reputedly the Klimataria and Constantinidis, both in King Constantine Square.

Komotini   A city whose 37,000 population is more or less half-and-half Christian and Muslim, and with a definite Anatolian atmosphere, Komotini is the commercial centre of the *nome* of Rodopis, with a number of mosques and an Armenian quarter.

It is hard to imagine why anyone should want to go there except to make money out of tobacco dealing, but those who do can reach it from Athens by air, rail or bus and stay in any of eight second- to fifth-class hotels with a total of 355 rooms. While Komotini is unavoidable for those driving to Turkey, overnight stays are more commonly spent at Kavala or Alexandroupolis.

Alexan-
droupolis

Alexandroupolis is a good place to spend a night, and a necessary place if your destination is the northern Aegean island of Samothrace – a three-hour voyage effected by two ferries a day in the summer.

Getting
there

Alexandroupolis can be reached from Athens by air, train and bus, and from Thessaloniki by train and bus, and has its own bus connections to Komotini, Xanthi and Kavala.

With a population of 35,000, Alexandroupolis is the last town of any size before the Turkish frontier, 43 km away. While the natural assumption would be that it took its name – the city, *polis*, of Alexander – from Alexander the Great, some Greek references ascribe the name to King Alexander, who visited it after its liberation in 1920 during a brief reign ended by the bite of a pet monkey. The version of the Great Alexander, however, appears to be preferred by publications dating from after the abolition of the monarchy in 1974: this kind of cloudiness is met with frequently in Greece, where even recent events can be subject to reinterpretation when political fashions change.

History

However, it is agreed that the present city was laid out by the Russians after they captured it from the Turks in 1877 during a war between czar and sultan. It was at that time called by the Turkish name of Dedeagatz, and it acquired its present name after its recovery by Greece in the aftermath of the First World War. Also, in 1860 there was not a single house where Alexandroupolis now stands, regardless of whether it is the same city referred to by Plutarch as founded by Alexander the Great.

Where
to stay

Its chief attraction today is its seaside promenade and wide sandy beach, along which a number of resort hotels have been built. In total, the city offers 556 rooms in eighteen units ranging from first class (the Astir Motel) to fifth. Two hotels on the beach are the Alexander Beach (second class, 116 beds) and Alkyon (third class, fifty-two beds).

Where
to eat

A couple of good restaurants back from the waterfront are the Elysee near the Olympic Airways office and the Klimataria alongside the railway station. Greeks returning from excursions to Istanbul descend on the seaside restaurants and cafés with cries of delight, since it is a matter of national pride that the attractions, though many and various, of what once was Byzantium, do not extend to Turkish cuisine. Even the most cosmopolitan Greeks tend to be chauvinistic about Greek cooking, despite the number of Turkish dishes on local menus; it is a chauvinism that is better justified if they are returning from Bulgaria.

The Kipi
Bridge

From Alexandroupolis onwards to the Kipi bridge, you are in no doubt that you are in a frontier region, and not one between particularly good friends, for all that Greece and Turkey are allies in NATO. The Evros River marks the border between Greece and Turkey, and in the middle of the Kipi Bridge, 810 m long, Greek and Turkish sentries confront each other.

Frontier formalities are apt to be as tedious there as at the

Promahonas crossing into Bulgaria, with the difference of a more specific focus on the search for drugs on the way into Greece and for money on the way out. It is government policy not to make it particularly easy for Greeks to spend a holiday in Turkey, nor indeed for European tour operators who would like to offer two-country itineraries; Greece sees no reason why it should help to relieve Turkey's equally pressing need for foreign currency at the cost of its own inflows. Also, it is a common secret that Greeks do smuggle money on that particular route, since they are unlikely to have secret accounts in Turkish banks and would not go far in the Istanbul bazaar on the travel allowance for Turkey.

This is not to suggest that the tourist faces any particular difficulties or identifiable attempts at discouragement. Simply, it will not be quite like crossing from other EEC countries into such non-members as Switzerland or Austria.

The Evros wetlands   Between Alexandroupolis and the frontier you pass along the edges of the Evros wetlands, the river estuary that forms Greece's only real nature reserve as distinct from 'sea parks' for the protection of seals, turtles and such. If you have time to ramble, you could look for some of the 263 species of birds believed to be resident or transient; even without looking, you should catch glimpses of the occasional stork and heron.

Soufli   A short diversion of about 30 km (simply ignore the right turn to Kipi) will take you to Soufli. This will save you the cost of a flight to Bangkok if it is silk that lights a glint in your eye. Greece is not nor is ever likely to be a major centre of the silk industry, but Soufli (population 5,600) has carved its little niche. You will be told by shopkeepers there that the craft, along with the ancient ancestors of the present worms, was brought to Soufli some 300 years ago from Constantinople and took root because the climate was particularly suitable for mulberry. It is very much a cottage industry, unusual rather than economically significant.

In the folk museum in Soufli you can see how silk is made, from worm to loom, and then stroll along the stone-paved main street to shop for lengths or garments. Soufli has three third- to fifth-class hotels, with twenty-nine rooms.

Didimotichon   Some 30 km beyond Soufli on the same road, Didimotichon, population 8,400, is a remarkable little Byzantine town that would certainly have acquired a tourist movement if only it were more accessible. As it is, its eighty-four rooms in two hotels are rarely filled.

Founded in the late eighth and early ninth centuries AD, Didimotichon means 'twin walls' and takes its name from the double walls that used to surround it, parts of which still survive. Two Byzantine emperors and one Turkish sultan were born there, and another Byzantine emperor was proclaimed while in the city. Its showpiece is the oldest and biggest mosque in Europe, built in 1368 by the Sultan Murad I.

Orestias   Another 20 km along the road, at the very end of Greece, Orestias, known also as Orestiada, is a modern town of 12,700 inhabitants which dates from the 1920s and offers 157 rooms in four third- and fourth-class hotels. It is remote indeed even from the unbeaten track, and scarcely worth the effort unless you want to say that you got as far as possible from Athens without actually leaving the country.

Greece's 'north-west frontier'

If you have no objections to disfiguring your map of Greece, draw a straight line from Thessaloniki to Ioannina and then two right-angles, one from Thessaloniki to the Yugoslav border and the other from Ioannina to the Albanian border. You now have a rectangle that, for the crow, would have a top and bottom of about 200 km and sides of about 70 km.

This area, made up of central and western Macedonia and a piece of Epiros, essentially comprises Greece's north-west frontier region; one of spectacular views but little tourist development. The question is whether it is worth exploring, in depth, an area that the Greeks themselves would scarcely consider for a holiday unless returning to family villages. The answer is to some degree affirmative, because of the towns of Kastoria, Edessa and Florina; the archaeological sites of Pella and Vergina; the Prespa lakes, and the mountain ranges of Vermion, Pindos, Gramos and Vitsi where the communist guerrillas made their last stand in 1949 before melting away across the frontiers into Yugoslavia and Albania, taking with them thousands of abducted children to be brought up as soldiers for the next round.

The proposed route will take you along the base of the rectangle to Kozani, from there up to Kastoria, and then along the top through Florina, Edessa and Yannitsa. By the time you are back in Thessaloniki you will have covered approximately 500 km, on roads that are adequate though in no way comparable to motorways. You will also have achieved something unusual for Greece: after the first couple of hours you will not have caught even a glimpse of the sea.

The obvious place for an overnight stay would be Kastoria, a little beyond the half-way point of the journey. If you can afford two nights, you could spend the first at Kastoria and the second only 70 km away at Florina, so as to allow more time for Greece's lake district.

You leave Thessaloniki along the Athens motorway and then, after about half an hour or rather more if the traffic is heavy, take the right fork for Veria and the archaeological site of Vergina.

Veria   Veria, population 37,000, is an attractive old town on the eastern

foothills of the Vermion mountains which has had a chequered history even for Greece. Occupied at one time or another by Macedonians, Byzantines, Bulgarians, Normans, Franks, Turks and Serbs, it was liberated only in 1912. St Paul went there in AD 56 or 57. Today it offers Greek and Roman remains, along with fifty-one churches.

It can be reached by bus from Athens (eight hours) and Thessaloniki (one and a half hours), and by train from either city, and has bus services to Edessa and Kozani. It has five hotels of third and fourth class, with 197 rooms.

Vergina   Vergina, fifteen or twenty minutes' drive from Veria, does not yet have much to show but may eventually have more; considerable excavation remains to be done. The site is open from 9 a.m. to 3 p.m. but the treasures that made it famous have, of course, been removed to the Thessaloniki Archaeological Museum.

Naoussa

An 18-km side trip from Veria, along a route that you would have to retrace later, would take you to Naoussa, a town of 19,300 inhabitants built at an altitude of 330 m. It is best known for its red wine, fruit and vegetable canneries and textiles, particularly blankets. Its Square of National Martyrs commemorates the beheading of 1,241 of its inhabitants in the early stages of the 1821 Revolution. Though the Naoussa municipality has built a holiday complex at Aghios Nikolaos, 3 km outside the town, if it ever acquires a holiday movement it will need more than its present sixty rooms in four hotels, including the twenty in the second-class Vermion at Aghios Nikolaos.

Kozani and Ptolemaida

From Veria you have to drive to Kozani, a distance of 61 km, before deciding which route to take for Kastoria. Kozani, population 31,000, and nearby Ptolemaida, population 22,000, are sometimes described as Greece's 'little Ruhr', rather because of the mines than the metallurgical industries. Ptolemaida, written also as Ptolemais, is named after the general of Alexander the Great, and is Greece's principal centre for the production of electricity from lignite. At most, Kozani might be regarded as a place for a quick lunch; Ptolemaida does not have even that much to offer.

The more attractive route to Kastoria is through Siatista, 25 km from Kozani and 66 from Kastoria. At Siatista, population 5,700, you will see a little of what you will see much more of later: the processing of fur.

Kastoria

Kastoria is what makes the whole trip worth while: it is the one really lovely town of north-west Greece, and the only one in which the Greeks could imagine themselves spending part of their holiday.

Getting there

Kastoria can be reached by air from Athens, and by bus from Athens (ten hours) and Thessaloniki (four hours), over distances of 555 km and 219 km respectively. It has bus services to Edessa, Kozani, Florina, Larisa and Ioannina.

History

It is built on a promontory jutting into a lake of 33 sq km, invariably known as Lake Kastoria although it is more properly called Orestias after the town's legendary founder, Orestes, the son of Agamemnon. The wooded hills around it are particularly beautiful in autumn.

The town, originally Keletron, was renamed Justianoupolis after the Emperor Justinian in Byzantine times, and takes its present name from the Greek for beaver, *kastoria*. Beavers flourished in the lake until the end of the nineteenth century, but are now extinct. As well as a lakeside it is a mountain town, built at an altitude of 628 m. It is one of the coldest places in Greece in the winter and, at least during the days, one of the hottest in summer, though rarely humid. There are three reasons why you should allow yourself at least half a day in Kastoria: the setting, the architecture and the furs.

With a population of 20,600, Kastoria spills down the slopes of the promontory towards water of a paler blue than the sea, with an ever-changing delicacy of hue. On the lake, the fishermen work from blunt-ended boats of almost biblical simplicity to supply fish for the tavernas and ouzeries along the banks.

The archontika

There are seventy churches, some dating from the eleventh century and not all in use, in the narrow streets leading up from the waterfront. The explanation for their profusion is that many of them were originally the private chapels of the great houses, *archontika*, which may have been large for the times but are no longer so in comparison with a modern villa. The Kastoria *archontika* are three-storey structures, the top floor of which juts out over the street. The ground floor, with small, high windows, was used for livestock and storage, the low-ceilinged second floor was the family's living quarters, and the spacious third floor was the equivalent of the Victorian 'front room', to be opened up for celebrations or the entertainment of guests. The overhang, with its casement windows, served as a kind of solarium.

Dating mostly from the eighteenth century, the *archontika*, with their wooden ceilings, open fireplaces and carved panelling, are unusual examples of eastern influences on Byzantine tradition. One of them, that of the Nerantzis family, has been turned into a folk museum; many of the others are fur workshops.

Little bits of mink

The city's fame and present prosperity rest on minute fragments of mink, the waste of New York workshops, which in Kastoria are reunited into bolts of fur that eventually become coats, jackets, stoles, hats, gloves and purses.

There are conflicting accounts of exactly how fur came to Kastoria. Most authorities date it from the settlement in Kastoria of Jewish furriers, refugees from persecution in Europe, who were attracted there by the availability of beaver. Another version holds that during the Middle Ages migrants from Kastoria, who had already learned to work with beaver, settled in southern Russia and supplied Russian pelts to Constantinople and scraps to Kastoria for more elaborate processing, so shifting the emphasis there from whole skins to pieces.

Though mink are now raised in Kastoria on a small scale, the trade is still essentially based on the import of scraps, which are first sorted according to the part of the animal from which they come, colour, quality and length of hair, then stitched into bolts of fur mainly for shipment to Athens. The resulting garments, retailed by furriers in the Ermou–Mitropoleos–Philhellinon district around Constitution Square, are considerably cheaper than those manufactured from whole skins. In the absence of meticulous scrutiny, the only apparent difference is the far greater weight resulting from the amount of stitching that has gone into them.

This explains why you see more mink in Athens in the winter than in the capitals of far richer or colder countries, and why a fur coat is a realisable ambition, not a daydream, of any working girl. Men with fur hats in their wardrobes have been known to pray for snow despite the cost of central heating.

Purchases can be made in Kastoria itself; however, the fashion-conscious maintain that there is a greater variety in the Athens stores, though at somewhat higher prices.

Where to stay and where to eat

Unusually for Greece, all eleven of the city's hotels, with a total of 319 rooms, are open throughout the year, indicating the popularity of Kastoria for winter excursions. Easily the best hotel is the Xenia Du Lac, first class, where a double room is priced at about Dr 4,000 a night. Other favourites are the Tsamis, 3 km outside the town, and the Maria motel, both second class, at around Dr 3,500 a night.

While you can eat well at the Omilos restaurant in Nikis Street, Kastoria residents like the peace of the lakeside tavernas just outside the town: the Panorama 3 km away is said to be the best, if a little expensive.

Florina and the Prespa Lakes

From Kastoria to Thessaloniki by way of Edessa is a drive of about 220 km along secondary, mountainous roads for which five or six hours should be allowed. This means there will be time for a side-trip to Florina and Prespa (at least an extra 150 km), only if you leave Kastoria early in the morning or can spare a night for Florina. Florina alone, a mountain town of 12,500 inhabitants close to the Yugoslav and Albanian borders, is not worth the effort; its six hotels with 249 rooms are there solely because Florina is the closest you can stay to Prespa. The two best are also accorded the two best restaurants – the King Alexander in Nikis Street (seventy beds) and Lyngos (seventy-six beds) in Tagmatarhou Naoum Street, both second class. For a taverna meal, try the Hira in Omonia Square.

There are actually two lakes, Little Prespa, which is in Greece, and Great Prespa, which is shared by Greece, Yugoslavia and Albania; the borders are lines on a map of the lake. Little Prespa is a matter of setting and wildlife. At an altitude of 850 m and up to 50 m deep, it is a place for birdwatchers – the many species that nest there include wild duck and pelicans – and fishing; you can also swim if you don't mind very cold water.

Edessa

The attraction of Edessa, not one to be missed, lies in its water-falls, Greece's largest. With a population of 16,000, Edessa was until recently considered the site of the lost city of Aiges, the first capital of Macedonia before its transfer to Pella in the fifth century BC; this, however, is now being questioned as a result of the finds at Vergina, which are held to indicate that Vergina itself must have been the ancient capital.

Deprived of its awe, Edessa is left only with its cataracts, an unusual clock tower from the Turkish period, several good restaurants, and 208 rooms in seven hotels for travellers overtaken by night.

Pella

Pella, roughly half-way between Edessa and Thessaloniki, is not a particularly impressive ancient site despite its associations with Philip II and Alexander the Great; the non-specialist visitor will generally be content to see the ruins of an acropolis and the mosaic depicting a lion hunt. Finds from Pella are housed in the museum there; both it and the site itself are open from 9 a.m. to 3 p.m., though the museum is closed on Tuesdays.

Yannitsa   Just off the main road, about 4 km back, you will catch glimpses of Yannitsa, a modern market town of 21,000 inhabitants constructed on the bed of a lake drained during the 1930s. A wave in passing is sufficient.

You would have to go a long way, in any country, to find a stretch of road as dull as the 68-km motorway from Thessaloniki to Evzoni, forming the right side of the rectangle. The only possible reason for taking it is the reason for which it was built: to link up with the Yugoslav *autoput* to Belgrade and beyond.

Useful Reading

There is no shortage of books and guidebooks on modern Greece. A highly personal choice would include:

Guidebooks

Blue Guide to Greece – Stuart Rossiter.
Fodor Guide to Greece – Editors: Peter Sheldon and Richard Moore.

Works of Literature

Henry Miller's *The Colossus of Maroussi* (for bubbling enthusiasm).
Nicholas Gage's *Hellas – A Portrait of Greece* for general information.
Patrick Leigh Fermor's *Roumeli* and *Mani*.
Mary Renault's novels provide an excellent feel for Ancient Greece.
The third volume of Olivia Manning's *Balkan Trilogy* is set against a background to Greece in the Second World War.

Background Information

Sir Steven Runciman's *Mistras* and *Byzantine Style and Civilisation* for more specialised information.

You will also find in the larger Athens bookshops well-translated and lavishly-printed editions of Greek publications on specific periods of ancient history, archaeological sites and museums.

Index